Women
in Cross-Cultural Perspective

WOMEN
IN CROSS-CULTURAL PERSPECTIVE

Edited by
Leonore Loeb Adler

Foreword by
Harriet P. Lefley

PRAEGER

New York
Westport, Connecticut
London

Library of Congress Cataloging-in-Publication Data

Women in cross-cultural perspective / edited by Leonore Loeb Adler.
      p.   cm.
    Includes bibliographical references.
    Includes index.
    ISBN 0-275-93658-9 (alk. paper)
    1. Women—Cross-cultural studies.   2. Sex role—Cross-cultural
studies.   I. Adler, Leonore Loeb.
  HQ1154.W8833   1991
  305.42—dc20   90-7376

British Library Cataloguing in Publication Data is available.

Library of Congress Catalog Card Number: 90-7376
ISBN: 0-275-93658-9

First published in 1991

Praeger Publishers, One Madison Avenue, New York, NY 10010
An imprint of Greenwood Publishing Group, Inc.

Printed in the United States of America

The paper used in this book complies with the
Permanent Paper Standard issued by the National
Information Standards Organization (Z39.48-1984).

10 9 8 7 6 5 4 3 2 1

To my grandchildren, who carry on the traditions and promote innovations that enhance the experiences of a vital quality of life.

Contents

Acknowledgments

As the editor of this book, I would like to extend my thanks to each of the 26 authors without whose contributions this volume would not exist. This book brings together internationally renowned authors from around the world. All of them are active and involved people who make the work of the editor more pleasant. And then my hearty thanks and high regard go to Paul Macirowski, Psychology Editor at Praeger Publishers, whose expertise and calm reassuring manner gave rise to some very enjoyable interactions during this endeavor. I am also most indebted to my son, Barry P. Adler, for his readiness to help in many ways, any time, especially to get the manuscript camera-ready. My sincere appreciation is gratefully extended to my daughter-in-law, Karen Adler, who outdid herself to work on the actual process of the production; she put in many long hours to meet the book's timetable, for which I thank her wholeheartedly. And last, but by no means least, I acknowledge the patience and understanding of my husband, Dr. Helmut E. Adler, which he extended to me during the time-consuming activities that kept me busy and occupied with the manuscript for many months. I must also mention the support and encouragement that I received from my daughters Dr. Beverly Adler-Gross and Mrs. Evelyn Renee Agostini together with their husbands Madison R. Gross and Pedro J. Agostini. I recognize that I am very lucky to be surrounded by such a wonderful and warm family, which of course includes my sister and brother-in-law Margo and Eric Kahn, as well. Before closing, I want to acknowledge the unknown and uncounted readers of this book to whom I wish good reading, increased knowledge to foster understanding and tolerance of persons who live in other cultures and environments—and most important, to help promote harmonious existence with people everywhere.

Foreword

Harriet P. Lefley

As we approach the end of the twentieth century, students of human behavior are beginning to abandon the old nature-nurture controversies and to focus on the complex biopsychosocial human being in cultural context. In this process, an understanding of women's role in society has become central for understanding the parameters and interactions of biology, social role, and culture. This book is therefore far more than an interesting description of the evolving lives of women in different parts of the world. By demonstrating the diversities and commonalities of the female experience, these chapters add new ways of understanding how gender-in-culture affects the human condition.

Anthropologists have long known that gender evaluation and role specificity are culturally patterned. Although women in agrarian societies typically do heavy physical labor, along with or even replacing men, there generally seems to be an inverse relationship between sex-role differentiation and economic development. With industrialization and advances in technology, societies offer greater opportunities for women of all classes to become more educated, assume productive roles in the labor market, demand equal rights, and reduce the distance between male and female prerogatives. Under these conditions boundaries become more permeable and there is greater acceptance of equal privilege for both sexual and sex-role behaviors. As we are finding in many of the Western countries, this begins to be manifested in the popular culture. Unisex clothes and hair styles merge with unisex education and even homemaking and childrearing responsibilities.

When one reads the chapters in this book, different cultures seem light years apart, particularly with respect to the view of females as commodities or to the rigor of constraints on sexual activity. Cultures differ, too, in the extent to which women accept, reinforce, and transmit values of male privilege to their sons and daughters. Although the voting franchise would seem to be related to women's ability to control the events that shape their lives, the degree to which this option is exercised autonomously, in separation from the views of significant males, appears to be an aspect of culture. Culture also determines the options for female leadership roles and positions of power in the political calculus.

It would seem that the only remaining biological given is that women give birth physically (sometimes, as in couvade, with painful imitation by males). After that, their essential roles in infant nurturance, even in breast versus bottle feeding, and in the childrearing process itself, are culturally and economically determined. The vital statistics of their lives, health, morbidity, and mortality are similarly affected. Across cultures, there are differences among rural and urban women, women of different socioeconomic classes, women of different religions, and women from societies that vary in levels of technological development. Within these subgroups, women vary as a function of generation—and not always in a progressive linear mode. But underlying these differences are cultural values and belief systems that determine both the parameters of the female role, and the degree to which those parameters can be modified through culture change or political action. In some countries with rapid economic development and accelerated social change, we may see women in respected leadership positions contiguous with women in degraded roles of sexual exploitation.

To what degree is gender asymmetry—male dominance, female subjugation—a transcultural fact of life? Anthropologists looking at women cross-culturally have generally studied female roles in social, economic, and political organization, focusing on kinship, childrearing, magico-religious, and commercial life. Women have been viewed as producers, owners, and commodities, but there are wide variations in female authority and power. P. R. Sanday (1981) speaks of dual-sex political systems, like West African Obamkpa, in which "each sex has its own autonomous sphere of authority and an area of shared responsibility" (p. 116). In many preliterate cultures women are reputed to have inordinate power, whether through an enduring magico-religious association between maternity and soil fertility, both assuring social continuity (Sanday, 1981) or through "blood magic," the power of female menstruation (Buckley & Gottlieb, 1988).

Identification of specific areas of power rarely can be generalized across other domains. Yet societies that seem to us blatantly sexist may contend that women have separate but equal roles. Cultures in which women's subordination is sanctified by religion and codified in law continue to maintain the myth of the mother-wife as shadow ruler: "the hand that rocks the cradle" or "the power behind the throne." Conversely, as is evident in this book, some cultures that have openly espoused equality of the sexes still seem to view gender-specific roles in a patriarchal family system as the natural order, and to delegate most leadership positions to men. As anthropologists S. B. Ortner & H. Whitehead (1981) have pointed out, despite considerable variability in degree or type of gender asymmetry across cultures, "everywhere, to the best of our knowledge, gender categories are hierarchically arranged with the masculine valued over the feminine" (p. 33).

As several chapters indicate, women's lives are affected by men's lives as well. There are cultures or subcultures in which it is normative for men to beat their mates, as in the lives of lower-class Latin American women described by Ruben Ardila, and where women even accept the myth that this is proof of sexual love. However, one must ask whether such beatings are not a function of the frustration and rage of impoverished lives, projected onto the weaker partner, and defensively justified by the male rights and honor of *machismo*. The maltreatment in turn generates the compensatory gender-linked value of *la sufrida,* the suffering female who sacrifices for those whom she loves. There are numerous situations of social change—rural to urban movement, agrarian to industrial economies, erosion of the hunting and fishing resources of aboriginal cultures—that result in few jobs for unskilled men and many more for unskilled women. Under these conditions, men idle and drink away their self-esteem, while women work for wages, raise children, and forebear. Erosion of marital and paternal bonding, self-denigration of males, female anger, and other social problems affecting the sexes and their children are almost inevitable under these circumstances.

Cultural myths both evolve from and serve to perpetuate gender inequities until such time as they are rendered socially dysfunctional. As we know, this may take many generations or even centuries of external social change. A persistent question, both for anthropologists and cross-cultural psychologists, relates to the ethical dimensions of being the instruments of culture change. These are typically changes that are extremely desirable within the value system of the observer, as in interference with wife-beating, or the saving of a sickly infant doomed to die (see Scheper-Hughes, 1987). However, the problem of superimposing one's own values, most particularly with respect to women's roles in traditional cultures, is an old issue in cross-cultural counseling and psychotherapy (Lefley, 1985). Too often it implies isolation and loss of solidarity with one's traditional group. Objective consideration of the self is alien to people from communalistic cultures, but this is certainly part of the consciousness-raising that occurs in recognizing gender roles. When women from traditional cultures present for counseling—and frequently these are educated women who are encountering culture shock in a United States of America or European university—there is always the dilemma of reinforcing a more self-assertive posture that may be in tune with our own values, but maladaptive in the culture of origin.

Paradoxically, expanding opportunities for professional training and careers outside the home have been accompanied by social changes that make it difficult for women to avail themselves of these options. Erosion of the joint family system and industrial work for women who formerly were restricted to jobs as maids or housekeepers, have reduced the pool of childcare resources. This is a critical problem for women who work—a problem that always had existed for the women who took care of other women's children, and now is being realized in the middle and even upper middle socioeconomic groups.

A related issue is the extent to which social changes ushered in by feminist initiatives are good for all socioeconomic strata. At a number of conferences of professional women, frequently held in luxury hotels, I have heard maids and waitresses snicker at the earnest speeches of affluent feminists and pronounce their great willingness to stay at home with the kids. In the United States of America, our increasing devaluation of home careers for women is not shared across social classes, particularly when women work for wages as a matter of dire need rather than conscious choice. Certainly in the long range, job access and equality of options will benefit all. However, poor women often have problems dealing with an emphasis on access to upper-echelon positions, as opposed to equalizing pay at the lower levels for gender-linked jobs of equal social value, or of providing financial entitlements to mothers who prefer to stay at home.

A rare and valuable feature of this book is that it is written, as Editor Leonore Loeb Adler points out, from the emic (insider's) viewpoint. Most unicultural and cross-cultural studies have been conducted by trained outsiders looking in, learning the rules, structure, function, and meanings of another's realities. To a great extent, the community of scholars must impose etic (outsider's) categories of discussion: male-female relationships, developmental life-stages, tradition and change, and the like. But the content of each contribution reflects observations within the conceptual and experiential boundaries of that particular culture. We rarely have an opportunity to read the contributions of so many knowledgeable professionals writing specifically about events within their own emic domains.

Within the context of emic values there is an inevitable diversity of opinion about feminist goals. The authors reflect the continuing ambivalence and ongoing realities regarding division of labor based on biological gender. They mirror cultural uncertainties about sex-role differentiation and specialization, linked both to biological parameters and to the persistence of cultural and religious values. There are fewer uncertainties about differential social roles of single and married women and the positive values of education and career options for females. Most contemporary authors seem to value achieved over ascribed status, in which women define themselves in terms of their own accomplishments rather than the shared status of significant males.

Above all, most depict a rapidly changing world in which male-female roles are linked to far-ranging ecological, economic, and political developments affecting the life-sustaining environment and traditional modes of production. Erosion of rural economies and moves to urban life have inevitably affected kinship structure, led to attrition of the joint family system, and reduced the influence of significant role models on children's socialization. War, poverty, and survival economies lead to father absence and female-headed families, variables that impact on the socialization and gender development of new generations.

In societies offering greater opportunities for women, in contrast, motherhood may be differentially viewed by women who value self-actualization outside of traditional mother-wife roles. Certainly many professional women want children, with or without husbands, and worry about outdistancing the biological clock. Florence L. Denmark, however, has raised a critical issue that is barely acknowledged, let alone researched: the negative aspects of motherhood. Taking care of infants and toddlers involves fatigue, curtailment of freedom, a damper on intellectual stimulation, and frustrated career options. This is a critical issue in societies that value higher education and professions for females, but fail to offer alternative or respite resources for childrearing. Although it is not yet culturally condoned, women in the United States of America have increasing options to reject marriage and the parenting role, or alternatively, to raise children without fathers in a climate of social neutrality. Poverty is most clearly associated with families of women and children unsupported by men. With growing divorce and separation rates, however, it is possible that at all points in the economic spectrum, female-headed households may become much more normative in the Western world.

Together, the chapters in this book paint a vivid picture of traditional and evolving socialization of females and cultural perceptions of women's role. Inevitably, as women become more educated and more oriented toward reducing the gender asymmetry of their cultures, changes will take place in the definitions and evaluations of male-female relationships. Although the move toward greater equality is a slow, uneven, and highly variable process, it seems to be happening in many places in the world. Concomitant developments in economic and political spheres may reinforce needed adaptations in female roles. How these changes will impact on family structure and childrearing, economic division of labor, female self-actualization, notions of ideal masculinity and femininity, and cultural belief and value systems remains for future social scientists to explore. This is an exciting period in history, for both men and women, and this book will add to our ability to understand, synthesize, and generate hypotheses about the future of the human adventure.

REFERENCES

Buckley, T., & Gottlieb, A. (Eds.). (1988). *Blood magic: The anthropology of menstruation*. Berkeley: University of California Press.

Lefley, H. P. (1985). Mental health training across cultures. In P. Pedersen (Ed.). *Handbook of cross-cultural counseling and therapy* (pp. 259-266). Westport, CT: Greenwood Press.

Ortner, S. B., & Whitehead, H. (1981). *Sexual meanings: The cultural construction of gender and sexuality*. New York: Cambridge University Press.

Sanday, P. R. (1981). *Female power and male dominance: On the origins of sexual inequality*. New York: Cambridge University Press.

Scheper-Hughes, N. (1987). Culture, scarcity, and maternal thinking: Mother love and child death in Northeast Brazil. In N. Scheper-Hughes (Ed.). *Child survival: Anthropological perspectives on the treatment and maltreatment of children* (pp. 187-208). Dordrecht, Holland: D. Reidel.

Introduction

Leonore Loeb Adler

Women in Cross-Cultural Perspective is a collection of chapters by authors from different countries and cultures around the world. All continents—except Antarctica— are represented in these 17 chapters. The sequence starts in North America with the "Women from the United States of America and Canada" (Chapter 1). The next chapter provides an illustration of life of "Women in the Arctic," in Alaska (Chapter 2). Then attention is focused on the South American continent and the "Women in Latin America" (Chapter 3). From there the discourse moves to Europe, which includes several chapters; the first one discusses "Women in Great Britain" (Chapter 4), which is followed by Chapter 5: "Women in Poland." The next chapter (Chapter 6) reports on "Women in the USSR," which is expanded in Chapter 7 on "Soviet Women" by the author's impressions gathered during a stay as visiting professor in the Eurasian USSR. The sequence of chapters continues with a focus on the Middle East and the "Women in Israel" (Chapter 8). From there the discourse proceeds to the next continent, Africa (Chapter 9), that deals with the life-span of women in the sometimes more and sometimes less traditional environments of Egypt and the Sudan. Another African country is presented from the mostly traditional point of view of the "Women in Nigeria" (Chapter 10). From there the spotlight concentrates on the versatility of women in different countries and cultures on the Asian continent. First it follows the life-stages in the development of "The Hindu Woman in India" (Chapter 11). Next in line is an introduction to the Tharus, the "Tribal Women of India" (Chapter 12), which provides information on a group of people who are not well known outside of India. The exposition continues with a chapter on "Women in Thailand" (Chapter 13), and is succeeded by an account of "Women in China" (Chapter 14), which covers women both on the Mainland and in Taiwan. This is followed by a report on "Women in Japan" (Chapter 15). The focus then moves south to the Insular Pacific region and "Women in Western Samoa" (Chapter 16). The final chapter centers its attention on the smallest continent, Australia, and "Women in Australia" (Chapter 17).

Not only do these chapters provide fascinating and informative reading, but each author also contributes a distinct and eloquent style of writing. The readers will be impressed by the pertinent comparisons that deal with the same orthogonal and parallel outlines of most chapters. Most of these include a short historical background sketch which is then followed by an elaborate life-span exposition of women in a chronological sequence from infancy, to school years, to marriage and pregnancy/childbirth, to adult activities, to aging. This book offers an overview of women in traditional societies and the changes that occur due to a worldwide trend toward modernization in the status of women.

A novel and interesting approach of this book is that each of the contributors presents the women in his or her own country and culture from an *emic* (an insider's) point of view, while the readers relate to the variety of ethnic backgrounds from an *etic* (an outsider's) point of view. This volume provides an opportunity to compare the ways in which women all over the globe function and live in different ecologies, that is, in different climates and a variety of cultures, representing specific customs, manners, and life-styles.

In the home women hold a central position, regardless of nationality or geographic area. However, in many developed as well as developing countries, more and more women are striving for a status of equality with men in the professions and in jobs in a variety of fields. They endeavor to transcend the polarized sex roles and eliminate the sex-role concept in the workplace outside the home.

Perusing the chapters of this book, the reader is confronted with the essence of similarities that are basic to the biological prerogative of womanhood. Superimposed then on their basic functions and traits are the cultural conditions which change the life-styles of women in a variety of environments. It is probably not remarkable that in all the countries and cultures sampled in this book, a trend to change toward modernization exists, even though each population goes about it in its own specific or idiosyncratic ways. All women want to be recognized in their own right and to come closer to a status of equality with men. In certain cultures women may achieve their goals earlier than in others. Some countries may offer better opportunities and more conducive conditions. Through the advent of communication—via telephone, radio, and television, and more recently via FAX machines and BitNet—messages can be sent instantaneously to transmit verbal as well as pictorial information all around the world, wherever modern equipment has been set up, as well as the know-how to maintain it. It could well be that—as a consequence of the efficient network of communication around the globe—women, in due time, will eventually achieve a greater behavioral flexibility, a kind of sex-role transcendence, when all people can act as individuals in their own right, regardless of biological gender.

However, in the meantime, there are enormous differences in the circumstances in which women live and function. For instance, in North

America, in the United States of America and Canada, where it is accepted that women can take jobs and work outside their home, there are still only few women holding top positions in business and industry, or in professional and academic occupations. However, women are visible not only in the arts and sciences, but in community work and in the government, as well as running for elected offices. (Of course the women in the Arctic encounter additional difficulties during the process of modernization and culture change.) On the southern side of the equator, in South America, the Latin American woman faces such traditional values as the concept of *machismo*. Yet today many of the social changes are in the hands of women, including aspects of socialization of children, the education of youngsters, the guidance of the young and often the adults as well, in achieving and keeping a balance between traditional customs and modern innovations.

In Europe the Liberation Movement is in full progress in Britain, although it appears that not all women want to fall in line. Some women still seem to prefer the traditional manners, in which men treated ladies with consideration and deference, rather than dealing with them as their equals. Nevertheless, in general women seek more independence, which includes marital relationships. The situation is somewhat different in Poland, where many women move from the rural areas to an urban environment. Many changes are inherent with such altered life-styles, which include full-time employment for greater economic and social freedom. While the demands are twofold—on the one hand the needs of and obligations to the family and homelife, and on the other hand, the responsibilities and fulfillment of duties to the job—Polish women have shown that they can handle such challenges and keep the balance by creating a successful interaction between their housekeeping duties and their jobs. For quite some years Russian women had the reputation for having achieved "Equal Rights with Men;" although on close inspection it appears that the equal status with men is not yet completely reached, neither at the workplace, nor at home where "Women in the USSR" take care of the childrearing duties and all the household chores.

Other situations face Israeli women. These include cleavages within Jewish society between immigrants from industrialized Western democracies, and immigrants from non-industrialized Islamic countries of the Middle East and North Africa. However, whether the young girl is raised in a kibbutz setting or within a traditional family fold, she faces a compulsory two-year tour of duty in the army. For a mother, the induction of a son or daughter brings about more mothering, or like an intensification of such activities, which results in a "crowded nest syndrome" when the soldiers return home one to three weekends per month. Women in Israel have made great strides in modernization, but equality with men has not yet been reached.

For the women in Africa the struggle to be recognized and to improve their status is also still in progress; there remains a wide gap between equal rights under the law and the actual circumstances. Even though the Women's Liberation Movement was started much earlier in Egypt than in the Sudan, the goals of women in Egypt have still to be realized. Specific issues need even greater disclosure to effect drastic changes with the traditional custom of the painful female circumcision, which seems more prevalent in rural regions than in the big cities. Another important issue is that of education. There are fewer girls going to school, especially in rural districts. But those girls that can get an education through to a university degree find it more difficult to get married. For instance, in recent years ads appeared in newspapers for men and women to meet possible future spouses. In general, men seem to specify that the women should be younger, shorter, and less educated than they are. In Nigeria each tribe follows more or less different customs for some of the same practices, which can include marriage arrangement for the yet unborn girls, and allows for provisions in cases of divorce (mostly for childlessness) and widowhood.

In the Hindu family in India the birth of a boy is still preferred to that of a girl. While both boys and girls get an education, a well-educated young woman has a better chance to meet a husband (as seen in the matrimonial ads in the newspapers, where the young women's education and beauty are emphasized); education also gives the parents of the prospective bride an opportunity to negotiate for a smaller dowry. However, Indian women generally—although they seem to be on the right track to secure a place of equality with the men, as well as an individual identity for themselves—still remain more or less subservient to their mothers-in-law in the family tradition. Yet there is another view of women in India which is found in the tribal communities, among them the Tharu women in the northern regions of India. These women have dominant positions in their communities. They are industrious workers in the fields and skillful artisans in the production of artifacts that can be sold in the markets. Tharu women have a unique place in their society: they hold a superior rank and are in charge of family affairs. However, the Tharu men rely on their women and do not function independently. Buddist Thailand is another country in which one finds traditional life-styles—such as birth and childrearing practices—co-existing with modern attitudes and values, especially among the working women in urban areas. Women's roles in agriculture and the rural economy have given them an important status in their communities. However, many move to the cities where they experience life in a modernizing society with many advances in technology that lead to sociocultural changes.

Not only are women's roles changing, but their countries are also in the process of transition. The two Chinas, the Peoples Republic of China on the Mainland, and Taiwan in the Western Pacific, are a case in point. While the Communist and the Nationalist governments officially established equality for Chinese women in education and career opportunities, women's economic status is not equal with men's. Marriage and motherhood—only one child per couple is allowed on the Mainland—are highly valued in the modern Chinas. But frequently the young mothers experience a conflict in their expected roles of factory or office workers and the traditional roles of homemakers and loving caregivers with their child or children. For example, the government on the Mainland provides daycare centers for working mothers—with time out for breast feeding the babies—while in Taiwan there exists a shortage of private daycare centers. However, the most progressive advances in modern China are that women no longer have to submit to their tyrannical mothers-in-law, and that marriages are no longer arranged by the parents. Laws stipulate that women can vote, and can receive up to 70 percent of their retirement benefits if they retire at the age of 50 years. While social benefits do exist for women, equality with men is still elusive. In the current society in Japan, which still recognizes traditional values, there have been many changes since World War II. Nowadays love-matches have increased for young people. Young couples live by themselves after their wedding ceremony—at a large hotel or in some public hall—for their honeymoon. However, the divorce rate has also increased since the war years. Interestingly, this trend is not only found in the young, but among older couples as well. Yet in present-day Japan, conditions are conducive for women to have a more pleasant and enjoyable life than was the case in the past.

Next in the discourse comes one of the largest, essentially pure Polynesian groups of people in the Pacific, the people of Western Samoa (although some Chinese and Europeans live among them). At least 400 women hold the title of "Chief" for their extended family, showing that women can manage the responsibilities and hold the respect for handling the family's affairs. Yet sex-stereotyped behavior is reinforced throughout the female's life-span. Great strides are being accomplished by women in the economy, especially in the monetized sector, that is, in working for wages or salaries. This rise in the economy is not true for the subsistence factor, which is identified as people who work to grow, gather, or catch food to eat. Few women work in the small farms, yet more and more women are engaged in social and personal service industries. However, in recent years the government has developed rural development programs and especially encouraged women to submit proposals for these government-funded projects. In addition, the Department of Agriculture has provided women with training in various specialties of food production and vegetable garden projects. These turned out to be successful ventures for improving both health and the family economy.

Last but by no means least is a report on the Australian woman. She is spirited and energetic in dealing with current conditions at home, and expresses her opinions on government issues and politics. The Australian woman is perhaps not a totally liberated woman, but she is moving closer to equal status with the Australian man. She has achieved recognition in the arts and sciences, and she is getting closer to conquering more fields of endeavor.

Women in Cross-Cultural Perspective gives the reader a better understanding and a more complete appreciation of the enormous varieties and great differences in the ecologies in which women live and function. At the same time, however, there exist striking similarities across cultures and climates, due to the biological prerogative of motherhood. These chapters allow the reader to get a glimpse of the hardships and difficulties women face and try to overcome in striving to fulfil their potentials, whether they live in a modern environment or in a traditional setting. Regardless of the geographical area, each chapter presents women from a life-span point of view in a cross-national, cross-ethnic, and cross-cultural perspective.

Women
in Cross-Cultural Perspective

S. Janet A. Fitzgerald, O.P., Ph.D. (left), President of Molloy College, and Leonore Loeb Adler, Ph.D. (right), Director of the ICCCES and Social Psychologist in the Department of Psychology, Molloy College

Photo credit: John Galaskas

1

Women in the United States of America and Canada

Florence L. Denmark, Laurel Schwartz, and Kathleen Maurer Smith

The United States of America and Canada are Western, industrialized nations that share a border, said to be one of the world's friendliest, which extends for 3,986 miles (Kane, 1976). These two countries, along with Mexico and the large island of Greenland, make up the North American continent. The United States of America covers an area of 3,618,770 square miles and contains a population of 244 million. It is the fourth largest nation in the world in both area and population. Canada, in contrast, is larger, covering 3,851,809 square miles (making it the second largest country in the world after the Soviet Union), but contains far fewer people, since its population is 25,700,000. As a result, Canada's population density is only six people per square mile, while in the United States of America it is 67 per square mile. The United States of America contains 50 states, 48 of which are contiguous on the mainland, as well as Alaska and Hawaii. Canada consists of ten provinces and two territories.

The United States of America is a federal republic while Canada is a confederation. The latter is a free, independent democracy with a parliamentary form of government, although Britain's Queen Elizabeth II is considered the head of state. Both countries had been under control of the British empire, but the colonies that were later to become the United States of America mounted a revolution in 1776 which resulted in their independence. Many residents of the colonies who were still loyal to the crown emigrated north and settled in Canada, which was still under British control. Instead of a revolutionary break with Britain, Canada's greater autonomy evolved during the nineteenth century. Both countries therefore have their roots in British culture, although Canada has a large French-speaking population as well, which is concentrated primarily in the province of Quebec (Kane, 1976). In spite of the initial British influence, both countries have become nations of immigrants, which contributes to their rich cultural diversity (Duggan, 1979).

The United States of America is recognized as the world's premier economic and political power. This has caused Canada to experience an identity problem due to living in the shadow of the United States of America (Malcolm, 1985). While their similar backgrounds, similar experiences (such as industrialization, urbanization, and economic prosperity), and close proximity to each other have led to a great similarity of culture between these two nations, Canadians dislike being thought of as exactly like the citizens of the United States of America. Some cultural differences do indeed exist. For example, Canadians tend to be somewhat more conservative and more conscious of social and economic differences than are people in the United States of America (Duggan, 1979).

MODERN WOMEN IN THE UNITED STATES OF AMERICA AND CANADA

In spite of Canada's desire for a separate identity, as well as the few differences that do exist between the United States of America and Canada historically and culturally, on the whole the experiences of women in these two countries have been remarkably similar. In both countries, for example, industrialization led to a shift from a household economy to a market economy. This has had a profound effect on the role of women in society, since the importance of the domestic role was diminished. This trend occurred because the economic significance of such a role in a market economy is not recognized to the extent that it was in the household economy which existed prior to industrialization when most families lived and worked on farms (Blumstein & Schwartz, 1985).

During World War II women entered the labor force in large numbers to replace the male workers who had gone to fight the war. This allowed women to experience new opportunities and develop new skills. When the war ended, however, women were expected to give up their jobs to the returning men. Women's resumption of the domestic role contributed to the great increase in population that has come to be known as the postwar "baby boom." The decade of the 1950s became very family-centered and child-oriented. Couples tended to marry young and begin their families right away. In the 1960s, however, this began to change. The development of reliable means of artificial birth control allowed couples to plan and limit their families (Blumstein & Schwartz, 1985). This, along with an economic recession and the spiraling inflation that was experienced during the 1970s, contributed to a marked decline in the birth rate from 3.6 births per woman of childbearing age (between 18 and 44) in 1960, to 1.8 births in 1980 (Seager & Olson, 1986). As a result, the family of today is generally smaller than it had been previously. In addition, many families have met the economic challenges of the 1970s and 1980s by having two wage earners. Women once again entered the labor force in unprecedented numbers (Clark, 1987).

In general, in both the United States of America and Canada, there has been an attempt to redefine women's roles in order that women may experience sexual equality in society. In each country, a feminist movement appeared in order to push for reforms that would lead to this equality. However, although women received the right to vote in both the United States of America and Canada in 1920, they still have not achieved political and economic equality. Those who hold elected office and positions of influence on federal, state, and local levels are still overwhelmingly male. In addition, the Equal Rights Amendment to the United States of America Constitution, which was to have guaranteed equal rights under the law regardless of sex, has never been ratified (Clark, 1987). It appears that although some changes have occurred with regard to the role of women in these countries, they still have quite a way to go before equality between the sexes is achieved.

INFANCY AND EARLY CHILDHOOD

Parent-Child Relationships

The United States of America and Canada are both very child-centered societies. Although children are no longer considered economic assets, as they had been when the economy was rooted in agricultural production, couples still desire to have children primarily for emotional reasons. As family size has decreased and general affluence has increased, the result is that, in general, there are more resources available to provide for each child. Parents often express the desire to bestow upon their children all the comforts and opportunities that they themselves may have missed as children.

As more children are being raised in dual-income families as well as single-parent families (due to the high rates of divorce and unwed parenthood), however, there has been some concern expressed about the amount of care and supervision that children are receiving from their parents today. Due to the lack of adequate childcare facilities and the limited number of employers who allow for maternity and paternity leaves and other such family-support measures, caring properly for children continues to be problematic for working parents.

Sex-Typing and Socialization

At birth, we are all confronted with expectations for our behavior as defined by the society in which we live. We are expected to adapt and conform to those behaviors that are designated appropriate to our gender. Although there are many aspects to the complete socialization process, acquisition of sex-role behavior is defined by some theorists as the most potent and long-lasting (Katz, 1979). Gender labeling cannot be avoided. It is a major determinant on the configuration of women's lives.

In recent years, a great deal of research has been done regarding the sex-role socialization that takes place in the United States of America and Canada. Studies have shown that sex-differential treatment begins at birth and continues throughout life. However, stereotypical attitudes toward what is considered gender-appropriate are evident even prior to birth. Many people believe, for example, that an active fetus is male, while a less active fetus is assumed to be female (Lewis, 1972b). Research also shows that among parents who want to select the sex of their unborn child, boys are preferred over girls. This preference is greatest for the first-born child and is based on the feeling that a girl should have an older brother, since it is often believed that a boy would be stronger and wiser and she would therefore benefit from his guidance and protection (Jaccoma & Denmark, 1974).

Another interesting observation is that, at birth, parents tend to view their female newborn as being small, delicate, and fragile. The male, by comparison, is described by his parents as being more alert, stronger, and better coordinated (Williams, 1983). These differing perceptions will certainly influence the way in which each child is treated by his or her parents.

The physical environment of infants is subject to sex-differential treatment as well. The girl's room differs from the boy's in that it is more likely to be decorated in pink with ruffles and flowers. The toys selected for her also differ, typically including dolls and soft stuffed animals (Katz, 1979). Her clothing is likely to be yellow, pink, or white in color as blue is reserved for the male. The style of a girl's clothing will often be one that is nonfunctional, such as a frilly dress, while the apparel that is commonly worn by boys is likely to be sturdier and less confining (Denmark, 1977).

Although most infant behaviors do not show gender differences (Hyde, 1985), males and females experience not only different physical environments, but different social environments as well (Katz, 1979). Prior to six months of age, boys receive more physical stimulation than girls and are handled more roughly (Maccoby & Jackson, 1974). After six months, however, it is the females who are touched more frequently, which is a pattern that continues throughout their lives (Lewis & Rosenblum, 1974). Males might initially receive more physical contact due to their being more valued, or due to their greater irritability and longer hours of wakefulness (Denmark, 1977). The decline in physical contact that occurs later is generally attributed to cultural influences which lead mothers to expect that their sons should be more independent (Alberle & Naegele, 1952; Lewis, 1972b).

At the age of 13 months, boys spend longer periods of time away from their mothers and venture longer distances than girls of the same age. Nursery schools receive more applications for boys than for girls, suggesting that mothers are more willing to separate from sons than from daughters (Sherman, 1971). Another difference that has been observed in the ways in which parents interact with their young children is that girl babies are looked at and talked to more than boys (Lewis, 1972a). The female's subsequent superior verbal skills, something she maintains throughout her lifetime, may be attributed to this greater verbal stimulation. That she is looked at more than a male may be responsible for the greater sensitivity to social stimulation and greater self-consciousness about her physical appearance that is common among females in society (Katz, 1979).

A father's relationship to his infant is also affected by sex. He has a tendency to spend more time with his infant son than his daughter. As a matter of fact, by the time the child reaches the age of two, the father spends only half as much time with his daughter as with his son. In addition, fathers are generally more prone to sex-type the activities of their children than mothers (Denmark, 1977). A consequence of this is that daughters often attempt to win their fathers' attention and approval by engaging in stereotypical female behavior such as passivity and dependence (Williams, 1983).

By the age of two, most children have learned gender concepts and are capable of gender self-classification. At a later age, gender concepts include psychological traits. Young children of both sexes tend to view males as being more dangerous and punishing than females. One study (Kagan & Lemkin, 1960) showed that six-year-old boys were more likely to designate their fathers and themselves as larger, darker, more angular, and more dangerous than their mothers and other females. These qualities are generally thought of as being stereotypical male traits.

By the early preschool years, the number of observed sex differences has increased. Aggression, which first appears at the age of two, is found to a greater degree in boys than in girls. Boys are more likely than girls to engage in physically rougher play activities (Denmark, 1977). Girls, however, demonstrate more verbal and milder forms of aggression (Feshbach, 1970), suggesting that, although viewed as a male attribute, aggression may simply be expressed differently by the two sexes (Denmark, 1977).

Sex differences are also observed in toy and game preference. Two- and three-year-old girls sew, string beads, and play at housekeeping, while boys play with guns, toy trucks, and carpentry (Maccoby & Jackson, 1974). Boys' play is active and imaginative and is involved with the acquisition of skills, whereas girls' play is often passive and sedentary. The difference in orientations may be attributed to stereotypical concepts of appropriate gender behavior, which are culturally and socially promoted (Denmark, 1977).

THE SCHOOL YEARS

The Educational System

In the United States of America and Canada, education has always been viewed as a means of increasing one's social status and improving one's economic position. Elementary and secondary education are considered so essential that they are currently provided free of charge by the state or provincial governments in the form of public schools. Higher education is provided by colleges and universities. It is interesting to note that in 1982, the proportion of women students enrolled in college was 51 percent in both countries. This is roughly the same proportion that women represent of the total population. Prior to 1982, women had been underrepresented in colleges and universities.

Achievement and Socialization

The differential socialization that children receive according to gender continues when they attend school. In nursery school, girls are found to be more emotionally mature, adapting to their new environment with greater ease than boys (activity levels and longer attention spans), to interact more with teachers, and to seek help more frequently. However, this behavior coincides with the expectations held by teachers and parents. Girls are docile, sociable, and dependent, and therefore such behaviors often are inadvertently encouraged and reinforced (Katz, 1979).

In grade school, boys still experience difficulty in the school environment and are referred for psychological evaluation and found in remedial classes more often than girls (Dreger et al., 1964; Spivak & Spotts, 1965; Werry & Quay, 1971). This variation in male and female behavior can be explained by the boys' view of school as a feminine place administered by female teachers who value behaviors that are gender-appropriate for girls, including obedience and the suppression of aggression and motor activity (Kagan, 1964).

Although the stated sex-role expectations for boys and girls in the school environment are similar, sex-role stereotypes are reinforced through textbooks, course content, teachers, and career counseling (Levitin & Chananie, 1972). When children attend school they are exposed to the subordinate position of women in the educational system itself. Elementary school teachers are overwhelmingly female (almost 90 percent), but nearly 90 percent of all school principals are male. Men also make up the great majority of other administrators and schoolboard members.

Gender-role stereotypes have been found to be perpetuated by school textbooks in which females are frequently shown in dependent or domestic roles, while males are shown to be active and competent. Boys are overrepresented in action and adventure stories while girls are more frequently portrayed as onlookers who are seen as passive and ineffectual (Katz, 1979). In addition, history textbooks have consistently omitted references to the achievements of women.

Boys have been found to benefit from the remedial programs that they are referred to in larger numbers than are girls, as well as the additional time that teachers and volunteers are willing to spend with them to upgrade their verbal skills, which tend to lag behind those of females. In junior high and high school boys continue to benefit from this additional attention. Junior high teachers of both sexes initiate more positive contacts with boys, provide boys with more opportunities to respond, and are more likely to facilitate more interactions of all types with boys. Some of these interactions are thought to be significant in promoting higher achievement motivation and more analytical skills for the male students (Good, Sikes, & Brophy, 1973).

Teachers and guidance counselors often steer students into career choices that are deemed appropriate for their sex. Girls are often encouraged into fields such as nursing and teaching, while boys are directed toward medicine, engineering, or business (Chafetz, 1978).

While no sex difference in self-esteem is found to exist during middle childhood, by the end of grade school girls begin to evaluate themselves more negatively, with this difference indicating either greater maturity or greater conflict (Silvern, 1978). At puberty, achievement and femininity often become incompatible for the female. Rewarded for her intellectual performance throughout her life so far, competence in areas outside of the domestic arena now becomes antithetical to what is considered appropriate gender-role behavior. As a result, while her school performance up to this point has been superior to that of males, now a reverse trend is seen, with her performance declining and his improving (Lynn, 1972).

In recreational activities, girls are more likely to associate with one or two close companions than to play in large groups, perhaps due to the fact that the relationship takes precedence over the activity (Denmark, 1977). Boys are encouraged to participate in group activities and sports. It is through these media that they are taught achievement skills and competitive behavior skills (Denmark, 1977). Competition and winning remain fairly unfamiliar experiences for females (Denmark, 1977). Girls who are taught competitive behavior will often experience negative consequences, especially in mixed-sex situations (Horner, 1970). The only competition that is considered gender-appropriate is either for a mate or for the approval of others (Boslooper & Hayes, 1973).

Values and Interests

For girls in middle childhood and throughout adulthood, there is a preference for the masculine role and greater ambivalence regarding a clear-cut identification with the feminine role. Boys are more likely to identify unequivocally with the male role, and thus do not show this cross-sex preference. Girls have greater freedom to state a cross-sex preference and engage in cross-sex activities, especially prior to adolescence, but the preference for the male role could also be attributed to the female's perception of the male role as being invested with higher status, greater rewards, and greater opportunity for self-actualization (Williams, 1983).

Although femininity is desirable and necessary if the young girl is to be viewed as successful, albeit in her own limited sphere, the price she pays is her competency. She is asked to reduce her physical and intellectual skills, whereas the boy is expected to increase his (Rosenberg, 1972). Her status is determined more by her attractiveness than by her accomplishments, as she becomes increasingly self-conscious and people-oriented (Hyde, 1985).

The male grows up anticipating a career, with education and work emphasized in his development. The female, however, has not been encouraged in this direction to a great extent, since it is in direct contradiction to the expectations held for her by society. She is encouraged to see her future role as a wife and mother with home and family her priority, even if she also has a career (Hyde, 1985).

MARRIAGE

Patterns of Mate Selection

In the United States of America and Canada, mate choice is considered to be free and people marry because they have "fallen in love" with each other. In reality, however, parents have a great deal of informal influence regarding those whom their children ultimately choose to marry. Since people can marry only those whom they meet, parents can affect these possibilities by deciding what neighborhoods to live in, what schools their children attend, and with what friends they are allowed to associate. In addition, throughout the child's upbringing, they convey to him or her the characteristics that are considered by the family to be highly desirable in a spouse. They also will express approval or disapproval regarding whom their children choose to date (Goode, 1959). As a result, people in the United States of America and Canada tend to marry people who are socially similar to themselves, especially with regard to race, religion, and social class (Eckland, 1968).

Marriage Arrangements

Male expectations of the marriage arrangement have traditionally included the idea that their wives will be responsible for domestic life (Katz, 1979). Society has expected women not only to take on these domestic duties, but to perform them gladly (Williams, 1983). This expectation, however, often places many women in a role that underutilizes their abilities and restricts their development (Williams, 1983). Many young wives suppress achievement urges in favor of accomplishing the wife-mother role (Lipman-Blumen, 1972; Papanek, 1973). In addition, housework, for most women, is largely viewed with dissatisfaction due to the loneliness, monotony, long hours and lack of structure (Oakley, 1974).

Marriage is still thought of as giving a woman status and economic security, although this status is generally dependent on her husband's occupation and activities rather than her own (Williams, 1983). This is true even when the wife is also a wage earner, as is the case in a growing number of families today.

Families

Due to the economic realities that have created a need in recent years for women to work outside the home, the traditional "ideal" family, which consists of a father who is the sole breadwinner and a mother who is a full-time homemaker with two or more children to take care of, has faded from prominence (Masnick & Bane, 1980). Even though there are greater numbers of women in the work force, United States of America and Canadian cultural values still uphold the idea that a woman's top priority should be her family (Kane, 1976). This has led to the creation of a new role to which women are expected to aspire. This role is that of a "supermom" who works full-time in paid employment yet continues to take full responsibility for the care and feeding of the family (Hewlett, 1986). As women have moved rapidly into the occupational sphere, there has not, as of yet, been an equal movement of men into the domestic sphere. One study showed that between 1965 and 1985, while employed wives had reduced the amount of time that they spent caring for the family (e.g., cooking, housework, childcare, etc.) from 29 to 25 hours per week, husbands only increased their time spent in these activities from 9 to 9.7 hours per week (Robinson, 1977).

There is potential for a fundamental change in the marriage relationship with a movement toward greater equality and a concurrent demise of the patriarchal family structure in which the man is the head of the household and the wife and children are subservient and economically dependent. This change can be attributed to the "ESE factor," which consists of three components: educational, sexual, and economic freedom for women (O'Neill & O'Neill, 1972).

Divorce

One marriage in three now ends in divorce (Williams, 1983). As income becomes available to women and the stigma of divorce lessens, more women initiate divorce and separation than do men (Chodorow, 1978). Even though the increased financial burdens as well as the change in status and roles are stressful, many women experience new advantages as a single parent such as increased autonomy and independence (Hyde, 1985). It should be noted, however, that divorce usually creates greater economic hardship among women than it does among men. Studies have shown that after divorce, economic conditions generally improve for men while they deteriorate for women. Women are more likely to retain custody of the children, and many of them are faced with partial payment or nonpayment of alimony and child support. This contributes to the feminization of poverty, since single-parent families that are female-headed are disproportionately represented among families that have incomes below the poverty level (Weitzman, 1985).

PREGNANCY AND CHILDBIRTH

Attitudes and Practices

Most individuals anticipate that parenting will be a central experience in their lives. For a woman, however, motherhood is viewed as the ultimate feminine fulfillment. It is a source of personal identity and self-esteem, and a way of attaining adult status. For many women, competence is not defined in terms of academic and occupational accomplishments, but rather in terms of their ability to conceive, gestate, deliver, and nurse a baby, thereby proving their feminine identity (Katz, 1979).

The centrality of motherhood to a woman's identity has been called the "motherhood mandate" (Russo, 1979). This mandate states that a woman should have at least two children and immediately attend to their every need. If infant care comes before any other interest, she is a "good mother." The image of the ideal mother is full of self-abnegation (Denmark, 1977), and the belief that a mother of young children who does anything else on a regular basis is guilty of neglect is still widespread and influential (Williams, 1983).

The actual practice of birthing was exclusively handled by women until the middle of the nineteenth century in the United States of America and Canada (Wertz & Wertz, 1979). Physicians, most of whom were male, then began to include the delivery of babies as one of their services and transformed birth from a social event to a medical one. This is reflected in the fact that the caesarean delivery rate increased almost 300 percent over a ten-year period to the point where, in 1981, almost one out of five babies born in the United States of America was born by caesarean. This rate has continued to rise, with middle- and upper-class women at higher risk for this type of delivery than lower-class women (Hurst & Summey, 1984). Even the event of natural birth moved from the home to the hospital and became defined as a pathological process. In the last few years, however, aspects of this medical model have been challenged (Williams, 1983).

Preparation for Childrearing

Little is taught through formal education about being a parent. Frequently, women are psychologically unprepared for the biological aspects of pregnancy and childbirth and the subsequent care of the infant (Rossi,

1968). It is not unusual for a woman to experience her first pregnancy with very little knowledge about the physiological changes or what to expect during labor and delivery.

In regard to maternal skills, no formal source of instruction or training exists. Most women learn maternal skills through vicarious modeling and the observation of mothering figures, which often leads to insecurity and ambivalence for the first-time mother (Denmark, 1978). Some negative aspects of motherhood include the curtailment of personal freedom, tedium associated with the extended care of young children, loss of privacy, fatigue, and a frequent lack of interaction with other adults (Denmark, 1978).

The view of motherhood as a woman's ultimate fulfillment, as well as the fixation on only its pleasurable aspects, often has negative consequences for women who have attempted to conform to this view. It has led them to have enormous expectations that cannot be met. It has left them with very little to look forward to after their childbearing years. It has also made it difficult for women to express any negative or ambivalent attitudes toward motherhood. Since she has been led to expect only joy and happiness from motherhood, she has often been left feeling disappointed, inadequate, guilty, and anxious (Denmark, 1978). It is not surprising, then, that there is a prevalence of depression among women with young children (Richman, 1976).

Although negative or ambivalent attitudes toward motherhood are met with social disapproval, there are women who are making a conscious choice not to have children or to have smaller families (Katz, 1979). These women generally have high levels of autonomy and are achievement-oriented (Houseknecht, 1979). Interestingly, married couples without children report greater happiness than do married couples with children (Campbell, Converse, & Rodgers, 1975).

Mother-Infant Bonding

All infants have certain emotional needs that must be met, including the needs for affection and approval. This is essential to the development of the child's self-esteem. Since cultural tradition dictates that mothers should be the primary caregivers with regard to children, they usually find themselves assuming the responsibility for their children's emotional well-being. This cultural expectation has led to the myth of the "maternal instinct," which assumes that women come naturally by their ability to provide for their children and that men do not. This is simply not the case (Hoffman & Nye, 1974). Studies show that fathers, when given the chance, are able to display nurturant behavior as well as mothers do (Parke & Swain, 1976). It appears, then, that being in the role of primary caregiver has more to do with parent-infant bonding than does the sex of the parent.

ADULT ACTIVITIES

Career Opportunities

In 1950, 29.6 percent of the civilian labor force in the United States of America were women. In 1970 this proportion had increased to 38.2 percent, and by 1985 the figure grew still further to 43 percent. Similarly, in Canada women now comprise 41 percent of the total work force. In both countries, more than half of all adult women are employed (Masnick & Bane, 1980).

Even though women have increased their participation in the occupational world in the last few decades, inequality still exists with regard to wages (Smith, 1979). Median salary figures in the United States of America for 1981 indicated a gap between men's and women's wages. White men earned $21,160, while white women earned $12,287. A gap also exists between black men and women since black men's median wage that year was $15,119, while black women earned $11,312 (Russo & Denmark, 1984). The wage discrepancy between the sexes is also reflected in the fact that the average male high school dropout earned $1,600 more a year than the average female college graduate (Friedan, 1981).

At present, women earn only 62 percent of men's wages, which has hardly improved over the 61 percent that women earned as compared with men in 1960. Much of this can be explained by the fact that approximately 40 percent of all women working today are concentrated in nine sex-segregated job categories. Such jobs include that of typist, bookkeeper, household worker, secretary, elementary schoolteacher, waitress, cashier, seamstress, and nurse (Blau, 1978). Most women work in the clerical and service sectors. These jobs tend to be low-paying, low-status jobs with little opportunity for advancement (Kahl, 1983). The Equal Pay Act of 1963 in the United States of America has obviously not been able to deal with this structured inequality, although laws mandating equal pay for comparable worth would be effective in eliminating such wage discrepancies. At present, there is no such federal law in the United States of America. In Canada, however, a comparable worth measure was passed by the legislature in Ontario in 1987. Stereotypes involving women and work include the idea that women work only for pin money, when, in fact, they work out of economic necessity. Women have been accused of higher turnover rates and absenteeism. According to the United States of America Department of Labor (1969), however, the rate is higher only in low-paying, low-skill level jobs. When given the same job and the same pay as men, women compared favorably with them (United States of America Department of Labor, Women's Bureau, 1969).

One prevalent notion is that a woman who is truly ambitious and qualified can get ahead. In reality, women face outright job discrimination in the work force today (Hyde, 1985). Women start with lower-ranking jobs and are less frequently promoted. In addition, sex-role stereotypes often influence personnel decisions, with males tending to discriminate against women in decisions involving promotion, development, and supervision. There appears to be a biased tendency to minimize or to completely ignore female ability (Denmark & Fernandez, 1985).

External barriers, however, are not the only obstacles that need to be overcome. Women themselves often contribute to their lack of success in the occupational sphere. While males tend to give higher estimates of success expectancy, females generally do not, regardless of how well they performed the task in the past (Crandall, 1969). The conflict between achievement and femininity is again evident, with women expecting some kind of societal rejection for what they consider to be gender-inappropriate behavior (Horner, 1969).

AGING

Since women have been socialized to be as sexually attractive as possible in order to find a mate, marry, and become a mother, aging is particularly difficult for them. Their most socially valued qualities have dwindled and many of them have never acquired any other emotional or professional resources (Williams, 1983). When children leave home, many women experience a lack of meaning and purpose in their lives. The term "empty nest syndrome" has been used to describe the depression that some women experience at this time (Hyde, 1985). For many women, however, the predominant feeling that they experience at this time is one of relief (Rubin, 1979).

The average age of menopause in women is 49 (Perlmutter, 1978). Only 10 to 15 percent of women have physical or emotional problems that are severe enough to require medical care. Yet menopause, too, may promote feelings of depression, depending on the extent to which the woman has identified exclusively with her roles as a mother and wife and invested in them her self-esteem and value (Shafer, 1970).

Despite the loss of her reproductive capacity, a woman's sex drive remains stable and less susceptible to the effects of aging than a man's. In their forties and fifties women frequently have a renewed interest in sex due to release from the strains of childcare and fear of pregnancy (Williams, 1983). One of the most significant factors influencing sexual behavior in older women is the problem of the availability of a partner. As they age the ratio of men to women declines drastically. Women have a longer life expectancy than men and are therefore more likely to be widowed (United States of America Department of Commerce, 1973). Among adults over 65, 14 percent of men are widowed as compared with 52 percent of women (Marquis Academic Media, 1979). With the average age of widowhood at 56, it is fairly common for a woman to face the next 15 to 20 years of her life alone, since life expectancy for women is 78 years (Bernardo, 1968). Another factor that affects the availability of a partner is the double standard of aging (Sontag, 1972; Berman, O'Nan, & Floyd, 1981), whereby men, unlike women, are still viewed as attractive as they get older. Although men have lost their youth they still maintain a significant attribute—power. As a result, many of the few available older men will pair off with younger women, diminishing the numbers of men available to older women even further.

As a woman grows older, she becomes less restricted to the mother role when her children leave home. Since she is often younger than her husband she may still be working while he is retired and maintaining the household. It is interesting to note that as people age, the gender roles that once had been so critical in forming and defining their identity become more relaxed and, in some cases, even reversed (Hyde, 1985).

WOMEN TODAY: TRADITION AND CHANGE

Women in the United States of America and Canada have always been faced with cultural expectations that have shaped their lives. The effects of these expectations on women have created limitations for them in social, economic, educational, and political spheres. Changes have been occurring in these areas in recent years, however, that have led to a reexamination of traditional gender roles in the family and society. As women's participation in the spheres outside of the family increases, this will necessitate change in their familial roles as well. This has not yet been accomplished, however, since for many women their roles outside the family have simply been added onto their unaltered domestic role, thus placing extraordinary demands on them. In addition, it appears that the traditional socialization that females experience while growing up will have to undergo some alteration as well, in order that women may be adequately prepared to be successful in performing roles outside of the home as well as within it.

CONCLUSION

The effects of gender labeling as it applies to the acquisition of sex-role behavior and its effect on women's lives have been examined. Although generalizations may be made as to the ways in which women's lives are shaped and influenced by these societal and cultural expectations, women must also look within themselves. They must examine and then change the expectations that they, too, have held, whether self-imposed or not, as they strive for further development as individuals and full contributors to the world in which they live.

REFERENCES

Alberle, D. F., & Naegele, K. D. (1952). Middle-class father's occupational role and attitudes toward children. *American Journal of Orthopsychiatry, 22,* 366-378.

Berman, P. W., O'Nan, B. A., & Floyd, W. (1981). The double standard of aging and the social situation. *Sex Roles, 7,* 87-96.

Bernardo, F. (1968). Widowhood status in the United States: Perspective on a neglected aspect of the family life-cycle. *Family Coordinator, 17,* 191-203.

Blau, F. (1978). The data on women workers, past, present, future. In A. Stromberg & S. Harkness (Eds.). *Women working: Theories and facts in perspective.* Palo Alto, CA: Mayfield.

Blumstein, P., & Schwartz, P. (1985). The American couple in historical perspective. In J. M. Henslin (Ed.). *Marriage and family in changing society* (pp. 34-42). New York: The Free Press.

Boslooper, T., & Hayes, M. (1973). *The femininity game.* New York: Stein and Day.

Campbell, A., Converse, P. E., & Rodgers, W. L. (1975). *The quality of American life.* Ann Arbor, MI: ISR Social Science Archive.

Chafetz, J. S. (1978). *Masculine, feminine or human?* Itasca, IL: F. E. Peacock Publishers.

Chodorow, N. (1978). *The reproduction of mothering.* Berkeley, CA: University of California Press.

Clark, J. F. (1987). *Almanac of American women in the twentieth century.* New York: Prentice-Hall Press.

Crandall, V. (1969). Sex differences in expectancy of intellectual and academic reinforcement. In C. Smith (Ed.). *Achievement-related motives.* New York: Russell Sage Foundation.

Denmark, F. L. (1977). *What Sigmund Freud didn't know about women.* Paper presented at the Convocation, St. Olaf's College, Northfield, MN.

Denmark, F. L. (1978). Psychological adjustment to motherhood. In B.B. Wolman (Ed.). *Psychological aspects of gynecology and obstetrics.* Oradell, NJ: Medical Economics Company.

Denmark, F. L., & Fernandez, L. C. (1985). Psychological issues of women and work. In G. M. Vroman, D. Burnham, & S. G. Gordon (Eds.). *Women at work: Socialization toward inequality. Gene & Gender, Vol. 5.* (pp. 102-114). New York: Gordon Press.

Dreger, R. M., Lewis, P. M., Rich, T. A., Miller, K. S., Overlade, D. C., Taffel, C., & Flemming, A. L. (1964). Behavioral classification project. *Journal of Consulting Psychology, 28,* 1-13.

Duggan, W. R. (1979). *Our neighbor upstairs: The Canadians.* Chicago, IL: Nelson-Hall.

Eckland, B. K. (1968). Theories of mate selection. *Eugenics Quarterly, 15,* 17-23.

Feshbach, S. (1970). Aggression. In P. H. Mussen (Ed.). *Carmichael's manual of child psychology.* New York: Wiley.

Friedan, B. (1981). *The second stage*. New York: Summit Books.

Good, T. L., Sikes, J. N., & Brophy, J. E. (1973). Effects of teacher sex and student sex on classroom interaction. *Journal of Educational Psychology, 65*, 74-87.

Goode, W. J. (1959). The theoretical importance of love. *American Sociological Review, 24*(1), 38-47.

Hewlett, S. A. (1986). *A lesser life: The myth of women's liberation in America* (p. 35). New York: Morrow.

Hoffman, L. W., & Nye, F. I. (1974). *Working mothers*. San Francisco, CA: Jossey-Bass.

Horner, M. S. (1969). Fail: Bright women. *Psychology Today, 3*,(6), 36ff.

Horner, M. S. (1970). Femininity and successful achievement: Basic inconsistency. In J. M. Bardwick, E. Douvan, M. S. Horner, & D. Gutman (Eds.). *Feminine personality and conflict*. Belmont, CA: Brooks/Cole.

Houseknecht, S. K. (1979). Childlessness and marital adjustment. *Journal of Marriage and the Family, 41*(2), 259-265.

Hurst, M., & Summey, P.S. (1984). Childbirth and social class: The case of caesarean delivery. *Social Science and Medicine, 18*, 621-631.

Hyde, J. S. (1985). *Half the human experience: The psychology of women*. Lexington, MA: Denison University.

Jaccoma, G., & Denmark, F. L. (1974). *Boys or girls: The hows and whys*. Unpublished master's thesis, Hunter College, CUNY.

Kagan, J. (1964). The child's sex-role classification of school objects. *Child Development, 35*, 19-51.

Kagan, J., & Lemkin, J. (1960). The child's differential perception of parental attributes. *Journal of Abnormal and Social Psychology, 61*, 446.

Kahl, A. (1983). Characteristics of job entrants in 1980-1981. *Occupational Outlook Quarterly, 27*(1), 18-26.

Kane, R. S. (1976). *Canada A to Z*. Garden City, NY: Doubleday.

Katz, P. A. (1979). The development of the female identity. In C. B. Kopp & M. Fitzpatrick (Eds.). *Becoming female: Perspectives on development* (pp. 3-26). New York: Plenum Press.

Levitin, T. E., & Chananie, J. D. (1972). Responses of female primary school teachers to sex-typed behaviors in male and female children. *Child Development, 43*, 1309-1316.

Lewis, M. (1972a). Culture and gender roles: There's no unisex in the nursery. *Psychology Today, 5*, 54-57.

Lewis, M. (1972b). Parents and children: Sex role development. *School Review, 80*, 229-240.

Lewis, M., & Rosenblum, L. (Eds.). (1974). *The effect of the infant on its caregiver: The origins of behavior* (Vol. 1). New York: Wiley.

Lipman-Blumen, J. (1972). How ideology shapes women's lives. *Scientific American, 226*(1), 34-42.

Lynn, D. B. (1972). Determinants of intellectual growth in women. *School Review, 80*, 241-260.

Maccoby, E. E., & Jackson, C. N. (1974). *The psychology of sex differences*. Stanford, CA: Stanford University Press.

Malcolm, A. H. (1985). *The Canadians*. New York: Times Books.

Marquis Academic Media (1979). *Sourcebook on aging*. Chicago, IL: Marquis Who's Who.

Masnick, G., & Bane, M. J. (1980). *The nation's families: 1960-1990*. Cambridge, MA: Joint Center for Urban Studies of MIT and Harvard University.

Oakley, A. (1974). *The sociology of housework*. Bath, England: Pitman.

O'Neill, G., & O'Neill, N. (1972). *Open marriage*, New York: Avon.

Papanek, H. (1973). Men, women and work: Reflection on the two-person career. *American Journal of Sociology, 78*, 852-872.

Parke, D., & Swain, D. B. (1976). The father's role in infancy: A reevaluation. *Family Coordinator, 25*, 365-371.

Perlmutter, J. F. (1978). A gynecological approach to menopause. In M. T. Notman & C. C. Nadelson (Eds.). *The woman patient: Medical and psychological interfaces*. New York: Plenum Press.

Richman, N. (1976). Depression of mothers of pre-school children. *Journal of Child Psychology and Psychiatry, 17*, 75-78.

Robinson, J. P. (1977). *Changes in Americans' use of time: 1968-1975*. Cleveland, OH: Communication Research Center.

Rosenberg, B. G. (December, 1972). *Sex, sex role, and sex-role identity: The built-in paradoxes*. Paper presented at the annual meeting of the American Association for the Advancement of Science, Washington, DC.

Rossi, A. S. (1968). Transition to parenthood. *Journal of Marriage and the Family, 30*, 26-39.

Rubin, L. (1979). *Women of a certain age*. New York: Harper and Row.

Russo, N. F. (1979). Overview: Sex roles, fertility, and the motherhood mandate. *Psychology of Women Quarterly, 4*, 7-15.

Russo, N. F., & Denmark, F. L. (1984). Women, psychology and public policy. *American Psychologist, 39*(10), 1161-1165.

Seager, J., & Olson, A. (1986). *Women in the world: An international atlas*. New York: Simon and Schuster.

Shafer, N. (1970). Helping women through the change of life. *Sexology, 36*, 4-56.

Sherman, J. A. (1971). *On the psychology of women*. Springfield, IL: Charles C. Thomas.

Silvern, L. E. (1978). Masculinity-femininity in children's self-concepts: The relationship of teachers' judgments of social adjustment and academic ability, classroom behaviors, and popularity. *Sex Roles, 6*, 929-949.

Smith, R. E. (1979). Movement of women into the labor force. In R. E. Smith (Ed.). *The subtle revolution: Women at work*. Washington, DC: The Urban Institute.

Sontag, S. (1972). The double standard of aging. *Saturday Review, 55*(39), 29-38.

Spivak, G., & Spotts, J. (1965). The Devereux child behavior rating scales: A study of symptom behaviors in latency age atypical children. *American Journal of Mental Deficiency, 69*(6), 839-853.

U. S. Department of Commerce (1973). *Some demographic aspects of aging in the U. S. growth of the population 65 years and over*. Washington, DC: U. S. Government Printing Office.

U. S. Department of Labor, Women's Bureau (1969). *Facts about women's absenteeism and labor turnover*. Washington, DC: U. S. Government Printing Office.

Weitzman, L. J. (1985). *The divorce revolution: the unexpected consequences for women and children in America*. New York: The Free Press.

Werry, J. S., & Quay, H. C. (1971). The prevalence of behavior symptoms in younger elementary school children. *American Journal of Orthopsychiatry, 4*(1), 136-143.

Wertz, R. W., & Wertz, D. C. (1979). *Lying-in: A history of childbirth in America*. New York: Schocken.

Williams, J. H. (1983). *Psychology of women: Behavior in a biosocial context*. New York: W. W. Norton and Co.

Beth Rachel Adler, clarinetist of the Brick Memorial High School Marching Band

Photo credit: Peter J. Orabonl

2

Women of the Arctic (Alaska):
A Culture in Transition

Margaret Fischer

Alaska in the Arctic zone is an immense land of snow, three million lakes, and 5,000 glaciers. To give a basis for size comparison, the Malaspina glacier is larger than Switzerland. There are one million acres of land and an average of one person per square mile. It is one-fifth the size of the continental United States of America and 120 times larger than Rhode Island. It is the farthest east (because the Aleutian Islands reach beyond the dateline, beyond longitude of 180°), north, and west state in the union. In fact, Attu, on the Aleutian Chain, is in tomorrow ("Time Out," *Anchorage Times*, 1985).

The permanent population of Alaska is about 525,000. Of that number approximately 70,000 are native Eskimos and Indians (U.S. Census Bureau, 1985). Eskimos inhabit the Arctic coastline and western Alaska. The Indians inhabit the interior and the southeast parts of the state. While there are seven distinct language groups, children learn in English, and it is the common tongue.

The Eskimos are descended from the Thule people who migrated from Asia through Siberia and the Bering Strait to North America about 3,000 years ago at the same time that many now-extinct animals were passing to and fro over the land bridge that once existed between Asia and North America. There are four subdivisions of Alaskan aborigines: the Aleuts who inhabited the Aleutian Islands and the western part of the Alaska Peninsula; the Eskimos who frequented the Arctic and Bering Sea coasts; the Tlingit-Haida Indians who dwelled along the southeastern coastal region; and the Athapascan Indians of interior Alaska. With the exception of the Tlingits and Haidas, these groups have the almost unique distinction among neighboring peoples of never having warred against each other. While their tribal ways have largely diminished, the subdivisions still apply.

The physiognomy of the Arctic native peoples is, in general, remarkably uniform, having the appearance of a mixture of Mongol and Indian. Eskimos are powerfully built. Their trunks are comparatively long; their arms and legs are short in proportion to their height (Ho, Mikkelson, Lewis, Feldman, & Taylor, 1972).

The way of life of Arctic natives for many centuries was subsistence fishing and hunting in an often harsh and inhospitable climate. Living in the Arctic required that each person share in the work. Marriage was essential. An unmarried man was virtually helpless since he needed the work that a woman could provide. A woman's role was to cut and tan hides, take measurements, and sew skins, sometimes using thread from flour sacks. She maintained the home, gathered, prepared, and preserved food. In the subsistence life-style, food was the measure of wealth. When a bird or duck was caught or muktuk from a whale was shared it conferred on those so blessed a feeling of prosperity.

The woman played many roles. She was the doctor and the nurse. She brewed wild herbs to cure pneumonia and learned to use swamp tea, seaweed, and stinkweed for medicinal purposes. She bore a large family and was assisted in child delivery by a midwife.

MARRIAGE

Marriages were frequently arranged between families in the same community. When an agreement was made the parents of the girl made a gift to the boy—a knife, harpoon, or parka—while he in turn came to their house to work for them. Such bride service was of short duration since the boy might merely catch a seal and give it to his prospective parents-in-law. The marriage might be consummated at any time during these proceedings. And once consummated it was viewed as marriage. If a girl refused marriage, and her freedom of choice was clearly recognized, her suitor might marry another.

Marriages were more or less a lasting state, since a couple learned to adjust to each other's ways and a strong bond of affection might arise. While the state of marriage operated largely on economic terms, and was permanent on that basis, it was defined sexually. When a man and a woman had sexual relations, a state of marriage was considered to have existed between them. The criterion of permanent marriage was co-residence; divorce was simply the breaking of the residence tie (Spencer, 1959).

There was no taboo against premarital sex and no stigma was attached to an unwed mother. Rather, it was common for the relatives of the father of the child to claim the child instead of rejecting it, because increasing family size and creating a potential worker for the family was always desirable. Unwed mothers, in fact, enhanced their chances for marriage as a woman who was known to be fertile might have a choice of prospective husbands. But a girl who was sexually free was not considered too desirable because she spent too much time in her romantic affairs and too little in being busy. The chiding was not for her morals, but for her laziness (Spencer, 1959).

FAMILIES

The lines of social status were derived from a woman's husband's position or rank in the village. If he was a leader or elder she played an important role in village ceremonies. If he was a common laborer her social status was congruent with that of the lower echelons of that society. A widow was viewed as poor if she received no support from her relatives or her former husband's kin. A woman who acquired wealth, perhaps in the form of a reindeer herd, a team of dogs, or domesticated animals, was accorded power and influence in the village. Yet there was an inherent bias in the native cultures that placed more stress and conflict on women than on men. Women's roles carried less prestige than those of men, and relatively great psychological deprivation.

Childrearing

The dwellings of the Arctic natives were small. As a large portion of the Arctic region was above the tree-line, the typical home was semi-subterranean. They contained one to three rooms with walls of turf and soil. Entrance was through a hole in the roof or through a narrow tunnel. The lack of timber created a dependence on animal fat provided by the blubber of seals or whales for fuel and light. Often a family would sleep side by side on a large platform that was raised above the floor. Foodstuffs were stored beneath the platform.

A mother was responsible for training her daughters to trap, hunt, and fish, to haul twigs and branches for the stove, and ice and snow for fresh water. The female children tended to the household chores while the male children accompanied the father on hunting and fishing trips. Girls as well as boys learned to shoot when quite young. The rabbits and ptarmigan for many meals were shot or trapped by schoolboys and schoolgirls. During the spring and summer months the women and older children gathered willow buds for greens and cranberries and blueberries. Small boys were lowered over the cliffs on sealskin ropes to gather birds' eggs from the nests in the rocks. Often the women and children jigged for tomcod while the men did the harder work of hunting, lifting fish traps, and hauling wood.

EDUCATION

In the early years of the twentieth century there were two schools, the territorial school for Caucasians and mixed Caucasian/native students who could pass, and the Bureau of Indian Affairs school for the native children. Students who came from isolated communities were disadvantaged as their culture patterns emphasized noncompetitiveness, class equality, communal use of property, an absence of social tension, and respect for individual rights (Brooks, 1983). Assertiveness was not a part of the culture and so the children acceded to the prohibition against speaking their native language in school and performing many traditional rituals and dances.

Most of the teachers were non-natives who could not relate to the students' way of life, environment, culture, and traditions. Curriculum materials were often irrelevant. The reading texts depicted children living on farms or in an apartment that were vastly different from the sod huts with which students were familiar. It is not surprising therefore that when large numbers of villagers, particularly women, emigrated to urban settings they were ill prepared educationally to compete in the job market where they were matched with a highly educated labor force.

OUTMIGRATION

Many native women came to reject their low-status roles. Factors such as male dominance, depreciation of the female, females' subservient role, the suppression of competitive and assertive impulses, and the inability to deal openly with hostility constituted important reasons for migration (Bloom, 1973). The female's rejection of her old role was a major factor in the potential breakup of native societies and the subsistence life-style.

The coming of Euroamericans to Alaska for furs, the discovery of oil in Alaska, the shortening of distances to the outside world by air travel, the impact of television, and improved education and technology hastened the acculturation process and the shift from subsistence living to a cash-based economy. It was understandable that Arctic natives were ready to embrace the new technology as environmental conditions were so harsh that anything that made life easier would have been welcomed.

Women left their villages in large numbers to find equality, prestige, and dignity in the larger villages and cities. The emigration to urban settings and the change from subsistence living to a cash economy required rapid social adjustment. Females seemed more adaptable than males in the cosmopolitan atmosphere. The lure of a higher standard of living, the hope of marrying a non-native man, and the glamorized picture of life in the big city made the change attractive for females but created a new phenomenon for males left in the villages. Native bachelors, depressed because the women were leaving, spent their days "hanging out," drinking, and watching television. Although subsistence hunting and fishing were generally available, fewer young people were interested in it. The idea of adapting to city life was a difficult prospect for many because, by history, most Arctic natives were nomadic peoples and not city dwellers.

Yet women who rejected old roles still carried with them part of the negative self-image that was important to the psychological integrity of the traditional native culture. The native women who migrated often served as sexual objects to the non-native men who came to the Arctic seeking their fortunes. These unions between native women and non-native men were often based on movie-like romanticism for the women and frequently ended in separation, depression, and suicide attempts. Thus women who were suffering from confused identity in their rejection of former roles failed in achieving a new sense of identity in the new communities (Spencer, 1959). The results of prejudice and stereotyping, which were often the rule in the new urban settings, contributed to the stresses associated with the acculturation process, as the new environment did not always welcome the native migrant. Unsatisfactory integration into the new culture appeared for some to lead to increased psychosocial dysfunction and psychopathology.

Nevertheless, native women moved into the work force at a much faster rate than did white women in Alaska. During the 1970s labor force participation of native women increased by an amazing 50 percent. By 1980, the labor force consisted of 40 percent native women and 60 percent white women (Thomas, et al., 1983). More natives, however, were in lower-paying occupations than white women. The majority were employed in service and support occupations. Only 17 percent of native women who worked held managerial, professional, and technical jobs. The average annual income of native families was 56 percent lower than that of white families in the state.

The proportion of women raising families without husbands was twice as high among natives as it was among whites in Alaska, and native women on the average had more children. Their fertility rate was among the highest in the world. Pregnancies among native teenagers occurred faster than among adolescents in most nations (*Anchorage Times*, 1989). Infant mortality was no longer the problem it once was, so the native population increased. The greatest threat to infant health was the fetal alcohol syndrome, as alcoholism remained the single most serious problem for both native men and women. It was one of the major pitfalls in the transition from traditional life-styles to a cash-and-carry economy.

Change caused stress, as evidenced by the skyrocketing alcoholism and suicide rates in Alaska. While natives comprised less than 15 percent of the population, they accounted for 33 percent of the total admissions to the state psychiatric facility (1988 figures: Anchorage, AK: Alaska Psychiatric Inst.). Large-scale outmigration to the larger towns, where there was a lack of control over one's personal destiny, inadequate income opportunities to match rising consumer expectations, growing tension in white-native contacts, deep-seated resentments, and feelings of personal inadequacy on the part of natives were some of the factors that hindered adaptation. Recognizing the immensity of the problems of a culture in transition, the Alaska Federation of Natives asked the U. S. Congress to help natives surmount the social and economic upheaval facing rural villages (Fahys, 1989). In response, the National Research Council in 1989 called for more social science research on the rapidly changing communities of the Arctic to study the effects of rapid social change on physical and mental health, and the limits of people's cognitive and emotional resources to deal with change.

It has been said that attitudes of people toward change help determine their survival or extinction. The desire for change and the trend toward modernization among natives was unmistakable. For many of them the age of subsistence living was a part of the past which they revered but did not want to experience. They identified with Western cultures in their dress, music preferences, and fast-food appetites. Young people replaced the kuspuk with blue jeans, the traditional native chants with rock and roll music, and the muktuk with tacos and pizzas.

A cross-cultural emphasis is a necessary starting point in the orientation and training of all persons working on Arctic problems if their work is to be effective. The government's handling of problems of Indian populations in the United States of America was fraught with difficulties in the past because the changes were legislated with little concern for the culture, heritage, or autonomy of the Indians. We hope that these mistakes will be rectified when legislators seek solutions to the acculturation problems of the Arctic natives.

Completing the transition to a modern life-style may take a decade or more, but eventually Alaska natives in general, and native women in particular, will gain the acceptance, self-respect, and equality they seek. Their struggle mirrors that of women around the world. It just had a later start.

REFERENCES

Alaska teen pregnancy rate higher than most countries. (1989). *Anchorage Times,* Sunday, October 1, p. B-3.

Bloom, J. D. (1973). Migration and psychopathology of Eskimo women. *American Journal of Psychiatry, 130,* 446-449.

Brooks, M. (1973). *Women's oral history collection.* Anchorage, AK: Alaska Historical Society.

Fahys, J. (1989, March 2). AFN seeks help: Asks Congress for new ideas. *Anchorage Times,* pp. A-1, 8.

Ho, K. J., Mikkelson, B., Lewis, L. A., Feldman, S. A., & Taylor, C. B. (1972). Alaska Arctic Eskimo: Responses to a customary high fat diet. *The American Journal of Clinical Nutrition, 25.* 737-745.

Spencer, R. T. (1959). *The North Alaskan Eskimo.* Washington, DC: Smithsonian.

Thomas, C., Worl, R., Smythe, C. W., & Lane, T. (1983, September). The economic status of Alaska native women. *Chilkat Institute & the Institute of Social and Economic Research,* Anchorage, AK.

Time out. (1985, July). *Anchorage Times.*

U. S. Census Bureau. Personal communication, July 31,1985.

Erica Abt with iguana

3

Women in Latin America

Ruben Ardila

The status of women in such an extensive and heterogeneous area as Latin America cannot easily be covered in a short chapter. There exist many differences between the daily life-style of a woman in a large city such as Buenos Aires or São Paulo and the daily routine of a woman in a little rural town of Guatemala or Ecuador. Nevertheless, there are many similarities that allow us to refer to the woman in Latin America in a generalized way, to her current life and her prospects for the near future.

Latin America is a gigantic continent. It has 430 million inhabitants and 23 countries. It includes the continental part and the Caribbean. This gigantic area of the planet receives diverse names; Latin America is probably the most adequate. It is comprised of populations that speak Spanish, Portuguese, French, English, and numerous native languages. Sometimes this part of the globe is called "Latin America and the Caribbean."

Generally, it is talked about as Latin America, including the important Caribbean zone. H. Herring (1968) is probably the most important source concerning its history. G. Arciniegas (1967) is the main thinker with regard to its culture. There are books dealing with the area's social and psychological problems; in this respect, see my book on psychology in Latin America (Ardila, 1986a).

Latin American women are a subject of enormous importance for which a historical, psychological, anthropological, social, and economical analysis would be necessary. Latin America is not homogeneous, and neither are its women. There are great differences between each country. In order to study Latin American women, keep in mind that a woman from Rio de Janeiro (Brazil) and others from Tegucigalpa (Honduras) have many points of divergence. However, more convergence than divergence will be discovered, as well as the differences of social classes, of the educational levels of urban-rural environments, and of historical epochs.

AN OVERVIEW: LATIN AMERICAN WOMEN

Perhaps the most distinctive characteristics of Latin American women derive from the fact that Latin America has traditionally been a continent distinguished at the social level by *machismo* and centered on men. The role of women has been a secondary one. Home has traditionally been considered as her place to stay, and childrearing as her main role. Very few women have been presidents of a Latin American country, few Secretaries of State, medical doctors, engineers, or scientists. Women have not worked outside the house and they hold a low status. The second characteristic in this analysis of women in Latin America is the result of the accelerated social change that the area has experienced. The accelerated urbanization, the decline in the birth rate, industrialization, improvements in communications, and so on, have contributed to changing the place of women in society. Now women go to the university, have a political career, work outside their home, or divorce; in some cases they are unmarried mothers, or study professions previously considered "masculine," such as engineering and veterinary science.

In an analysis of women in Latin America—as in the rest of the world—social class is a decisive factor. Upper-class women lead lives that are very different from those of middle-class and lower-class women in urban environments and women in rural areas. Upper-class women are generally the wives or daughters of top executives, or they may be professionals who do not need to work in order to live. Many upper-class men consider it a disgrace that their wives work. Many women have decided to become professionals, to break the traditional schemes of their society, to set their own pace, to disobey the cultural demands of their social group, and so on. These women are not really interested in getting married and having children, which they generally do mainly because of social pressure and not for personal reasons. The life of an upper-class woman is quite free. Her husband does not interfere too much in her activities, she has an adequate educational level as well as good information, so she does what pleases her. She travels alone; her children are not an obstacle in her personal or professional activities. Although she decided to break partially with the traditional world and follow her own life, this change was not difficult or traumatic. She feels badly because she does not devote enough time to her children and husband, but she knows there are other things to do apart from complying with the traditional roles of Latin American women.

The middle-class urban woman has a more difficult life. She must work in order to contribute to the support of her family. In many cases, she is a secretary, a teacher, a salesclerk, or works in a similar job, with a reduced salary and many responsibilities. Her husband also has a difficult life with economic and personal pressures. Their children stay alone at the house or with the maid. The middle-class woman would prefer to stay at home and not go to work as a bank teller or a business secretary, but money is urgently needed, expenses are progressively bigger, and the salary of her husband is not enough to support the family. Economic difficulties are normal, everyday occurrences. She must dress according to fashion, maintain a good appearance, have an acceptably comfortable house, and "stretch" the salary in order to satisfy all those needs. Her children are looked after by the grandmother, the maid, or the neighbors.

The lower-class urban woman considers work the normal thing to do, and not something imposed by circumstances. People from her social group have always worked. She is usually either a factory worker or a maid. Her husband is also a wage earner, for whom life is full of stress and privations. Frequently there are episodes of physical violence in the family, and alcoholism on the husband's side. It is not an enjoyable or pleasant life, but hard and bitter. This is the life her people have always followed and it is not expected that social change will modify it. Economic deprivations occur every day. If this woman works as a maid, she must tolerate her employer's bad treatment, the sexual approaches of the husband and of his adolescent children, and transportation difficulties (in many cases commuting to work takes more than two hours, especially in the large cities). This woman earns the lowest salary, which does not compensate the effort and time required for that work. She knows that she has to abandon her own children in order to look after those of her employer, and as a consequence feels a deep resentment against her life, her work, and the impossibility of changing her world. Due to her low educational level, she does not believe that there will ever be any social improvement or any way of improving her own life.

The rural woman leads quite a different life as compared with the upper-, middle-, and lower- class urban women. Technically, she is part of the lower class, but belongs to a different subclass. Country women do not have as many economic deprivations as the lower-class women of the large cities. In rural areas, there is much poverty, and a lack of medical services, employment, and education. But there is no deprivation of food and it is possible to live in the country without experiencing the great privations of the lower-class people of the cities. Rural women are more traditional, more religious, and simpler than urban women. Their life is more elementary and less stressful. Deprivations are almost always of an economic and educational character.

The life cycle of men and women in Latin America is closely related to their educational level, social mobility, social class, and rural or urban cultural environment.

INFANCY

Families generally prefer boys. In rural communities it is considered a disgrace to have only female children. It is believed that men are more intelligent, are hard workers, and have a rich and interesting life. This belief is common in Latin American small towns, and sometimes even in bigger cities. Such a preference for male children is maintained overall by the mother. She is the one who grants privileges to her sons and denies them to her daughters. Although she is closer to her daughters than to her sons, she prefers her sons and she is proud of being the mother of males. All this is found in the *machismo* context, which is one of the characteristics of the traditional Latin American family (Giraldo, 1972) and which, despite the accelerated social changes, has not disappeared completely in any of the Latin American countries. *Machismo* exists from Mexico to the American Southern Cone (Argentina and Chile), including the Caribbean.

Chileans, Colombians, Costa Ricans, and also populations with little Spanish ancestry are *machistas*. What is *machista* is not exactly what came from Spain to the Latin American culture, but its development in the New World.

The socialization of girls is quite strict, as we have found from our investigations on patterns of childrearing (Ardila, 1986b). The sex-typing is very strong. Girls must help their mothers with the house-keeping tasks, look after their smaller brothers and sisters, go to school, and be good members of the family. Boys, on the other hand, must become independent, smart, and manly, play outside the house, and acquire the manly characteristics that they have seen in their fathers, grandfathers, and ancestors.

THE SCHOOL YEARS

Schools for girls are quite different from those for boys; the tasks are less demanding, and emphasis is given to sewing, cooking, religion, and decorating and keeping a nice home. In the high social stratum, these traits are associated with "glamour" and are helpful in getting a husband. To get married in one's own social and economic class continues to represent the goal of Latin American women.

At the present time, there exist many integrated schools where not only men but also women attend. Public schools are generally mixed. In the decade of the 1970s, integrated schools were the exception and not the rule; however, all schools will be integrated in the future. There will probably be no single-sex schools.

MARRIAGE

The problems of mate selection have changed significantly in Latin America. One hundred years ago nobody thought that a marriage by choice could be more successful than an arranged marriage. Today everybody prefers a marriage in which the decision to start life together is no longer arranged by parents or other relatives. Most people in Latin America think that a woman's place is in the home. Given a choice between becoming a wife and mother on the one hand or becoming a high executive on the other, the first option is much preferred.

There exists lately an increasing number of unmarried mothers in the cities. These women decided they wanted to have a child but not a steady partner, and consequently acted accordingly. Many of these women are highly educated, intelligent, widely traveled, and quite self-reliant in decision making. No doubt, unmarried mothers are at the vanguard of what we could call "the new Latin American women." There are also many single women who decided to devote their time to their profession.

Another complex aspect of marriages in Latin America concerns economics. Formerly, the husband worked while the wife looked after the children and took care of the home. Today she looks after the children, keeps house, and additionally, must be gainfully employed. Her husband does not help much with the household chores; these have been and are still the wife's business. The family's economic support was the husband's business, but now it is a joint responsibility. Women's liberation is very worthy and important in stressing sexual equality. In fact, women have more responsibilities now than they had before; but it appears that they have not been liberated from household duties.

It is also important to point out that in many cases men and women who perform the same work do not earn the same salary. There are almost always specific laws which stipulate that there must be the same salary for the same activity, regardless of the sex of the employee. But the truth is that this almost never occurs. Typically, women earn less money than men even when both perform the same work.

The woman who works becomes independent and wins prestige at home. Children regard her more highly and this can lead to difficult situations with her husband.

DIVORCE

In almost all Latin American countries, divorce exists for civil marriages. A very few countries still are ruled by the "concordat" with the Holy See, which regulates many aspects of the relations between the Roman Catholic Church and the state. In these Latin American countries, divorce is more complex and difficult to get. Latin America is a continent with a high percentage of Roman Catholics—in some countries 90 percent of the population, or even more. The Catholic marriage does not allow divorce, since it is considered indissoluble, according to the rules of the Roman Catholic Church. The Latin American woman has struggled successfully to make divorce possible. Nonetheless, to get a divorce is a very complicated matter, with many financial, legal, psychological, and familial parameters. Many women tolerate an alcoholic husband who does not respond to domestic needs, who physically abuses his wife and children, or is a womanizer because a divorce is a serious social disgrace. A woman with a difficult marriage is better off than a divorced woman. It is not thought that a divorce is a solution but rather that it is a necessary evil for extremely serious cases.

PREGNANCY AND CHILDBIRTH

Attitudes toward pregnancy are very positive. Latin American women want to be mothers. They have their children when they are too young. However, the age of first pregnancies is increasing. It was common in the past—a generation ago—that women had their first children before they were 20 years old, but now they can have them when they are 28, 30, or more. In this respect, a woman's educational and social level have great influence. Educated women have their children later than those who are not educated.

Grandmothers help a great deal with the preparation for maternity. From one generation to another, values, attitudes, and patterns of behavior are transmitted with certain uniformity. The mother teaches her daughter how to bring up her child, how to adequately feed and discipline the child, and how to transmit cultural values. If this instruction does not coincide with the modern doctors' teaching, it does not matter. For instance, the age of weaning, the age at which solid food is given to babies, whether children are to be physically punished or not, all these are matters determined by the grandmothers and not by science. In this sense, the Latin American society is too conservative; grandmothers wield great influence even with educated groups of professional women.

Latin American women are generally tender and loving. They devote as much time as possible to their children and worry about their physical and psychological well-being. In this sense, we can affirm that they are "good mothers." They do not overprotect their children or neglect them. They try to keep a unified family, and strive so that their children become healthy adults and useful members of society. Children almost always adore and respect their mothers but not necessarily their fathers. Due to the accelerated social change that takes place mainly in the cities, mothers almost never have an educational level as high as that of their children; nevertheless, their viewpoints are respected by the children, who listen to their mothers' advice. Latin American women are very good mothers and their offspring admire and consider them as such.

ADULT ACTIVITIES

The potentialities of Latin American women are not easily realized. Even despite some current progress, feminine roles are limited and poor in relation to the masculine roles. The social change that we observe in Latin America today is due to the fact that a high percentage of women work outside their homes. This implies that the nuclear family has replaced the extended family. In the larger cities in Latin America the "family" includes the father, mother, and children (nuclear family), but not so much the grandparents, uncles, brothers-in-law, cousins, nieces, and nephews (extended family). In rural areas and small towns, the extended family is the rule.

Mothers who work have very limited time for their children. Small families are perhaps closer and enjoy better communication. Personal development is emphasized in men and women. There is nobody at home when the children arrive from school, which is an important limitation to the well-being of the family in its traditional sense; on the other hand, the mother who works has better social relations and more knowledge of the world in which she lives.

Less than 50 years ago the first Latin American women who went to the university generally studied medicine, philosophy, and law. They had to face many obstacles in order to have a university education, to find adequate employment, and to achieve a place in society.

The situation is very different today. Latin American women study all careers in all universities. There are women studying engineering, agronomy, physics, veterinary science, and other fields that were supposed to be only for men. In fields such as in medicine, dentistry, and law, women are performing very successfully. In many Latin American countries there are more women than men dentists, and more female than male lawyers. There are women who study nuclear physics, advanced mathematics, systems engineering, and all fields of scientific activity.

Arts and literature also benefited from the entry of women in the world of work. There are painters, writers, sculptors, and poets, whose reputations are as good as or better than those of men.

Politics has been a complex area and very difficult for women. Generally, women interested in a political career in Latin America belong to the upper or middle classes, which have more influence and more real possibilities of social promotion. But it is also at this social level that the activities of women in politics are not readily accepted.

In Latin America there are now many women devoted to politics, and they practice it with great efficiency and much success. There have been women presidents, and nominees for president. There are women secretaries of state, prime ministers, majors, ambassadors, members of Congress, and so on.

Eva Perón (1919-52) was probably the first Latin American woman to achieve international recognition. She was the wife of Juan D. Perón, an Argentinean military man and president of the country. "Evita" had great influence on her husband's government and she changed in a radical way many regulations in Argentina. The educational system and many aspects of the Argentinean economy were transformed because of Eva. She struggled to make her country great. This occurred at a time when it appeared impossible that a woman could perform such an important political role. It looked even less possible in Argentina, a Third World country. Eva died of cancer when she was only 33 years old. Her popularity even increased after her death, and reached levels never before achieved by any other Latin American woman. We could affirm that Argentina would not be what it is today without Eva Perón's mediation. In fact, Latin American women's roles would not be the same without her. Eva Perón has a place in history as the first Latin American woman with world impact.

Gabriela Mistral, the pen name of Lucila Godoy (1889-1957), was an influential Chilean woman. She received the Nobel Prize for literature in 1945, and was one of the few women to be awarded a Nobel Prize. She was a poor girl, with no important names, ancestry, or influence. She reached the highest levels of intellectual achievement by her own capabilities and not by her family's support.

Lower-class women previously worked as maids or had jobs in factories. Every day there are fewer domestic employees but more female factory workers. This trend implies progress, since factories offer better salaries, social benefits, relative possibilities for promotion, fewer daily working hours, and laws that regulate labor activities. None of these benefits exists with regard to domestic work. In any event, maids preferred employment in factories rather than as servants. The trend is quite clear. In the near future the situation of domestic employees will probably be similar to that existing in the United States of America and Europe.

AGING

To become old in Latin America is not as hard or bitter as it is in some other parts of the world. No doubt it is easier to be an elderly person in South America than in North America. Due to the respect and affection that Latin Americans feel toward their parents, the possibility that an elderly person is abandoned to his or her luck, is much less likely here than in the United States of America or in Europe.

With industrialization and urbanization, the traditional values are changing. It was not possible before to conceive of the idea of residential homes for old people, or that someone would leave his or her father or mother in such a residence. Today, this is not a frequent situation, but it does exist and will tend to increase. The situation here is not as bad as in the First World, but it is changing.

On farms, there are no such residences for old people. The status of the elderly is high, not only in rural areas but also in the city.

The majority of the elderly population are women, both in Latin America and in the rest of the world. The proportion of 51 percent of women and 49 percent of men in the adult population changes considerably after the age of 60 years because of their relative life expectancies.

The problems of getting old are different in this part of the world, due to difficulties of getting employment. An older person who lost a job is not always able to find another. Due to the *machismo* that exists despite efforts to eliminate it, employers prefer men workers to women. An elderly woman has a doubly difficult time to find a job. The fact of being a woman, as well as elderly, combine to make this situation worse (Dulcey and Ardila, 1987). If an elderly woman looks for a job, it is because she has important economic needs and urgency to work.

Leaving aside the economic aspect, aging in Latin America for women also has other problems. Due to accelerated social changes, elderly women have not adapted themselves to the world in which they now live. For them traditional values are still valid. They find, however, that their children and grandchildren do not share their values. They cannot accept the fact that a son may get a divorce, or a granddaughter an abortion, that a family member does not attend religious services, or that a niece has several lovers simultaneously. The world has changed in matters of great importance to the daily life of people and she does not understand such changes.

The loneliness of elderly people is something about which people talk a great deal and which is probably real. (The same thing is true with regard to economic problems and their implications.)

Nevertheless, in Latin America the elderly are not in as lonely a situation as in some other parts of the world. In addition, these changes occur in accordance with the social class and the educational level. Aging is more positive in Latin America than in many other countries of the First and Second Worlds.

WOMEN TODAY: TRADITION AND CHANGE

Social change is one of the most distinctive characteristics in our times. To live under social conditions of constant change is somewhat difficult. Life in Latin America is not easy for women in any event. The situations of women are full of ambiguities and rules that are not always clear. On one hand, the traditional roles of mother, wife, and home-maker are valued but are considered insufficient. On the other hand, the new roles of student, professional, executive, or independent woman are only partially accepted and tolerated.

Psychology has contributed greatly to the understanding and orientation of the social changes that are associated with women. In this regard, see for example Brody (1987); Larwood, Stromberg, & Gutek (1985); and Matlin (1987). In the specific case of Latin America, it is worthwhile to mention A. N. Rivera (1985); Thomas (1986); Londoño (1981, 1983, 1984); and Díaz-Guerrero (1974). These are examples of psychological research that has relevance to the present work. The importance of psychology and other behavioral sciences in the analysis of the situation of women in the world of today is very great.

Cuba presents an interesting case of social change. During the last decades, one of the greatest transformations of Latin American history has taken place there. This transformation—in behavioral terms—is still to be evaluated. But the transformation has major implications at individual, familial, and childrearing levels for the roles of both sexes. The change has occurred not only with regard to production levels, but also in many other fields. The role of the Cuban woman was very different before the revolution of Fidel Castro. No doubt, these changes have been very positive. Women have gained access to positions of power, of decision-making, such as they had never held before. In the health and educational fields, women's labor has been decisive. The new generation of Cuban youths who were born during Castro's revolution will hardly understand what those changes meant.

To return to the general subject of women in Latin America, there is no doubt that many aspects of social change are in the hands of women. They are the ones who transmit the values, attitudes, and patterns of behavior from one generation to the next. Women manage aspects that are very central and important in the life of people. Those elements that make life good are in the hands of women. A large part of the socialization of children is in the hands of mothers and teachers (who are usually women). If we consider that learning explains the largest part of the behavior of people, and that learning is the work of women, the conclusion is that the children and young people of Latin America are the responsibility of women.

CONCLUSIONS

The present chapter emphasized the shared characteristics rather than the differences among the women in Latin America. However, there are important differences described, such as those among the social classes, among age-ranges, and among individual countries.

These differences are probably the consequences of the heterogeneity of Latin America. This continent of 430 million inhabitants and 23 countries, with many diverse ancestors and a variety of different histories, cannot be homogeneous. It was said by Arciniegas (1967) that this discourse dealt with the "continent of seven colors."

Half of the people belong to the feminine sex. Their situation has special and different characteristics from those of men. Many patterns of behavior exist in common between men and women; this is identified as "androgyny." But here the attention centered on the differences between the sexes. Latin American society has greatly changed during the last decades, but by all accounts many traditional values have been kept. This balance between tradition and change has been difficult for Latin American women to achieve.

The Latin American woman continues her integration into the labor force. She perseveres in securing her place as a person in her own right, and not only as wife and/or mother. She continues to respond and adapt to the changes of her culture, her social class, and her country. In future years, there will be major personal developments of women and better communication among generations, and finally the desired balance between the genders will be reached. Latin American women have performed important roles in their society, in their time and in the world in which they live.

REFERENCES

Arciniegas, G. (1967). *Latin America: A cultural history*. New York: Knopf.

Ardila, R. (1986a). *La psicología en América Latina, pasado, presente y futuro*. Mexico: Siglo XXI.

Ardila, R. (1986b). *Psicología del hombre colombiano*. Bogota: Planeta.

Brody, D. M. (1987). *Women's therapy groups*. New York: Springer Publishing.

Díaz-Guerrero, R. (1974). La mujer y las premisas historico-sociocult-urales de la familia mexicana. *Revista Latinoamericana de Psicología, 6*, 7-16.

Dulcey, E., & Ardila, R. (1987). Work and retirement in Latin America. In G. L. Maddox & E. W. Busse (Eds.). *Aging: The universal human experience* (pp. 609-614). New York: Springer Publishing.

Giraldo, O. (1972). El machismo como fenomeno psicocultural. *Revista Latinoamericana de Psicología, 4*, 295-309.

Herring, H. (1968). *A history of Latin America*. New York: Knopf.

Larwood, L., Stromberg, A. H., & Gutek, B. A. (Eds.). (1985). *Women and work*, Vol. 1. Beverly Hills, CA: Sage Publications.

Londoño, M. L. (1981). La sexualidad femenina como factor de cambio social. Paper presented to the University of Antioquia, Medellin, Colombia.

Londoño, M. L. (1983). El feminismo: Una aproximación a la esperanza. Paper presented for the International Women's Day, Cali, Colombia.

Londoño, M. L. (1984). Actitudes hembrimachistas. Paper presented to the Third Colombian Seminar on Sexology, Bucaramanga, Colombia.

Matlin, M. W. (1987). *The psychology of women*. New York: Holt, Rinehart, and Winston.

Rivera, A. N. (1985). *La mujer puertorriqueña: Investigaciones psicosociales*. San Juan, Puerto Rico: Centro para el Estudio y Desarrollo de la Personalidad Puertorriqueña.

Thomas, F. (1986). *El macho y la hembra*. Bogota: Universidad Nacional de Colombia.

Helen Laemle, an active octogenarian working at her computer

Photo credit: Lois E. Clarke

4

Women in Great Britain

Ludwig F. Lowenstein
and Kathleen Lowenstein

As in many parts of the world, the role of the women in Britain is influenced by a number of factors including their traditional way of life, religion, customs, and the influences of their own families and community. There are also natural biological factors such as the birth of children and their subsequent care that form an integral part of most women's lives. While there have been changes in attitudes over the past 30 to 40 years due to the fact that women are taking a more prominent part in wage earning and thus financial support of the family, paid employment, for whatever reason, is still considered a secondary aspect of the role of womanhood in Britain today.

The role of women is partly defined by a division of labor which has a historical as well as biological origin. Part of this distinction is due to physical factors in women; woman carries and breastfeeds the infant while man is unable to perform this function. The tradition of British culture for centuries has acknowledged unquestioningly that man's primary task is to support the family and offer control in the form of discipline and leadership.

Within Britain there are certain regional differences, with the traditional masculine and feminine roles being somewhat more defined in the northern part of the country than in the southern part. In the southern part of Britain, no stigma is attached to a woman who works or who is the family breadwinner, but in the northern part, where there is a somewhat greater masculine cult which believes in male dominance, women, although they may be allowed to work, are expected to play a secondary role to the male. Northern men have a great pride in being able to financially support their wives and children, and are less able to understand the psychological need of some women to achieve success and stimulation in work outside the home.

AN OVERVIEW

In addition to regional differences there is a considerable overlap even within the regions in the role of male and female figures in the family. Social as well as biological influences determine the roles played by the sexes. Despite the concept of equality, the feminist approach has never taken root in many parts of Britain. Hence, there is still a differentiation between the types of activities and occupations practiced by women as compared with men. This is naturally based on customs and traditions as well as biological aspects. Women are likely, on the whole, to possess less physical strength, and hence are less likely to be occupied in tasks that require strong muscular effort such as in agriculture, building, and so on. Although there are exceptions to this, jobs of this type are almost all male-dominated, despite the fact that technology has reduced the physical effort previously involved. Domestic work and housework are still considered the main task of the female but in some households there may be shared tasks, especially if wives are also actively working and contributing to the family income.

The class factor has had an influence on the role of women. Since the Victorian era, women of the middle, upper middle, and upper classes spend relatively little time on the whole in caring for their young children, passing this task on to a variety of paid nannies. Hence the relationship between mother and child tends to be, on the whole, more formal rather than intimate. In contrast, in the lower middle or lower classes and working class, the relationship between mothers and children is close and intimate.

Another influence on the role of women in Britain is the increase in democratic thinking due to the strong feminist lobby, as a result of which women have become almost equal citizens with their male counterparts.

Today there is a lack of understanding or tolerance of the viewpoint that maternal love and the typical role of women is not always a part of every female, and indeed some women actively resent the role of playing the caretaker and bearer of the young. Conversely, we now recognize the fact that childcare within the family can be and often is provided by the father, either due to the absence of the female in the relationship or because a couple has made a conscious choice to reverse the traditional roles. While this may be a relatively rare phenomenon, it is one that is becoming increasingly more common and receiving new attention.

What has particularly been affected is the role of the male as protector of the female, the young, and the whole family. In the past, this was essentially what many women sought when looking for a partner, while they were quite happy to play the role of a less conspicuous domestic power within that family. Efforts have been made to raise the status of the housewife, and to emphasize the importance of her efforts on the next generation to counteract her need to seek gratification and power in what was previously designed to be the male's domain. The attack on clear gender identification among young people has resulted in some females adopting an androgynous mode of hairstyle and clothing, and in this way partially or totally deny their femininity.

The first feminist manifesto was by Mary Wollstonecraft in her book *Vindication of the Rights of Woman* during the late eighteenth century. This text advocated equality of the sexes and became an important volume for women seeking such equality for many years to come. The ultimate tone of the feminist movement in Britain was John Stuart Mill's *Subjugation of Women* during the end of the nineteenth century.

The nineteenth century and the Industrial Revolution in particular made a dramatic impact on the role that women were to play. Many women (as well as children) were exploited by having to work long hours under severe conditions. Factories were built to replace the old cottage industries and women were forced by circumstances to leave their families to seek work in these large "sweatshops."

In the meantime the middle classes prospered. Women in that class were served by numerous handmaids and servants, and hence had much time on their hands. Middle-class women displayed peculiar talents and roles indicating their lack of capacity to work, their chastity, and their propriety as their major virtues. It was also the time of the colonial empires developing throughout the world, making life—at least for the middle and upper classes of Western Europe—easier and easier. The gap between working-class women and middle- and upper-class women widened tremendously. There was even during that time a surplus of women unable to seek male partners.

The surplus of women in the middle classes led to an idleness that required activity to pass the time. The activity chosen frequently was education. The first women's college in Britain was Queen's College, established in 1848. It was established for the purpose of educating young women not for practical purposes, but as an amusement and occupation of somewhat idle lives. On the whole, admission to more advanced universities, which men usually attended, was far more difficult for women in Britain. British colleges such as Girton (founded in 1869) and Newnham (1871) allowed women to sit for local examinations, but it was not until 1948 that these two colleges became part of Cambridge University. This was undoubtedly due to the fact that they were women's colleges and there was a reluctance to admit them into a system that was a former prerogative of the male.

Allowing women into the professions such as medicine or law took even longer. They were only allowed to become infant school teachers, which was the most poorly paid of the teaching areas. Women began to clamor for greater opportunities in the educational spheres, and in improving social services, prisons, and hospitals. Nursing became an approved profession. Women became avowed fanatics in seeking to improve the welfare not only of themselves but of their children and less fortunate individuals, such as prostitutes. They also worked hard to reform current marriage and divorce laws as well as property rights.

Interestingly enough, it was Victorian conservatism that held women back from developing their interests in many other areas. Women were usually kept separate from men when they worked as members of the Civil Service.

Increasingly, women took the jobs formerly held by men, including office positions such as clerks and typists, and areas of business such as post office work and banks.

With the passage of time, women have made inroads into a variety of technical, engineering, and scientific professions. They have clamored for woman's emancipation and searched for equality. They have also played an increasing role in social and political as well as economic spheres.

Political equality was granted to women rather late in Britain. British women were first enfranchised by the Representation of the People Act of 1918 and finally achieved the vote in 1928, although this was subject to a number of limitations by age, marital status, and so on. The Houses of Parliament today can only boast of a 3 to 4 percent representation of women as MPs (Members of Parliament), although a woman was chosen Prime Minister. Margaret Thatcher was the first woman Prime Minister since Parliament was established.

INFANCY AND EARLY CHILDHOOD

Parent-Child Relationships

Most psychologically oriented investigators have indicated that there is an important role played by parents in determining the way in which a girl identifies with one sex or the other. This influence has tremendous ramifications as to the role such an individual will play in the future. It has long been accepted that a girl's capacity and desire to identify with the female figure, her mother, while having a close relationship with the father, is likely to be helpful in the future socialization process. It provides the individual with an identity and favorable impressions about herself and the human environment. Later, there will of course be other individuals with whom she will form some kind of relationship, such as grandparents, siblings, and other relations. The initial bonding, however, is due to the prevailing presence of one individual, usually the mother, with whom the child spends the greatest amount of time and the closest degree of intimacy.

Sex-Typing and Socialization

Parents are almost unaware of the way in which they imprint or condition the sexual role their children will play. On the whole, boys are treated in a different way from girls virtually from birth. Parents, consciously or otherwise, reinforce the sexual orientation through a variety of rewards and punishments which further encourage development along certain sex-stereotypical lines. Girls are usually treated gently, while boys, who are expected to be more robust, are treated more firmly, possibly to engender a more hardy or masculine outlook. In

Britain, there is still a sharp differentiation between male and female roles and a considerable amount of pressure is applied to develop feminine females and masculine males. A considerable amount of ostracism occurs when women adopt a more masculine role and behave aggressively or with an excessive dominance.

THE SCHOOL YEARS

As in most Western countries, Britain has witnessed a tremendous increase in interest in education by and for women. Education has been seen as a way of achieving not merely equality but self-actualization. Hence, where previously women were thought to have only a secondary or tertiary need for education because of the impending likelihood of their role as mother and wife, this has changed drastically in the last 50 to 100 years.

This change developed in association with the career opportunities being made available to women as they sought and were given greater equality with men. At the same time, educational opportunities were seen as an important way for women to find a potential partner for marriage. Although women were less ready to enter educational studies that were totally dominated by the male, they are continuing to make inroads into areas such as engineering, the sciences, and so on.

The Educational System

The educational system in Britain consists of a private as well as a state system. The private sector of education is commonly termed a "public" or "independent" school or "private school." At the younger end, preparatory schools and pre-preparatory schools exist for boys and girls in which parents who have chosen private schools for their children may begin the educational process, usually at the age of five. School is compulsory in Britain up to the age of sixteen for both boys and girls.

The majority of children attend state schools, again starting at the age of five and ending their education at the secondary level at approximately sixteen years.

The educational system of Britain and much of Europe has undergone significant changes in recent years with the introduction of comprehensive education in the state sector. In Britain there has been a tendency to retain the public school system. In some cases, grammar schools, which were part of the old system, have survived and continue to develop high academic ability in a relatively segregated atmosphere.

In the state sector, prior to the introduction of comprehensive schools, children attended infant schools, commonly termed primary schools. The only part of the old tripartite system which still exists in some areas is the grammar school. Under the old system children who were selected at the age of 11 or 13 for specialized education of the highest academic type were placed in grammar schools. Under both the tripartite system and comprehensive school system, there was free entry to a university for the higher levels of education, providing that the students met the academic requirements of institutions of higher learning. Entry to the grammar school was limited to approximately 15-20 percent of the population, either boys or girls who had passed some form of entrance examination.

Economic wealth, as well as ability, has frequently meant that some children, be they boys or girls, were able to attend private schools, which in Britain were called public or independent schools. In most cases the curricula for the different sexes were based on the expectations of society, traditions, values, and customs. With the greater liberation of women and higher expectation in academic performance, there has been an increasing tendency to provide a curriculum for boys and girls that was virtually identical. This has occurred both in the state system of education and in the private sector.

In Britain there exists a special network which caters to children with special needs, be they emotional, intellectual, physical, or behavioral. These schools tend to be day schools, but a number are also residential. Some of the schools are coeducational while others cater for one sex only. Comprehensive schools, with rare exceptions, are coeducational.

Achievement and Socialization

The achievement level of children in Britain, whether they are boys or girls, depends largely on their intellectual ability, their motivation toward studying, and encouragement from home.

The purpose of most schools is to provide education of an academic type, although efforts are also made to socialize children, to help them to live with one another and the staff of the school and eventually to be part of society outside the school system.

Most classes are carried out with both genders attending simultaneously. There are exceptions allowing for the fact that certain sports are provided for boys separate from girls and vice versa. Boys tend on the whole to be part of more robust activities such as football, rugby, and in some instances, wrestling, judo, and boxing. Girls participate in sporting activities such as swimming, cricket, netball, hockey, and so on. Certain sporting activities, however, are carried out by both sexes simultaneously.

Although girls and boys are encouraged to associate socially with a considerable amount of freedom, there is still some tendency to make certain that situations are supervised in which social intercourse occurs. In some instances, social activities such as dances, parties, attending theaters and other places of entertainment are equally attended by both genders.

Both boys and girls, providing they have enough academic proficiency and interest, can attend higher levels of education, including polytechnics which provide degrees as well as universities.

Universities, such as Oxford and Cambridge, are very much in demand by both sexes; certain colleges within those universities deal exclusively with either men or women students and house them in separate dormitories. However, the social activities, as well as most academic societies, cater for both sexes.

Values and Interests

Whatever values and interests are acquired by children are the responsibility of the parents, the school, and society as a whole. Customs, traditions, and influences within the neighborhood and through the mass media are important vehicles for the transmission of values.

Britain is a democratic society in which a great variety of influences occur. Unlike a one-party state, a variety of ideas exist within society and the environment in which the young reside.

In recent years, the influence on girls has undoubtedly been their need to compete effectively with their own sex, as well as with members of the opposite sex. At the same time a considerable amount of cooperation has also been considered to be important. There is little doubt that many girls were in some conflict as to the role they might play in the future.

Some girls seek to compete aggressively and on equal terms with all other members of society. This is partly due to the women's liberation movement, as well as to pressures applied by parents and schools. Other girls prefer to adopt the more traditional role which prepares them eventually for marriage, childbearing, and childrearing. Other girls see their role as being in neither one "camp" nor the other but seek to achieve some compromise between the expectations from past traditions and present demands. Certainly, it is true to say that the typical career woman is no longer as frowned upon by society or seen as an anomaly as was the case in the past. The choice of what values and interest a woman will follow after leaving school are predominantly left to herself.

MARRIAGE

In Britain today there is no longer a stigma attached to illegitimacy, as more and more couples choose to live together and bear children out of wedlock. However, in the main, marriage for the female as well as the male is one of the milestones of adult development. Prior to marriage there is a period usually of experimentation which leads to the selection of a mate and eventually to marriage. However, in Britain and other countries in the West, one in three marriages ends in divorce, although most women remarry sooner or later.

Patterns of Mate Selection

The selection of a mate is as accidental or calculated as the individuals who are involved in the process. Whether the choice of a mate is based on mutual interests, expected financial support, romance and love, or passion, it varies with the individuals participating in the interaction. The fact that many marriages are eventually dissolved indicates that the process is anything but perfect. Despite this, however, both men and women strive to fulfil their sexual and social roles of conformity or their need to continue to relate within a family system.

In Britain and Western Europe as a whole, the mate selection process is left to the partners concerned, rather than being arranged by a third or fourth party. Freedom of choice within the limitations of one's own personal choice dictates that responsibility must therefore be taken for such selection, whatever the outcome. One's parents, relations, and friends may add to the selection process by giving opinions. These may or may not be taken into consideration by the partners concerned.

Most marriages and most mate selection processes occur within the immediate vicinity of the home and can include work or institutions of learning at which social contacts can take place with others and where meetings of a number of young people occur. Frequently in Britain, the original meeting takes place close to home, at social events such as dances, or recreational centers, centers of education, in the workplace, or in the neighborhood close to home.

When selecting a mate, on the whole, it is usually considered that such a selection is for a lifetime, but as already mentioned, many marriages do not last and further mate selections occur, even after one or more failures.

Marriage Arrangement

Marriages are not arranged in Britain or Western cultures, except in some ethnic minorities where such customs have existed for a long time. It is for this reason that minority groups usually marry within their own area and among their own people, while those who belong to the predominant population follow the customs of self-selection.

Although freedom of choice between partners may seem preferable, marriages are often, albeit not always, strengthened by the involvement of some members of the families who help to arrange, and hence support to a large degree, marriages of arrangement rather than choice. There is, of course, also the element of choice taking place even with an arranged marriage among minority groups living in Britain. It is fully understood by relatives that unless the partners are "in tune" or have some degree of attraction for one another, it is less than sensible to arrange this kind of liaison.

In Britain, among the general population it would seem inconceivable that any relatives, including one's parents, should have a great deal to say in the choice of a mate. Hence, arrangements are typically between the partners concerned, with relatives playing a peripheral, if any, role.

Long courtships are rare in Western cultures. There tend to be frequent changes of partners until the marriage or relationship is finalized. In a few cases, there may be long periods of engagement and "getting to know one another." However, the importance of romance and sexual attraction still predominates among most young people, rather than a calculated attempt to find a partner who possesses more enduring qualities.

The influence of education, television, films, and literature has in many ways changed the pattern in Britain since World War II to approximate more closely the rapid pace of living, and this has emphasized the relative superficiality of relationships. This trend has gradually changed the psychology of women who now, less than formerly, see themselves as passive creatures in the selection of mates, or in the relationship between men and women.

FAMILIES

On the whole, families and children are born to young couples, but as already mentioned, with the frequency of divorce men and women may have two or even three families that exist in parallel.

With the greater understanding of the role of mothers and fathers in families, there has been a tendency in recent years in Britain and the West to encourage fathers to play a more prominent role in influencing and directing the lives of their children. Many fathers provide regular physical care for infants, especially if the wife is working, and this has brought about favorable repercussions in many ways. Children see the father's role extended into what was formerly the maternal prerogative, while they see their mother performing many of the functions formerly reserved for the male. This has helped children to see their parents not as distinct opposites, each performing a specific role, but rather as a merging of roles. It has undoubtedly also influenced the way that children see their own future in the identity they assume as well as the part they play in relationship with children of the opposite sex.

Hence the father may see himself as the authority within the family in certain areas or as a whole, and this may or may not be accepted by the mother. Certainly, there has been a breakdown in the convention of male dominance and in females' acceptance of this. Women have striven for equality or, in some cases, greater power in family decision-making. This has put significant strain on the marriage and family cohesiveness; however, if such difficulties are overcome, the relationship between the partners and family as a whole becomes stronger and is more likely to endure. Certainly, there is a greater need for tolerance and understanding and a "giving and taking" among the partners now than in the past, when the roles of male and female were more precisely defined.

Today in Britain the father rarely holds an autocratic role in the family, as in Victorian times when he would issue directives that were obeyed without question. Many families now have been constructed on a more democratic basis with input from the wife as well as the children, with decisions being made on the basis of unanimity whenever possible. Since roles are often interchanged now with the woman playing the dominant role or adopting a cooperative democratic position in relation to the male, there has come greater freedom for individuals to play roles determined by their own nature rather than by tradition. The disadvantage, of course, is that there may well be disharmony and a lack of purpose and decision because feelings of equality may lead to a stalemate situation in which neither will yield. While such difficulties are often resolved through mutual discussion and compromise, there are also occasions when this is not possible and disharmony persists, and may well destroy the marriage and ultimately the family. There are few difficulties in areas in which the male automatically makes the decisions concerning his own work, job progression, and so on; similarly, the woman at home looking after the children frequently makes decisions that are felt to be in her own domain. Such a division of labor and control is frequently acceptable to both partners since each has at least some sphere wherein their own ideas and needs prevail.

Divorce

As previously mentioned, in Britain at the present time, one marriage in three ends in divorce. On the whole, the law provides that unless there are severe restrictions to a mother retaining her children, it is the woman who will keep the young in her care. Frequently she will also retain the home wherein the family resided before the divorce. Modern divorce laws have given a considerable amount of equality and even advantage to the woman in a divorce. It has even been felt in Britain that the law has favored the woman rather than being equal in every way. Unless the woman remarries, for instance, she may well cohabit or have relations with other men following divorce, or even during the process of divorce, although she retains all her rights and privileges as well as financial aid from the husband.

Once remarriage occurs, the former husband is still responsible for the welfare and financial support of the children but no longer for that of the wife. It is for this reason that many relationships that could lead to marriage are often carried on surreptitiously without marriage, so that the former wife can have financial aid through the former husband's income, while enjoying a new relationship.

PREGNANCY AND CHILDBIRTH

Attitudes and Practices

While there are individual variations in attitudes and practices to childbirth and rearing, in general in Britain and the West, pregnancy and childbirth is seen as a natural concomitant of a lasting or relatively lasting relationship with a man. Childless marriages, of course, do occur either due to a lack of preference for the bearing of infants or the inability to do so. The statistics are incomplete but the general trend appears to be that one in six marriages are childless for biological or physiological reasons rather than from a lack of desire to bear children. The couple's recourse is usually to tend to adopt or foster children. Many women in Britain, as in many advanced countries, are prepared to spend vast sums of money to become mothers. Extreme measures such as surrogacy and in vitro fertilization demonstrate the desperate need of a woman to fulfil her biological role.

Preparation for Childrearing

Preparation for childrearing is a very haphazard affair. There is no actual preparation as such from the point of view of educational processes or formal training. Preparation therefore is learned on the whole from observations in the home of infants being born, although many are born in hospitals and hence the birth is not directly observable. Very few young mothers have read books on childrearing, or are indeed influenced by them. The generally accepted view is that rearing children is a natural process.

Mother-Infant Bonding

Mother-infant bonding or as psychoanalysts use the term, "cathexis," is very highly regarded in Britain. The natural process of childbirth and the immediate closeness of the infant to the mother in a physical as well as emotional sense begins at birth or even before to develop a connection by which the mother feeds the child not merely physically but emotionally. Mothers too derive a considerable amount of gratification from this process of bonding and fulfilling a deep need within themselves. Hence the two processes are beneficial for all concerned.

They are undermined only by a few abnormal situations such as the death of a parent, marital disharmony, or in some cases, the incapability of the mother herself in dealing with the important responsibility of child nurturing in the physical as well as emotional sense. It has recently been regarded as a form of child abuse to deprive children not merely of physical necessities but also of the emotional warmth which mothers, on the whole, show their infants.

ADULT ACTIVITIES

After marriage and childbirth, a woman's most important adult activities are careers and vocational interests. Careers are often closely associated with educational aspirations and achievements. It is also during periods of education or vocational activities that young women meet males with whom they become friends or with whom they eventually settle down to have families. Many young women are indeed attracted to the educational scene not so much by what it offers them in the area of education, but rather in the opportunities of meeting eligible men with backgrounds and aspirations that are somewhat above the average of the male population.

Status is gained by becoming educated and by obtaining qualifications or degrees. This makes it easier to find an appropriate male partner with whom they can share not merely the usual sexual and marital interests, but intellectual and artistic interests as well. Furthermore, education opens up career opportunities that in previous years would not have existed for women.

Career Opportunities

With the increase in opportunities in education there has come a parallel improvement in career prospects for women. Even in the most primitive of societies women have always contributed their labor, not merely in domestic areas and childrearing, but also in agricultural work. In the preindustrial societies, of course, women were not paid as such, but performed their labor as part of the family demand for everyone to be working to support life. Following the Industrial Revolution many women went out to work and the ratio tended to be, on the whole, one woman for every two men working in most areas.

Perhaps the newest trend is for married women with children to work. In industrialized societies such as Britain and many other parts of Europe, nearly 60 percent of the women employed are married and often with families. With this trend has come a reduction in the size of the family and an increased standard of living. (Another interesting aspect of the typically industrialized society is that one-third of the population is under the age of 15 or over the age of 65; this portion of the population, which is not working, needs to be supported.) However, some believe that the problems of today's children, such as drug taking and glue sniffing, may be attributed in part to the reduction of supervision by working mothers.

Women work primarily for economic reasons, but also for social and moral reasons, which dictate that they give more toward the financial support of their family than was previously the case. A recent census in Britain revealed that over one-third of married women were working. In addition, many women return to work after their families are more independent, which usually occurs between the ages of 30 and 50. Two peaks appear to exist for women working: between the ages of 18-20, that is, before marriage, and from 35 onward, following the rearing of children and their independence. Modern domestic aids have reduced the housewife's work to a routine, quickly and easily completed task.

Some women initially do part-time work while continuing with their domestic responsibilities. Many women enjoy the prospect of returning to work and indeed may not have left it at all. Work provides not only economic sustenance but also stimulation. It provides what may be the only source of social relations that frequently become very important to them.

Despite the equality gradually being achieved by women in a variety of occupations, their pay for equivalent work done by men is still somewhat below parity. "Equal pay for work of equal value" still does not have true meaning. The argument frequently used against such equality is that women rarely perform the same kind of work as men, but this does not apply to many occupations any more. Another argument against giving equal pay is that women frequently only work for a short period of time before entering marriage and having children; this interrupts the continuity of work and frequently appears to waste a considerable period of training that they may have received. The same may, however, be said of men who change jobs in order to seek promotion.

Vocational and Leisure-Time Interests

Perhaps one of the greatest changes for women has been the tendency overall for greater leisure activity to promote their chance for participating in a variety of pursuits. Many more women now than in the past participate in sports throughout their lifetime and frequently in the company of, but also occasionally in competition with, males. In Britain and the West as a whole, women frequently attend courses that are not related to their day-to-day life or work, have hobbies, or participate in social events.

In addition to more leisure time being available, the life-span of both women and men has been extended as a result of better health conditions and improved medical care. Since women generally live longer than men and frequently retire before them, there is an even greater need for women to be provided with and to seek leisure-time activities and interests in hobbies that will sustain them and enrich their lives. Over the past ten years there has been a growth of leisure-time centers throughout Britain and the West to fill the time left by shorter working hours and labor-saving devices at home. Women have simply more time for such interests

WOMEN TODAY

There is little doubt that women today have a considerable degree of equality although not total equality with their male counterparts. Women are engaged in a great variety of occupations, often alongside men and reaching high positions of authority and expertise. Their pay, while not equal in every occupation and profession to that of men, moves closer to parity year by year.

Although women have now greater opportunities to advance themselves through further education and become professional or scientific leaders in their field, many prefer their role as housekeepers and mothers to becoming breadwinners or sharing the breadwinning role with their husbands. On the whole, there is a correlation between the educational level reached and the employment rate for women. Women who have achieved high levels of academic qualifications are more reluctant to give up work than those who have had very little educational opportunities or who have not taken up these opportunities for various reasons. Hence the education gained by women is not squandered following the attainment of their education and qualifications. In more highly educated families, husbands tend to be proud of the fact that their wives are achieving more than mere financial support for the family but are developing their own potential. This is certainly a change from the past when men on the whole felt demeaned by women who worked or who shared in academic attainment and honors through professional achievements.

CONCLUSIONS

The women of Britain, very much as the women of Western Europe in general, have gone through a period of change in recent history which may be termed as more than revolutionary. From being in positions of inferiority and accepting in part these positions, women have increased their influence in every sphere of life from politics to industry. This has led from the Women's Liberation Movement to a more secure position of viewing their own function in relationship to men, the family, and society more rationally. It is therefore anticipated that in the future women, while seeking in many cases to compete effectively with their male counterparts, will also examine their own particular roles in the light of tradition as well as biological function.

The pendulum has certainly swung from women being in a very subordinate position in relation to men and in society generally to one in which women are, if not equal, approaching equality and, in some cases, have usurped the role of the male totally. The question is now: where will women be or where should they be in the century to come? When we speak of women, however, we cannot speak of them in isolation from the rest of society and in particular their male counterparts.

While it is vital that equality of opportunity for women exist, it is also important for women (and for men also) to accept the fact that women are biologically created to perform certain roles that are unlikely ever to be performed by the male. These include childbirth and, on the whole, the initial nurturing of infants. Leaving aside the biological factors of childbirth and the initial caring, it is unlikely that there will be a great deal of difference between the sexes.

Dr. Halina Grzymala-Moszczynska and Johanna

Photo credit: Janusz Podlecki

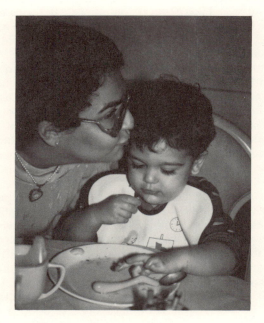

Dr. Beverly Adler-Gross and Harrison

Photo credit: Maric Productions

5

Women in Poland

Halina Grzymala-Moszczynska

The name "Polska" (Poland) was derived from a Slavic tribe, the Polonians, which inhabited the territory of what is known as Great Poland (Wielkopolska), the present-day Poznan region, in the early Middle Ages. In the early eleventh century, after the Polonians succeeded in uniting the lands in the basins of the Odra and Vistula rivers, the name "Polska" began to be applied to the entire state. Since 1952 the country's official name has been the Polish People's Republic. Poland covers an area of 120,733 square miles, which makes it the seventh largest country in Europe. Administratively, Poland is divided into 49 voivodships and 2,070 rural communes. In terms of surface area and population respectively the largest voivodships are the Olsztyn in northern Poland (with an area of 4,760 square miles), and the Katowice (3,806,000 inhabitants).

Poland has more than 36 million inhabitants. Polish society is among the youngest in Europe with one-third of the population being under 20 years of age, and more than half under 30 years. Over a half (59 percent) of all Poles live in towns. The average population density is 44 inhabitants per square mile, with the highest population density being recorded in Lodz (288 per square mile), followed by Warsaw (238 per square mile) and Silesia (over 220 per square mile). The most sparsely populated is the Suwalki voivodship (15 per square mile) in northeast Poland.

Poland is an ethnically homogeneous country, with people of non-Polish nationality comprising 1.5 percent of the population. Most of these are of Byelorussian, Ukrainian, Lithuanian, and Jewish extraction. These ethnic communities have their own cultural associations and publications in their respective languages. At least ten million Poles live outside of Poland. In the United States of America there are some 6,500,000 persons of Polish descent, in the USSR about 1.1 million, in Brazil 840,000, in France 750,000, in Canada over 300,000, in Britain 145,000, in the Federal Republic of Germany 132,000, in Argentina and Australia 120,000 each, in Czechoslovakia 72,000, and in Belgium 45,000, to name just a few countries.

The 1952 Constitution stated that the Polish People's Republic was a State of People's Democracy and that power belonged to the working people in the towns and countryside. That power was to be exercised directly by the representatives elected to the Seym and to the People's Councils. The social ownership of the basic branches of the national economy and the state monopoly of foreign trade were confirmed. The fundamental tasks of the Seym were to enact laws, supervise public administration, adopt long-term economic plans, and approve the state budget. The legislative initiative was vested in the Council of State elected by the Seym, the cabinet, and the deputies to the Seym. The cabinet (literally called the "Council of Ministers") with its prime ministers was to be the highest executive and administrative agency of the state. The Constitution guaranteed to the citizens of Poland the right to work and to rest, the protection of health, education, and access to cultural achievements. It also stated that women and men had equal rights, that the State would protect the family as a social institution, that all citizens would enjoy the same rights regardless of nationality, race and religion, and freedom of thought. There was separation of church and state. The Constitution guaranteed freedom of thought and religion to its citizens, as well as the liberty to perform religious functions to the churches and to the other denominational groups. At present, there are more than 30 regional churches and denominations in Poland. Traditionally the largest of them has been the Roman Catholic Church with 7,299 parishes and a total of more than 14,000 churches and chapels.

Among the socioeconomic changes that took place between the merger of the workers' parties and the passing of the 1952 Constitution the most radical was the drive (undertaken despite a shortage of agricultural tools and machineries, mainly tractors) to form collective farms. This was intended to unify the agrarian organization of the countries engaged in the building of socialism and rapidly to transform individual farms, which were concentrating on marketable products on a small scale, into socialist ones. The 1952 Constitution included both (1) a provision that promised support for the formation of cooperative farms; and (2) one that ensured protection to individually (privately) owned farms (*Panorama of Polish History*, 1982; Wojnowski, 1984).

Then in 1956, while emphasizing the unchanging observance of the principles of Marxism-Leninism, the necessity was stressed of democratizing political life and improving living standards. The concept of the rightist and nationalist deviation was totally abandoned. This event created a new political climate in the country and revealed—as had been the case immediately after the end of the war—the spirit of the masses.

The drive for industrialization, launched immediately after the war, was particularly intense in the period covered by the Six-Year Plan (1950-56), which led to the construction of many new industrial plants, including a number of new industrial town districts, such as Nowa Huta in Cracow, Nowe Tychy, and the new districts of Konin in Great Poland.

Accelerated economic growth through industrialization was then achieved mainly by the maximum use of labor, that is, by the virtual elimination of the latent unemployment in the rural areas, typical of the prewar period, and less by increased labor productivity. A considerable exodus of people from rural to urban areas could be observed.

In 1973, the level of industrial production in Poland was 20 times higher than it had been in 1938. The structure of industry changed too; the role of electrical engineering, chemical production, automobile and shipbuilding industries grew.

Industrialization and the growth of agriculture were closely linked to changes in the social structure. In that respect People's Poland had witnessed a far-reaching revolution. Before World War II the rural population accounted for 73 percent of the population in Poland, whereas in 1979 some 77.5 percent of the population lived on earnings from nonagricultural sources, the figure being 50 percent for the rural areas. This meant a high degree of urbanization of those areas, accompanied by corresponding changes in cultural patterns. If we take the years 1950, 1960, and 1979, the percentage of the population that lived primarily on agriculture fell from 47.1 to 38.4 and 22.5 percent respectively. Correspondingly, the percentage of the urban population was growing rapidly, from 39 in 1950, to 48.3 in 1960, to 58.2 in 1979. While the population of the country increased by 11.7 million people, the corresponding figure for the urban population was 12.5 million, which showed that the towns absorbed not only the whole natural increase of the population, but also some people from rural areas. In all, the population of Poland rose from 25 million in 1950 to 35.6 million in 1980, which equalled the prewar level. Next to the increase of the percentage of the population gainfully employed outside agriculture, the numerical increase of the working class, together with the changes in its structure, must be considered the other significant process. In 1970 there were 6.8 million workers, of whom 64.5 percent worked in industry and the building trade. The number of workers employed in modern industries, including the automated ones, had grown to about 40 percent and many of them were educated on the secondary vocational level.

The growth of the "intelligentsia" is to be noted as the third important change in the social structure, the more so since that group had undergone radical modifications, primarily because of the higher general standard of education. From being the traditional bearer of the national cultural heritage, it had come to be a much more heterogeneous group, comprising intellectuals, professional people, and white-collar workers in general; it had also become less hereditary than before World War II. The intelligentsia, decimated by the Nazis, accounted before the war for some 14 percent of all those gainfully employed outside agriculture; that number rose to some 25 percent in 1950, and to over 35 percent in 1973.

The process, as has been said, was closely associated with the increase in education: while between the two world wars some 85,000 persons acquired higher education, the analogous figure for 1945-65 was 368,900, with an additional 797,800 to be added in the following 14 years.

Further, more industrialization, urbanization, increased horizontal social mobility, a much quicker flow of information (via radio and TV), the effects of the educational system and advances in cultures, and higher living standards of the rural population all resulted, and continue to result, in reducing the differences between town and country. In most general terms, life has become in a sense urbanized, which can best be seen in the rural areas. The process has had two features: the adaptation of the people from the rural areas who have moved to towns to the life-styles of urban life, and the penetration by those life-styles into rural areas. Transitional folk culture has begun to vanish and changed into "folklore" in the sense of something "ornamental," deliberately revitalized in order to exploit local color. The most visible changes are observable in rural housing construction, which frequently imitated second-rate urban models, while folk patterns have become popular with well-to-do dwellers. The same trend applied to furniture. Here, modernization in the rural areas reached stoves and ranges first, spreading gradually to furniture and various household appliances (no more benches and chests, changes in interior decoration). There was a general trend to increase floor space, also in towns where—after the first period of reconstruction—housing conditions had been improving, although at too slow a pace.

Education was the basis on which culture could develop and spread. The postwar period witnessed a growth in the number of schools and students. The number of schools of higher education (both those of university levels and vocational) also rose. The number of pupils in secondary schools increased, as did the number of students attending universities. This illustrated the spreading of post-elementary education, and hence the better intellectual "equipment" of the population. In 1970-80 Poland had 10 universities, 18 colleges (institutes) of technology, 10 medical schools, nine agricultural colleges, and 46 schools of other types (concerned with teacher training, physical education, sports, art, and theology). Over 100 research institutes affiliated with the various ministries have been set up. The number of research workers increased significantly; while the average rise in employment in the socialized economy was 7.6 percent between 1970 and 1972, the analogous figure for the number of researchers and the academic staff was 55.7 percent (see *Panorama of Polish History*, 1982; Wojnowski, 1984.)

INFANCY AND EARLY CHILDHOOD

In spite of the fact that children of both sexes are equally welcomed by their parents, there is still some difference in approach to the newborn girl and the newborn boy. Usually fathers are prouder of their newborn sons than of their newborn daughters. They treat him as the prospective successor of the family name and family property. To that extent the son might be treated as proof of the real "masculinity" of the father. Statistics also show that sons are often more welcomed as the first child in the family than daughters. A daughter is treated somewhat less seriously, but almost always very much wanted as a second child as a boy was wanted as the firstborn. Usually it is the mother who wants daughters, since daughters are expected to help with the housework. All children, regardless of gender, stay close to their mother during the first year of life. Up to five years of age the relationship between the children and their fathers remains rather loose. It changes at about five years when the father becomes a more important authority than the mother; and finally at about seven years the attitudes toward both parents balance out.

From almost the first days of an infant's life, sex-typing and socialization to prospective sex-stereotypical roles are started. There are three aspects of children's life that are connected with sex-typing: the way of dressing children, toys, and the domain of home duties. According to tradition male and female infants are dressed in different colors. Boys' clothes should be blue and girls' are pink. Nowadays this tradition is limited due to difficulties in getting children's clothes. From the very beginning girls and boys wear clothes almost identical to the clothes of adults of the same sex. This is especially true for more festive occasions when children are expected to be little ladies or gentlemen. Girls especially are dressed like big dolls. In everyday life and among poorer people this is less popular, but otherwise it is the current tradition.

Concerning children's games and toys there is a very definite difference between the toys offered to boys and to girls, as well as between the games both of them are taught. Only girls are given dolls, doll carriages, doll dresses, or small kitchen appliances. Probably only they will be taught by their mothers how to sew doll clothes. In contrast, only boys get small cars, gadgets for tinkering, or balls for sports like soccer. Also during team games (cooperative play) both girls and boys are taught to take roles proper to their sexes. Girls play games that concentrate primarily on family topics. One favorite among girls is playing "house." Girls take on roles of mother and father, and with their doll carriages go for walks. Dolls "play" the role of the child in the family. On the other hand, the games and toys for boys concentrate mainly on cars, technical tools, and the ways to manipulate and use them.

THE SCHOOL YEARS

The Educational System, Achievement and Socialization, Values and Interests

Compulsory schooling starts in Poland at the age of six years. At this age a child has to attend kindergarten, which is located either within the preschool (for children who have previously participated in preschool) or within the school (for children who have never attended preschool). Kindergarten programs include a knowledge of general ideas of arithmetic, knowledge of the alphabet (printed only), and a general knowledge of specific work activities. Children are also taught to behave in school, school discipline, cooperative work, and so on. Teachers teach them to keep notebooks, and inform them about the general rules of school life. Since the 1960s all schools are coeducational. The only classes that are conducted separately are physical education and technical classes. For example, classes for girls offer more games, while classes for boys concentrate on soccer, basketball, and other sports. In technical education or home economic classes girls are taught to cook, make simple clothes, and embroider. On the other hand, boys are taught vocational skills, such as how to repair simple home utensils like irons, or electric heaters, and how to use basic tools like planes, grinding wheels, lathes, and so on. Although all other classes are conducted for girls and boys together, there still exist important differences in what teachers expect from the pupils of each sex. Usually teachers expect a better performance from girls in the humanities and from boys in the sciences. Teachers are stricter with girls with respect to dress or keeping well-organized notebooks. This attitude stems from the fact that girls are seen as prospective housewives who should know how to keep their surroundings clean and organized.

Primary school is compulsory for all children. Training in secondary school depends on individual decisions. Although the majority of children continue their schooling in the secondary school, there are major differences in the kinds of schools that are chosen by boys and girls. Most often girls, at least the wealthy or more ambitious ones, attend a general high school. The first choice for boys is a vocational high school which gives them, immediately after graduation, the opportunity to accept a job. Secondary schools are also coed. However, there are schools with very obvious majorities of men or women. For example, schools for dressmakers, nursery school or kindergarten teachers are almost exclusively attended by girls. In contrast, coal mining or metallurgy schools are exclusively for boys. Boys from rural areas usually end their education after the secondary professional schools, while girls finish after primary school. City boys usually stop after technical or vocational school. Girls very often go on to universities.

The time spent in secondary school is also a period of important decision-making for girls, especially concerning their plans for the future. Some girls who finish their education after secondary school start professional jobs, but wish (at least this is true of the majority) to get married. Girls who decide to continue their education go to universities, technical schools, and the like. University education in Poland became recently more and more "feminized." At the universities a definite majority of students are women; they are especially numerous in the humanities (liberal arts) and teachers' colleges. Specific technical colleges, such as for coalminers or metallurgical studies, have mostly men students; women students are very rare there, and sometimes they are semi-jokingly called "husband-hunters." Other faculties, such as civil engineering, architecture, and medicine, have an undifferentiated enrollment of men and women. Research results show very clearly that gender does not influence how successful a person is in his or her studies; another factor, however, which influences and predicts success is the person's IQ. Male students as a group had a higher IQ score than female students. In fact, after graduation it is almost only the men who receive proposals to work as assistant professors. Discrimination against women is usually very prevalent, possibly because of prospective pregnancy, motherhood, and maternity leave followed by many days at home because of the child's illnesses.

MARRIAGE

Patterns of Mate Selection, Marriage Arrangements, Families, and Divorce

The social background of a boy or a girl affects the selection of prospective spouses. According to tradition, men are supposed to play an active role in their choice of a future wife. Young women assume the passive role. They are asked to accept somebody else's proposal. Until World War I a marriage was completely arranged by the parents of the prospective spouses with the help of a matchmaker. In the period between wars fewer and fewer marriages were contracted in this way, and there was an increase in the number of marriages contracted by the spouses themselves. However, the more traditional way of contracting marriages prevails in the country. In spite of a great deal of relaxation concerning traditional norms, there are still many marriages contracted through the suggestions of parents or neighbors due, for example, to property reasons (a good way of joining the land of two neighboring farms). Before World War II, many girls never married because their parents could not afford to give them the proper dowry. But nowadays a girl's education can replace the traditional dowry. Good, practical professions like a tailor, hairdresser, or a university education can easily replace a girl's money and property even with the most traditional farmer families. There is an important difference between the village and the city in terms of the average age in which marriage takes place. Most girls in rural areas get married between 18 and 22, though in the city the ages ranged mostly between 21 and 26 years. Social pressure for early marriages is far stronger in rural areas, due to the fact that farm work requires real physical strength and as such is considered men's work. City life leaves much more freedom in this respect and late marriages are more common.

Pressure for a second marriage is also stronger in rural than in urban areas, due to the fact that farm life needs a "complete" family more urgently than is necessary for city life. Most marriages in the villages occur between young men and young women of rural origin. Many young farmers face difficulties in selecting a prospective wife. Girls in the country are afraid to assume the duties of a housewife on a big farm. Many girls "escape" to the city to find freedom and a less strenuous life. This makes it very difficult for men to find a wife. Therefore many young farmers ask for help from matrimonial agencies, but usually without success, because city girls are also afraid to start life in the country. Currently the problem of finding wives is one of the most important reasons for the mass escape of young adults from the country to the city. This, in turn, influences the so-called "aging" of the Polish village, where more elderly people remain.

In the city the selection of prospective spouses takes place almost completely without parental involvement. Due to the coeducational school system and coeducational employment, young women and young men have more opportunities to meet each other and to choose prospective spouses. Therefore young city women are much more independent in their choices of husbands. More than half of all couples have the same educational level, 45 percent have the same profession and 43 percent have the same social background. According to tradition in Poland, an important problem in the mate-selection process was a dowry, which the wife should bring to her husband's house. Usually it contained some money and some utensils for the future household. Almost obligatory for the wife's dowry was a featherbed (comforter), pillows, and kitchen utensils. More affluent families gave their daughters houses, some land, and a cow. Even a daughter who lived in the city might get a "symbolic cow" in the form of money from selling a real cow.

A financial agreement between both families covers the problem of the costs of the wedding party after the marriage ceremony. The bride's family should supply all meals, while the groom should pay for the drinks (alcoholic) and the band. Wedding parties are very expensive, since usually many guests attend such a party. In the country the guest lists include approximately 150 to 200 guests, although in the city there are most frequently from 30 to 100 guests. In the village the party takes place in the house of the fiancé, while in the city it is held at a restaurant or a club.

The traditional division of costs and dowry is far more popular in rural districts than in the city. Usually poorer families who live in the city cannot afford the traditional big party, so they often give a small reception for just a few persons at their home. Family life in contemporary Poland depends mainly on the education of both spouses.

At the top of the hierarchy, both partners represent the so-called "creative" professions, for example, the marriage of research workers. Usually there is a strong intellectual bond between spouses, with mutual concerns in their work, achievements, and interests. Sometimes this kind of marriage can be called a "compassionate match." Despite their mutual attachments, both partners are quite tolerant of extramarital sex.

The situation is different when only the husband has a "creative" profession. There are usually two possibilities for the wife: **(1)** she will accept her husband's work as most important and will subordinate her life-style and the family life to the husband's duties; or **(2)** she will pressure her husband to give her more time and a more active social life than he can afford (this situation usually results in marital conflict).

A third kind of family situation is the one in which both partners have university education, but work in "non-creative" professions. Spouses share their domestic duties, the care of the children, cleaning the home, and so on. The wife spends less time preparing meals or washing clothes than in any other type of family, because she utilizes outside services for these chores.

A fourth type of family is represented by the family in which both spouses finished their secondary school education. Husband-wife relationships are more strict. The division of labor between husband and wife is also far more defined than in any other type of marriage style. Many men work at a second job to earn more money. The wife is the only person responsible for home and children. These blue-collar workers' families have some very traditional characteristics. The husband and wife usually have only a primary education, but sometimes have also completed some vocational courses. The wife usually does not work. Family life is organized around the work schedule of the factory. Since the husband supports the family, the housework is done exclusively by the wife. Her responsibility is to run the household and see to the education of the children. The husband has several privileges, which include getting better food and exemption from the household chores. In spite of the strict delineation between the duties of the head of the household and his wife, there are some exceptions to the rule, especially in villages. Women share the men's work with regard to agriculture. She takes care of the horses, mows with the lawn mower or mowing machine, and ploughs. Men participate only in the "rush hour" duties, for example, in harvesting or digging potatoes. This family belongs to the most traditional type and is the least susceptible to cultural changes.

Another traditional life-style is found among farmers. Similar to the blue-collar worker's family, there is a strict division of labor between men and women. It is the most patriarchal type of family. The wife, as well as the children, depend very much on the father's and husband's wishes. This is the only type of family in which parents in a decisive manner decide on, or at least approve of, the prospective spouse for their child. In such a case the interest of the family has priority over those of the individual.

Tradition and the contemporary practice of church weddings are prevalent in Poland. More than 80 percent of the couples who register in City Hall also have church weddings; but only 40 percent fully accept the church wedding as a sacrament. The remaining 60 percent approach the church wedding mainly as a beautiful traditional ceremony with a very solemn atmosphere. Polish law requires civil registration prior to the church ceremony. Since the church wedding is not seen as a sacrament, the church and civil ceremonies are treated as being equal. The civil ceremony is accepted as a sufficient condition for having sexual relationships and consummating the marriage.

A second aspect of marriage secularization is the acceptance of divorce as a possible solution to marital problems. The divorce rate between 1949 and 1980 increased three times with city dwellers and two times in rural communities. The incidence of divorce increased with the educational level of the spouses and was concentrated mainly among young couples. Because of the continuous increase in the economic independence of women, the divorce rate has increased, regardless of the number of children involved. The courts usually give custody of the children to their mothers and not to their fathers.

Women apply for divorce more often in marriages of up to 15 years' duration, while more men apply in "older" marriages. More and more, divorces are accepted by the society.

Another prominent trend in contemporary marriages concerns the number of children. During the first decade after World War II the average couple had 3.5 children. Since then this figure was reduced to 2.1 children in 1975. Today's families in urban areas have 1.6 children and in rural areas 2.7 children. Thus the typical family in the city has 1 or 2 children and in the country 3 or 4 children. Less than one-tenth of all families have more than four children. The increased educational level of women is a major factor that correlates with the decrease in number of children. Women with a primary school education usually have 2.4 children, while those with a secondary school level have 1.6 children, and women with a university education have 1.5 children. A relatively large proportion (37 percent) of childless married women do not wish to have children. A trend exists among more affluent families to have one or two children.

PREGNANCY AND CHILDBIRTH

Attitudes and Practices, Preparations for Childrearing, Mother-Infant Bonding

Pregnancy gives a woman in Poland some special rights. She cannot be employed in difficult positions, for example, in jobs demanding physical labor or work at night. She can shop without queuing (standing in line) and after the third month of pregnancy women are very much encouraged to remain in continuous contact with their doctors. In most big cities childbearing classes are organized. At these classes women are taught proper physical exercises that will help them to keep fit during pregnancy, as well as the use of proper breathing and relaxing techniques during labor. Men are especially invited to attend classes devoted to basic childcare.

Almost 100 percent of the births take place in hospitals and clinics. It is prohibited for medical personnel to organize a delivery at home, even at the request of the prospective mother. Delivery wards are organized in all hospitals, except in rural communities where there are small delivery rooms with a midwife and part-time obstetrician in attendance. There is almost no literature concerning sex education, but there are many books on childrearing. These books very often are the only source of information on this topic for women who rear their child without contact with their family or outside the family tradition. Differences can be seen in this respect between rural and urban families. Tradition plays a more important role in rural than in urban communities. A three-months fully paid maternity leave is guaranteed for all mothers. After this period a mother has to decide whether she will continue her maternity leave (with part-payment) or return to her job. If she decides to return to work, she must arrange some type of care for her baby. An optimal solution would be if one of the family members (for example, a retired mother) could stay with the child at home. Otherwise, the mother may hire a babysitter, which is very expensive and difficult to find. Due to the limited openings at daycare centers (no more than 24 percent of daycare candidates are accepted) this solution remains a rather theoretical one (Adamski, 1982).

Usually bonding between child and mother is strong; however, due to the situation described above, in many families mother-infant bonding remains quite loose and time-limited.

ADULT ACTIVITIES

Career Opportunities

Although the law stresses equality between all members of the society, unfortunately there is no such thing for men and women with respect to career and salary opportunities. The average salaries for women are about 30 percent lower than the men's salaries for equivalent positions. To get the jobs, women must present better skills and higher abilities than men. There are several reasons for the lower level positions of women employees. Objectively, one could mention the physical and psychological reasons, for example, in professions such as coal mining or metallurgy. However, much more important are the jobs that are "appropriate" for women. Sometimes women refuse managerial positions because they lack self-confidence for such job opportunities. Even in factories or offices where mainly women work, managerial positions are usually held by men because it is felt that women are unable to lead other women.

There are some health-related professions with especially high percentages of women. Women constitute 50 percent of the medical doctors, 80 percent of dentists, 77.5 percent of pharmacists, 97 percent of nurses, 90 percent of laboratory technicians, 71 percent of all teachers, 81.2 percent of librarians, and 68.8 percent of psychologists, just to mention a few of the professions. Generally the average salaries in the "feminine" professions are lower than those in the "masculine" occupations. Also, men working in the feminine professions usually earn higher salaries than women do. Ten times more men than women occupy top positions, like directors or supervisors. The same is true in the sciences. Among full professors there are only 16.7 percent women.

AGING

In Poland women can retire earlier (at 60 years old) than men (65 years). After retirement they live a fuller and busier life than men. Women's activities with their children's family life constitutes a type of continuation of their own family life. A grandmother retired from professional duties is still the most wanted solution for the majority of families in which young adult women, in spite of being a wife and mother, wish to continue their professional careers. A high level of activity in the social family life, which characterizes the majority of retired women, seems to influence their better health, and the fact that the average life expectancy for women in Poland is 70 years, while for men it is 65 years.

CONCLUSIONS

The main factor that influenced changes in the traditional patterns of Polish women's life-style is their occupational involvement outside their home. Since World War II until now there was an increase of about five times as many women working in money-making jobs. This trend is illustrated by the following statistics: In 1931 there were 1,060,000 women with outside jobs; however, in 1980 the number had increased to 5,000,000 working women. Poland occupies the second highest position in the world (after the USSR) with regard to the number of women who are employed outside their home: 46 percent of all women have jobs, and 75 percent of the married women among them are gainfully employed.

The basic motive for these women is that of economic necessity (especially among those performing manual labor). Women with high school and university education list instead their personal involvement in professions.

Employment of women brought along several important changes to the social role of women. First of all, women who are only busy as a homemaker are far less appreciated than those who are employed outside the house. Second, due to the severe time limitations of the working mother, the primary function in the socialization process, that of shaping the children's attitudes toward life and continuing traditional family values, is now being transferred to the duties of the grandmother. Emotional relationships between the grandmother and the grandchildren therefore remain very often much warmer than the relationship between mother and children. The role of the father is markedly reduced in this respect (this is especially true for manual laborers' and blue-collar workers' families). This change is clear and important, because for a long time men (father and grandfather) were mainly responsible for preserving the family's traditions.

The Polish woman has had to pay a rather high price for her economic and social independence. This price included the necessity to accept full-time employment and then to respond to demands from both the family and the home, and her employment and the workplace.

REFERENCES

Adamski, F. (1982). *Socjologia malzenstwa i rodziny*. Warsaw: Wprowadzenie.
Panorama of Polish History. (1982). Warsaw, Poland: Interpress
Wojnowski. T. (1984). *A Polish American's Guide to Poland*. Warsaw, Poland: Interpress.

Two ''Big Sisters'': Natasha (left) and Lena (right)

Two ''Little Sisters'': Xenya (8 years) and Masha (6 years)

6

Women in the USSR

Lena Zhernova

Many problems are connected with women's rights, among them those concerned with the family, motherhood, and childhood, which are current in different countries irrespective of their public and social systems. Because of a mutual need for ways to find solutions, an exchange of experiences on the international level is important. The current political situation and the relaxation of international tension give us an excellent opportunity for an exchange of ideas and practical know-how from a cross-national and cross-cultural perspective.

I am not a specialist in the determination and solution of "women's problems"; I am a journalist writing on these themes. But I hope that my chapter will help give a clear—if only partial view—of a woman's life in the USSR today.

BACKGROUND AND HISTORY

Before talking of the current conditions it is good to take a look at the history of the USSR. October 1917 was the starting point of a new life for thousands of women who were oppressed and had no rights at all in Czarist Russia. The Great October Socialist Revolution significantly changed the history of the whole country as well as the destiny of women. A struggle for the social reconstruction of a society is impossible without a striving for women's rights of equality. Keeping this fact in mind, the Communist Party and the Soviet government took steps toward the solution of "women's problems" on all the stages of the country's history.

The way toward social achievements was a long and difficult one. On the one hand, the October Revolution provided Soviet women with equal rights with men in all spheres of the economy, as well as in political and cultural life. Real possibilities for the realization of women's rights in labor and education were created. All women were given the opportunity to work in any branch of the national economy and to study at any educational institution. Labor and education—the most important conditions of true equality—became vital requirements to millions of Soviet women. On the other hand, our state was going through decades of laying heavy burdens on delicate women's shoulders, and for this reason women could use their full rights only quite recently.

The need to deal with a great number of problems, such as the protection of pregnant women and young children, came into existence right after the foundation of the Soviet States. It was necessary to create conditions for giving women—often mothers—opportunities for useful employment to provide the essential measures for the care of health and welfare for the children. In order to counteract the consequences of the civil war, of starvation, and of the economic upheaval, the Maternity and Child Protection Department was organized within the Ministry of the State's Charity starting on January 1, 1918.

The First All-Union Congress on the Maternity and Childhood Protection was held in December 1920. In January 1924 the Children's Fund, concerned with childcare, was founded at the Second All-Union Congress of the Soviets, which was dedicated to V. I. Lenin's memory. In 1938 this Fund was closed, but it was reopened in October 1987. Of the Constitution of the USSR, which was adopted in 1936, it used to be said quite a few years ago, that it was responsible for the successes that were achieved in the protection of pregnant women and children during the childhood years. Now we know how far from real-life situations were these "successes" so declared in documents and papers. Anyone who is to the slightest extent acquainted with Soviet history knows how tragic and complicated was our past. There was the civil war, economic dislocation, reconstruction of the national economy, industrialization, collectivization, terrible starvation of 1931-33, the great Patriotic War—and again the economic dislocation and hard labor to restore a normal life—and all this took place during the Stalin's cult period up to the beginning of the 1950s.

AN OVERVIEW: WOMEN IN THE USSR

Nowadays the situation in the country has changed greatly. A woman in the Soviet Union possesses not mythical but real rights. Her interests are safeguarded by the State's law and guaranteed by the USSR Constitution, which was adopted in 1977. Article 35 of the Constitution says (freely translated):

Women and men have equal rights in the USSR.
Realization of these rights is insured by affording women equal access with men to education and professional training, equal opportunities in employment, wages and promotion, in social, political, and cultural activities, and by special labor and health protection measures for women; by providing conditions enabling mothers to work; by legal protection, material, and moral support for

mothers and children, including paid leaves and other benefits for expectant mothers and mothers, and gradual reduction of working time for mothers with infants, toddlers, and preschool children.

Mothers' and children's interests are well protected and regulated by different legislative acts, among them the laws for care and public health, labor, marriage and family. The Communist Party and many government agencies take care to look after these matters and then follow them with appropriate actions to improve conditions. It is appropriate to say that the place of women in the labor force in the national economy is substantial and fulfils the aim of attracting women into different areas of the industrial job market. This was proposed from the start of the Soviet State, and has been well established now. But when this aim is accomplished, which is important by itself, one could forget that a woman is mainly destined to be a mother and a homemaker. In an ideal situation both of these roles for women—at home and on the job—have to harmonize and compliment each other. However, it is necessary to create economic and social conditions conducive to achieving this. In practice it means that a woman must have an opportunity to choose optimal hours for the working day for herself, in order to have as much time as possible to spend with her family, and on the education and upbringing of her children. Such a point of view of women has begun to be recognized in our society; women are now being considered not only as workers, but as a source of life and the health of future generations. And it is important, because about 70 percent of the working women have children. Yet most of them will not want to be either only a homemaker, or exclusively an employee.

INFANCY AND EARLY CHILDHOOD

Infancy is the most important period of physical and cognitive development. During the first years of life a base is also laid for the child's emotional growth as well, and since the baby is exposed to environmental influences it requires loving and thoughtful care.

A child is born at a maternity hospital under favorable conditions, where a skilled doctor and a trained nurse assist with the birth. Approximately on the sixth day the newborn baby and the mother leave the hospital for home, where they are looked after attentively by a clinic's doctor. During the first week after leaving the hospital a trained nurse comes to see the baby at home every day. She makes recommendations, gives practical advice for caring for the infant, and looks out for the infant's health and needs. Every month until the child reaches the age of one year, mother and baby see the doctor who looks after the baby's progress, and refers the child to different medical specialists for examination when necessary and prescribes the appropriate treatment. All these medical services are rendered free of charge.

Since December 1989, women in the USSR are given a partially paid leave of absence to look after the baby up to the age of one and a half years, and an unpaid leave up to the time that the child reaches three years. During all this time the mother keeps her position and her employment.

It is quite natural that not all mothers have an opportunity to stay with their child during the first three years. In this case a mother has the choice to enroll the child in a kindergarten. The number of children attending kindergartens has reached 16.5 million. The State provides for the greatest part of the costs of keeping children in kindergarten (about 80 percent). The children's maintenance cost in preschool institutions depends on the family's income. Families with low incomes are exempt from the payment of the maintenance cost.

In the summertime children go to the country together with a kindergarten group. As a rule, those children who attend the kindergarten are prepared for studies at schools which they enter when they reach six or seven years. At that age a new stage in their life begins.

SCHOOL YEARS

Universal secondary education is obligatory in this country now. Boys and girls receive secondary education either at a secondary school, where the program lasts 11 years, or at a vocational school, which they can enter on completion of the ninth grade. There are also evening schools at which young men and women can receive a secondary education if they are employed during the daytime.

Instruction in regular secondary schools can be divided into three stages. The first stage starts with the primary school, which takes three to four years, depending on what age the child is enrolled (at six or seven years). School education for six-year-old children was introduced not long ago, and now the plan is to switch to six years as the age at which children start to go to school. The second stage also lasts four years (that is, from the fifth to the ninth grade). After finishing the ninth grade, children choose whether they want to go on studying in school or prefer to enter a vocational school where they will be trained in a trade, which is equivalent to receiving a secondary education. The third stage in education takes three years and includes the ninth, tenth, and eleventh grades.

The system of education in this country has been conservative for many years; mainly, it remains conservative even today. The relationship between students and teachers, with occasional exceptions, is based on authoritarian administrative principles. In the senior grades students receive practical training in various skills (which they are free to choose) working at factories, industrial enterprises, collective farms, or workshops combined with their schools.

What do school children do in their free time? They can attend affordable courses in athletics and various sports, art, and music. They can join different hobby groups, which are connected to culture clubs and the young pioneers' centers in a location near their homes.

In the summer, children from primary and secondary schools can spend time at pioneer camps. Trade unions pay for the greater part of a pioneer camp voucher's price. Students from senior grades can join work teams.

After finishing school, each student receives a General Certificate of Education, which entitles them to take the entrance exam at any college in any Soviet town. Those who do not wish to continue their studies will start working in an occupation they choose.

If students pass the entrance exam (which does not permit any discrimination on sexual grounds), they start their studies at the university. Throughout their studies, students participate in practical training in their fields as well, which helps them complement theoretical knowledge with practical skills. During the summer months students can volunteer to join construction teams that offer them the opportunity to enjoy a change of activity and earn some money at the same time.

The following statistics can sum up the current situation: Women make up 60 percent of all specialists with higher or secondary education. At the beginning of the academic year 1985-86, 55 percent of all students were women. Of these, 31,900 studied at postgraduate courses (33 percent of the total number of postgraduate students); girls made up 58 percent of all the students in secondary vocational institutions.

MARRIAGE AND DIVORCE

In this country men and women can marry at the age of 18, that is, at the time of their coming of age. Family relations are legally regulated by the Fundamentals of the Marriage and Family legislation (which serves, in a sense, as marriage contracts). This legislation stipulates the terms and procedure of marriage and divorce, the parents' responsibility for bringing up children, measures to protect the interests of children, and so on. A family is formed after marriage. There are over 70 million families in the Soviet Union. Over 2.7 million families form every year. The majority of men and women marry.

Nowadays young couples have only a vague idea of what family relationships should be like when they marry. Several years ago a subject called "Ethics and Psychology of Family Life" was included in school curricula after a long debate. The scientific approach to this problem is only just starting to be recognized.

Marriage is a serious business. "A strong nation starts with strong families," people say. Is the modern Soviet family really strong? The answer to this question is negative. Various surveys demonstrate that the modern family is in a state of crisis. This is a regrettable situation, because traditionally, Russian families derived strength in kin ties and the patriarchal tradition.

To start, we note the increasing number of divorces; every third (or second, in large cities) marriage disintegrates. In 1986, for instance, 2,727,000 marriages were registered in the Soviet Union, only to be followed by 934,000 divorces. Annually 700,000 children lose a parent due to a divorce. Recent years witnessed a steady tendency for early marriages and an increase of childbirth to a family of parents under 18 years. Most of such marriages are "forced" ones connected with an unwanted pregnancy. The number of unregistered marriages is on the increase too. In Moscow, for example, 20 to 25 percent of the young people between 24 to 30 years live in unregistered marriages. Eleven percent of adults are convinced bachelors who refuse to marry and start a family. The number of childless marriages is growing, and so is the number of children born out of wedlock. In the 1970s the percentage of such children was 5.8 percent; in 1987, however, the respective indicator was 14 percent (that is, every eighth child was born to an unwed couple). Illegitimate children constitute the bulk of the so-called "refused children," that is, those who are voluntarily abandoned by their mothers at the maternity centers. About 6,000 children are turned in by single mothers to special children's homes every year.

And how do the parents or parents-to-be behave? About 100,000 have been stripped of their parental rights in the past five years and 150,000 have been pronounced incapable. (The data were supplied by Albert A. Likhanov, chairman of the Board of the USSR Children's Foundation.) Sixty percent of all premeditated murders and attempted murders, as well as 50 percent of serious physical injuries, are committed in families on home grounds. The growing rate of crime and alcohol abuse among women has generated special concern. Can one seriously speak of the prestige of motherhood, of the restoration of femininity, of charity and kindness when 545,000 women, mostly women with children, are chronic alcoholics? Over 5,000 women are registered as engaged in prostitution, and this number is growing with every passing year. The decline of parental morality boosts juvenile and infantile delinquency, which has increased by 2.8 percent over the past five years. Irresponsible attitudes of parents and their ignorance in elementary issues of sexual matters result in a growing incidence of serious disorders in children.

These statistics do not require any further comment. It is absolutely clear that the family must be salvaged, that urgent and effective measures are imperative if the family is to be restored and stabilized. These problems are tackled in earnest today by the Family Council, which was established by the Children's Foundation of the Soviet Union. The country's best experts, including sexologists, physicians, psychologists, sociologists, teachers, as well as parents themselves, participate in the work of the Family Council with the objective not only of studying the problems and demands of families, but also of rendering concrete assistance.

In addition, economic factors directly influence family relationships and their stability. Among such factors are the low level of services, poor organization of trade, shortages of staple foods and basic consumer items, and the acute housing problem. Although we speak of equality in marriage, the bulk of housework is done by women. In fact, women work 13 to 14 hours a day: eight hours at a job and five to six hours at home. On the average women enjoy one-and-a-half times less leisure time than men. The reason for this is simple: it is women's greater involvement in household affairs (two to three times greater than men's). In this context, a woman has only 30 to 40 minutes a day to devote to her children.

Not surprisingly, divorce is a not infrequent result of such a strenuous life. If the couple has no children, their divorce can be registered simply at the local registry office. If they do have children, however, their divorce application is considered by a court of law, which protects in most cases the interests of the mother and the child or children. The father must pay monthly alimony to support his children until the age of 18 (as a rule, after the divorce children stay with their mothers). The alimony is 25 percent of all earnings for one child, 33 percent for two children, and 50 percent for three or more children. The alimony cannot be lower than 20 rubles a month. It must be noted that in general alimonies do not amount to much and are insufficient to raise a child. The country still lacks a reliable method for recovering alimony, which makes it possible for former husbands to shirk on the payments for their children by changing jobs often, or simply by going about the country doing odd jobs. The work of bailiffs, who are responsible for retrieving alimony, leaves much to be desired as well.

The Fundamentals of Marriage and the Family legislation also stipulates the procedure of stripping parents of their parental rights, the removal of children from such parents, and the adoption and trusteeship of children who have lost their parents.

The State offers a number of privileges to mothers who raise their children alone. They enjoy the right to priority housing distribution, priority accommodation of their children at kindergartens, and a small monthly allowance, among others.

PREGNANCY AND CHILDBIRTH

There is a direct connection between the health condition of a mother-to-be or a mother of a baby, and the baby's physical and cognitive development. This connection explains why protection of motherhood and childhood is one of the priority objectives of the Soviet health care system. For the mother and the child, care is secured primarily by an extensive network of women's outpatient and diagnostic clinics, maternity homes, sanatoria, and leisure facilities for pregnant women and mothers with children. Health care institutions must provide each woman with a free and high-quality medical examination at the initial stages of pregnancy, medical assistance at hospitals during childbirth, follow-up examinations, and treatment for mothers with babies.

The work of pregnant women, nursing mothers, and women with children under one year is especially protected by the relevant legislation. These women cannot be put to work overtime, at night, on holidays, or sent on business trips. In cases of necessity, pregnant women can be offered lighter duties, while their wages remain intact. Nursing mothers and women with children under one year enjoy additional breaks for time to nurse their babies, besides the usual breaks during the working day for meals and rest.

Women who work for industrial enterprises or collective farms enjoy a fully paid leave of absence for pregnancy and childbirth, which covers 56 days before the delivery of the baby and 56 days afterward. In the event of a multiple birth, the leave is extended. The allowance for pregnancy is paid to women independently of their seniority on the job and the total amount of the wages.

Besides the pregnancy leave, women are eligible for a partially paid leave to look after the infant until the baby is one-and-a-half years old; the mother also has the right to an additional leave of absence during which she is not paid the salary, but her job and seniority remain secure. All in all, women can stay home with their babies while retaining their jobs for a total of three years. The right to such leaves also includes women who adopt babies right from maternity homes. Besides these benefits, women receive a one-time allowance for the baby.

In case a child under 14 gets sick, the mother gets a fully paid leave of 14 days during which she can care for the sick child. Working women with two or more children under 12 years get three extra days off, which are fully paid, in addition to an unpaid time off for under two weeks per year.

According to the legislation on labor, women with children can work either part-time, shorter weeks, on a flexible schedule, or at home. If they choose to work in this way, they continue to enjoy all the rights and privileges of the full-time employees at their places of employment.

ADULT ACTIVITIES

As already mentioned, men and women have an equal right to work in the Soviet Union. The equality of women, however, does not mean that women must also do heavy physical labor. Taking into consideration the physical characteristics of the female body, the interests of mother and childcare, which the Soviet legislation stipulates—besides those of the general labor protection ordinates—specific rules and regulations protect working women. The system of specific measures designed to improve the labor conditions for women and the protection of their health includes a list of industries and trades with heavy and harmful working conditions, at which the employment of women is not permitted. Labor legislation also contains norms that bind the administrations of various industries to adjust and implement measures of mechanization for manual labor and to exempt women from work connected with heavy physical labor. In practice, however, these rules, norms, and regulations are often violated or remain unfulfilled, and women are actively employed in heavy physical labor. This is a serious problem, directly connected with poor automation of work and general technological backwardness. Obviously, this problem will not be solved soon, but every effort must be made to remedy it.

The right to work, which is guaranteed to women—but cannot completely rule out the discrimination in wages as compared with men's salaries—also stipulates equal career opportunities. Naturally, given the large share of women's work, many women are promoted to high positions (although it appears that it is far more difficult for a woman than for a man to succeed in a career). Over 500,000 women preside in business enterprises, organizations, and institutions. Over one million head workshops and departments in industries.

Women also play an active part in the State Administration and civic life. Women comprise one-third of all Supreme Soviet Deputies. Considerable progress can be noted, especially in comparison with pre-revolutionary years, when women were not only disenfranchised, but also enjoyed no civil political rights. And still, women—as compared with men—continue to play a lesser role in managing the affairs of the State. Mostly men are appointed to key State positions.

OLD AGE

Old age can be a difficult time of life. Most of one's life is past, illnesses become more frequent, and many people feel helpless and depressed. It is extremely important to provide support for the elderly in such situations, and to help them preserve their interest in life and to secure a place in the society.

Old age pensions are given in the Soviet Union to women at the age of 55 with the total seniority of no less than 20 years. Women who have five or more children enjoy additional pension benefits. Their old age pension is given to them at the age of 50 years, with the total seniority of no less than 15 years. Depending on the type of work and the labor conditions, the pension age can be lowered by five to ten years. But it must be noted that few women of retirement age receive pensions that allow them to live a comfortable life. Most women have to work even after they turn 55. In connection with the conditions for the aged, the government has advocated a decision to increase pensions. This measure is viewed as benevolent, but since prices are rising, even the increased pensions are hardly sufficient to make ends meet. Homes for the aged are available for the elderly who live alone.

Much will have to be done to help the elderly and those people who are approaching old age. We are all indebted to those who have worked all their life to better the society.

CONCLUSION

Naturally much has been left out of the confines of this chapter. Women in the USSR have difficult lives. The complex situation in the economy has only added to the negative phenomena and aggravated them. Endless queues have become part and parcel of our everyday life, as are chronic shortages of staple foods and basic consumer items, household problems, and housing shortages. And still we are looking into the future with optimism, which is inherent in the Russian people. I am sure that soon these constraints will give way to an emancipation of the spirit. Anyway, I hope my children will be like this.

"Hero Mother"

Photo credit: Brynn Bruijn/Aramco World

Classroom with Professor Harold Takooshian (center), Moscow University

Photo credit: Dr. Harold Takooshian

7

Soviet Women

Harold Takooshian

The Union of Soviet Socialist Republics (USSR) occupies 8,649,496 square miles, making it the world's largest country—some 2.5 times the size of the United States of America, and one sixth of the planet's entire land area. Its population is 286 million. It is a nation that prides itself on its economic and military prowess, health care, science, social system and, not least of all, the equality of Soviet women and men. Life expectancy at birth is 62 years for men, 73 for women. Literacy is 99 percent, with most Soviets educated to grade 11, if not beyond.

The USSR is a political union of 15 separate Soviet Socialist Republics—Russia, Armenia, Azerbaijan, Byelorussia, Estonia, Georgia, Kazakh, Kirghiz, Latvia, Lithuania, Moldavia, Tajik, Turkmen, Ukraine, and Uzbek. It originated after November 7, 1918, when the Bolshevik "October Revolution" overthrew the Czar. The Russian SSR remains far larger than the other 14 republics, containing 52 percent of the total population of the USSR, 76 percent of its territory, and predominance in its highly centralized politics. Similarly, of the over 100 distinct ethnic groups identified in the Soviet census, Russians are by far the largest (43 percent). Considering the striking dissimilarity of these ethnic groups in culture, religion, and history, the USSR is variously described as a huge, happy family of peoples (Novosti, 1987), or else as a tense empire of unwilling bedfellows (Glebov & Crowfoot, 1989).

It is common, yet inaccurate, for Westerners to use the terms "Russian" and "Soviet" interchangeably. Although the Russian people have predominated in the Soviet Union, non-Russians of the USSR were actually a 57 percent majority at the start of the 1990s, with their percentage steadily increasing (Halsell, 1990). This chapter discusses Soviet women in general, both non-Russian and Russian.

Discussion of Soviet women is complicated by at least three factors: **(1) Ethnic diversity.** Like many large countries with a history of expansionism (India, China, the United States of America), the USSR's 100-plus ethnic groups include some of the world's most dissimilar cultures, among which the status of women could not vary more widely. **(2) Rosy glasses.** The USSR is widely known for the yawning chasm between its noble word (laws, government data, media reports), and not-so-noble reality. Since 1987, one aim of Soviet *perestroika* ("restructuring") and *glasnost* ("openness") is to reduce this chasm. **(3) The times are a changin'.** Even before entering the 1990s, the USSR had experienced breathtaking paroxysms of social change—the Berlin Wall suddenly crumbled, one-party rule died, mass emigration surged, violent revolutions occurred, Presidents Gorbachev and Bush declared the Cold War "ended," and a bottom-to-top revision of the USSR Constitution began. These changes surely will continue to the twenty-first century, and impact the status of Soviet women.

What is it like to live in the Soviet Union today? The list of adversities as well as advantages are both long. The adversities of Soviet life are immediately apparent, even to the transient visitor: long lines for even basic necessities of life; scarcities and rationing; poor quality goods; a harsh climate; travel restrictions; an uncertain political environment; rampant and visible alcoholism; and the fact that almost every family has sacrificed members to wars in the past 50 years. Impressive features of Soviet life are quickly apparent as well: the hard-working attitude of many who toil tirelessly from sunrise to sunset; the obvious pride Soviets have in prospering despite adversity; that many wear their military medals on their daily clothing to indicate their intense patriotism; and their remarkable resilience in dealing with the adversities created by humans and by nature. In many ways, it has fallen on the shoulders of the Soviet women to bear the brunt of these national adversities.

OVERVIEW: SOVIET WOMEN

Of the 286 million people of the Soviet Union, some 53 percent (or 182 million) are female. Women also account for 51 percent of the USSR work force, occupying all sorts of occupations. One of the legendary leaders of the 1917 Russian revolution was Lenin's wife, Nadezhda Krupskaya, a respected intellectual and revolutionary in her own right, who consciously fought for the emancipation of Russian women. Indeed, the Soviet constitution guaranteed women a political vote, emancipation, and legal equality with men. The most detailed 1,100-page guidebook for travellers to the USSR advises:

> The women are able to do work that is reserved for men in the Western countries, a fact which sometimes surprises the foreign visitor. There is no reason for surprise, for the Russian woman regards this equality with man as a liberation and is proud of it. Those who doubt this need only listen to the cheerful laughter and chatter of the women . . . who work on building sites or the women of a *kolkhoz* carrying their heavy loads. (Nagel, 1986, p. 108)

Yet what appears at first blush as a "liberation of women" is more likely, on closer scrutiny, to be a double burden which economic necessity has foisted on Soviet women (Bridger, 1988). Just as economic problems in the United States of America and Western nations in the 1970s forced women out of the home to earn a second income thereby raising "latchkey" children, so also Soviet women have been required by the economy to work between (as well as during) the USSR's many wars.

CHILDHOOD

The USSR birth rate is 19.6 per thousand, slightly higher than that of the United States of America (15.7). At birth, the life expectancy for Soviet women is 73 years (79 in the United States of America), longer than the 63 years for Soviet men (72 for United States of America men). By law, Soviet girls and boys are treated quite equally in terms of childrearing, access to childcare, and so on (Azarov, 1983). Because such a large percentage of women work outside the home (51 percent of the work force), the Soviet Union has invested in an impressive system of daycare centers, which might well be the envy of other nations. It is common for preschool children to be left by mom at the nearby nursery on the way to work, where for little or no fee professionals (typically women) will tend for the youths in a building uniquely designed for this purpose. (The centers visited by this author were well equipped with rooms full of cribs, athletic equipment, craft supplies, and attentive caretakers.)

THE SCHOOL YEARS

Soviets pride themselves on their educational system, which has produced a 99 percent literacy rate. Each Soviet is fluent in the language native to his or her republic and/or Russian, the lingua franca of the Union. Youngsters are expected to complete at least 11 years of school, and encouraged to continue into postsecondary education in one of three ways: (1) universities, which are typically five-year academic diplomas, plus three more years for a postgraduate ("candidate") degree; (2) professional institutes (like medicine, engineering, teaching) which vary from three to six years; and (3) vocational or technical schools, which teach more basic skills such as carpentry or clerical work. —All school grades were heavily based on oral exams until *perestroika* in 1987, when there began a shift towards anonymous, standardized written exams. (In the Stalin era, 1935-53, standardized tests had been virtually outlawed as anti-Soviet and demeaning to the individual.) Admission to higher education is highly competitive, particularly for the 65 universities of the USSR. One reason is that education is entirely free; in fact, students receive a full-time salary (some 100 rubles per month) to attend college. Those not admitted into higher education enter the work force, yet can opt to attend free, part-time college courses after work if they like. In theory, Soviet women have opportunities identical with male students and, indeed, higher education is predominantly female. Any "tracking" that occurs is informal, where women seem to be steered away from careers in law, politics, and a few other "male" specialties.

WORK LIFE

By law, able-bodied Soviet men are expected to work for a living. Women are not. Soviet society recognizes "two types of women," homemakers and workers.

Homemakers

Women who opt for homemaking need not enter the work force, particularly if they have children (which the government encourages). Homemaking in Soviet families is more time-consuming than in most Western societies: "Dishes are washed by hand. Clothing is generally laundered in tubs, then hung out to dry. Disposable diapers are unknown. Floors are scrubbed with brooms wrapped in damp cloths" (Smolowe, 1988, pp. 29-30).

Workers

Women who opt for the work world are legally accorded the same opportunities for salary and advancement as men. This is a sharp contrast with the prerevolutionary Soviet nations, where women were often forbidden from school or work, and perhaps not even permitted outside the house without a face-cloth or male escort. Still, there are a few problems with this: **(1) Financial:** Even women who prefer homemaking still find themselves forced into the work force for that second salary to help make ends meet, so fully half the work force is female. **(2) Low pay and rank:** Although it is illegal to pay women less than men for the same work, it happens. Moreover, "women are expected to have low aspirations and . . . the worst-paying jobs, typically in the health and education sectors" (Zelkowitz, 1989, p. 1), and are not promoted as readily once hired. Like Western nations, the USSR shows gender imbalances among its occupations, albeit different ones. For example, women represent 50 percent of USSR engineers, 69 percent of physicians, 75 percent of teachers, 87 percent of economists, and 91 percent of librarians (Novosti, 1987; Smolowe, 1988). There is inequality in political life too. Of the total Soviet population of 286 million, Soviet women are 54 percent of the population and 51 percent of its workers, but only 32 percent of the 1,500-member Supreme Soviet, 29 percent of the ruling Communist Party, 4 percent of the 320-member Central Committee, and 0 percent of the Kremlin's 13-man Politburo. **(3) House chores:** In 1988, Gorbachev proposed that working women's hours be reduced two hours daily, to accommodate their "inherent functions" as wife and mother. However, leading Soviet feminists like Tatyana Mamonova decry this as tokenism: "Men feel no sense of duty to help out with shopping, standing in lines, preparing meals from scratch, and taking care of children" (Zelkowitz, 1989). Indeed, one Soviet survey found that even working women averaged three hours per day standing in line or doing housework.

MARRIAGE

Soviet society expects its women to marry and have children. Due to limited money and housing, it is common for newlyweds to live with one of the couple's parents until they can go on their own, and these elders often help care for their infant grandchildren. Traditional, family-arranged weddings are unusual in Russia today, yet remain common in the more conservative Christian regions to the South, and more so in Muslim republics like Tajik and Uzbek SSR. Yet in Russian families too, parents seem to sense the shortage of men and often encourage their daughters to marry early.

Marriage and a family are not always easy for women, who outnumber Soviet men. In fact, the imbalanced sex-ratio (113 women per 100 men) is greater in the Soviet Union than any other major nation today (McWhirter, 1989), a significant fact considering the general link between a culture's shortage of men and its increased sexism (Guttentag & Secord, 1983). Depending on the specific region within the USSR, the ratio may be as many as six women per one man. While the age of first marriage is rising in the West, it is dropping in the USSR. A Moscow University study found Soviet women marrying three years earlier in 1986 than in 1966, with 25 percent of women married at age 18. "If you are not married by 20, people think there is something wrong with you" (Smolowe, 1988, p. 35). Other sociological studies find that 25 percent of women are pregnant during their marriage vows, and that some 60 percent of young adults have unprotected intercourse before marriage. One Soviet feminist, Mamonova, claims only one third of pregnancies are conceived in wedlock. "Pervasive fatherlessness (*bezottsovshchina*, a term which arose out of the tragedies of World War II) is making a comeback" (Zelkowitz, 1989, p. 1). Soviet media themselves do not disparage unwed motherhood. Novosti Press Agency tells this tale:

Single Mothers. Statistics show that in Byelorussia women outnumber men by 200,000. Many of these "redundant" women have children. Among them is Lyudmila Snarkova from Minsk. Three years ago . . . all her friends were thunderstruck when they learned she was expecting a baby. One should say that it takes courage to do what she did . . . . 'Although I am raising my son without a husband,' says Lyudmila, 'I am not lonely. And I am much happier than before when

I did not have him. Now I cannot even imagine my life without my son.' (1986, pp. 170-171)

Birth control

Government policy has made birth control methods readily available to women and men; and they indeed frequently are used. So is abortion. One woman who was expelled from the USSR in 1980 for feminist activism noted, "Because men do not help take care of children, many women refuse to have more than one child" (Zelkowitz, 1989, p. 1).

Divorce

Divorce is on the rise among Soviet families, with about one out of three marriages breaking up. This remains below the United States of America figure of one in two. In 1987 there were close to 1 million Soviet divorces. A media survey by *Literaturnaya Gazeta* found that women initiated 7 out of 10 of these Soviet divorces, usually due to their husband's alcoholism. Though other external stressors on family life are long work hours, cramped housing, and lack of creature comforts, "alcoholism is rampant among men and the leading factor in half of all divorces" (Zelkowitz, 1989, p. 1).

PREGNANCY AND CHILDBIRTH

Like marriage, childrearing is admired. Particularly in the northern republics, including Russia, couples tend to limit expenses and effort by having small families, while the government encourages large ones. In fact, in 1944, to replace the tens of millions dead due to war and purges, Soviet leaders awarded women with seven children the Glory of Motherhood medal, and mothers who bore ten or more children were accorded the title "Mother Heroine." Whereas Western feminism is sometimes regarded as anti-mother, Soviet feminists seem among those who extol motherhood, and the birth rate today slowly continues to rise above two per family. Today the government offers a bonus of $167 for having a third baby, and early retirement benefits for women with five children.

This topic of motherhood is one of the clearest examples of an internal Soviet split, between republics in the northwest and those in the southeast portions of the physically immense Union. Of the 15 republics, the six Muslim republics in Central Asia, known collectively as Turkestan, have historically had a high fertility rate which, at present, is about four times that of the Soviet population in general (Arndt, 1990). Muslim parents prefer large families. One Western journalist noted that in Moscow and Leningrad:

most couples have no more than one or two children, whereas many Central Asian women have five, six, seven or more. These statistics mean that Muslims are no longer simply one of the Soviet Union's many "minorities," but the only rapidly growing segment of the country's population. (Halsell, 1990, p. 32)

The 53 million Muslims now comprise some one-fifth of the Soviet population of 286 million, and at their current growth rate will replace Russians as the largest ethnic group by the year 2017, the centenary of the 1917 Soviet Revolution (Arndt, 1990), a matter of apparent concern to non-Muslim Soviets. The result seems an odd double-standard in Soviet policy in the Muslim republics, which one journalist describes this way:

The Soviet government created the Order of Maternal Glory and began distribution of the medals representing the order's successive levels before the Second World War, to encourage the birth of more defenders of the motherland. Although they continue to hand out the medals, the Soviets are presently conducting a campaign urging Central Asians to practice birth control. Soviet writers in Central Asian journals extol the virtues of planned parenthood, and in the hospitals, one Uzbek [noted] "a Russian nurse will tell a Muslim woman, 'It is better to have a small family.'" (Halsell, 1990, p. 32)

Across all 15 Soviet republics, Soviet society provides special maternity hospitals, devoted specifically to the needs of its mothers-to-be. However, like Soviet hospitals in general, these are often criticized as understaffed and underequipped, with as few as one midwife for every 15 mothers. Gynecological clinics too are available, yet poorly staffed. As of 1989, negotiations were underway for an America-run factory to introduce tampons among Soviet women, to replace the coarse cotton batting now used for feminine hygiene.

WOMEN TODAY: TRADITION AND CHANGE

How do Soviet women compare with Americans in their feminist attitudes? In 1987, while living for some four months in the USSR, this author hoped to conduct an empirical survey to answer this question. This was largely because the Soviet woman seems a paradoxical image in the West. In one way, she has been liberated, given the vote since 1917, and seems very much the equal of the Soviet man. In another way, she continues to be the object of discrimination, perhaps dissatisfied with the expanded social role she plays in the work force. What does she have to say about this?

Together with Ardashes Emin, a noted writer at Erevan State University, we two researchers worked with *Garun*, a Comsomol (Communist Youth) magazine, and managed to survey a cross-section of

115 women in Soviet Armenia. Public opinion surveys are often frowned upon in Soviet society, yet the sponsorship by *Garun* facilitated respondents' trust and cooperation. The standardized 12-item question-naire that was used is the Ethfem Survey that already had been translated and used in North and South America to assess women's attitudes toward feminism (Beere, 1990). The scale yields a score of 0-24, so the higher a woman's score, the more she believes "in the total equality of women and men—social, political, and biological" (Takooshian, 1990). The study of Soviet Armenian women made it possible to directly compare these Soviets' scores with responses of American respondents on the same 12 questions.

Table 7-1 indicates the scores of "nonethnic" American women (those who did not identify with any ethnic group) averaged 13.8 on the 0-24 scale, whereas Armenian-Americans averaged a significantly lower 9.3. The 115 Soviet Armenian women averaged significantly lower than this, at 8.3. Responses on each item indicate Soviet women seem less feminist than Americans on almost all of the topics. Tables 7-2 and 7-3 confirmed the same demographic trends in American and Soviet women—that older and less educated women are less approving of feminism than their younger, more educated daughters.

To be sure, the population of Soviet Armenia seems more traditional than Russia SSR, yet we sense that on the topic of feminism the results in most northern as well as southern republics would concur.

CONCLUSION

The Soviet Union is a collection of over 100 diverse nationalities, united by one political system and Constitution. The image of the "liberated" Soviet woman seems only partly accurate, since her equality is only partial, the result of economic necessity more than political will. To be sure, Soviet women are far more equal with men today than in pre-1917 Czarist Russia, yet many of them seem to cherish the possibility of larger, more comfortable, and egalitarian families, in place of full equality in the workplace. Surely the Soviet reform called *perestroika*, begun in 1987, has already accelerated with breathtaking speed, and promises to change the lot of Soviet women in the next decade to the year 2000, perhaps more than in the prior seven decades, 1917 to 1987.

TABLE 7-1

A Profile of Feminism Responses of Three Groups of Women:
102 U.S. nonethnics (N), 45 Armenian-Americans (A), and 115 Soviet Armenians (S).

	N.	A.	S.
1. A woman should have more responsibility than a man in caring for a child.*	1.6	1.2	.6
2. Women should have more responsibility than men in doing household duties.*	1.6	1.2	.8
3. Unisex clothes are a good idea, so men and women can dress more alike.	.3	.4	.6
4. By nature, women are more emotional than men.*	1.1	.8	.4
5. By nature, women enjoy sex less than men.*.	1.6	1.0	.8
6. A woman should adopt her husband's last name when they marry.*	1.0	1.4	1.4
7. Married women with young children should work outside the home if they wish.	1.6	1.2	1.4
8. I'd say it's perfectly all right for a husband to stay at home while the wife supported the family.	1.1	.6	.1
9. I'd say women's liberationists "rock the boat" too much. *	1.2	.4	.9
10. Many women who deny their femininity are actually confused people.*	.8	.5	.5
11. The use of obscene language is more unbecoming for a woman than for a man.*	1.1	.5	.4
12. The needs of a family should come before a woman's career. *	.9	.5	.6
TOTAL (0-24) feminism score:	13.8	9.3	8.3

*Note: For the 9 items marked (*), "Disagree" is the feminist response; "Agree" is the feminist response
for the other three items.

TABLE 7-2

Women's Mean Feminism Score, by Education

	N.	S.
Grammar school:	-	1.8
High school:	9.0	7.5
Some college:	14.3	8.7
College grad:	18.1	8.8
Graduate school:	16.8	-

TABLE 7-3

Women's Mean Feminism Score, by Age

	N.	S.
Under 20:	14.2	10.6
20-29:	16.5	8.7
30-49:	14.0	6.8
40-49:	11.0	4.7
50+:	7.8	3.9

REFERENCES

Arndt, R. (Ed.). (1990). Muslims in the U.S.S.R. [Special issue]. *Aramco World*, *41*(1), pp. 2-3.

Azarov, Yu. (1983). *A book about bringing up children*. Moscow: Progress.

Beere, C. A. (1990). *Gender roles research: A handbook of tests and measures*. Westport, CT: Greenwood Press.

Bridger, S. (1988). *Women in the Soviet countryside: Women's role in rural development in the Soviet Union*. New York: Cambridge.

Chua-Eoan, H. G. (1988, June 6). My wife is a very independent lady. *Time*, pp. 38-43.

Glebov, O., & Crowfoot, J. (Eds.). (1989). *The Soviet empire: Its nations speak out*. New York: Harwood.

Guttentag, M., & Secord, P. (1983). *Too many women?* Beverley Hills: Sage.

Halsell, G. (1990, Feb.). A visit to Baku. *Aramco World*, *41*(1), pp. 30-33.

McWhirter, N. (1989). *Guiness book of world records*. New York: Bantam.

Nagel Co. (1986). *Nagel's encyclopedia-guide: USSR*. Geneva: Nagel Co.

Novosti Press Agency. (1987). *Yearbook USSR '87*. Moscow: Novosti Press Agency.

Smolowe, J. (1988, June 6). Heroines of Soviet labor. *Time*, pp. 28-37.

Takooshian, H., & Stuart, C.R. (1983). Ethnicity and feminism among American women: Opposing social trends? *International Journal of Group Tensions*, *13*, 100-105.

Takooshian, H. (1990). Feminism in cross-cultural perspective. In L. L. Adler (Chair), *Symposium on current issues in cross-cultural psychology*, at the annual meeting of the Eastern Psychological Association, Philadelphia.

Zelkowitz, J. (1989). Feminism and Soviet society. *Harriman Institute Newsletter*, *3*(3).

Modern Milkmaid in a Kibbutz

Photo credit: Maric Productions

8

Growing Up Female: A Life-Span Perspective on Women in Israel

Marilyn P. Safir and Dafna N. Izraeli

As feminism was gaining momentum in the early 1970s in the United States of America and other Western countries, Israelis were confident that they had already achieved equality between the sexes. There was justification for their confidence. Israel was one of the few countries in which a woman was Head of State, where military service was compulsory for both men and women, and where the Declaration of Independence (1948) promised to maintain equal social and political rights for all citizens, irrespective of sex. This commitment to equality was in keeping with the legacy left by the founding generations of modern Israel when in the 1920s, men and women pioneers jointly engaged in activities of national reconstruction. Together they built roads, constructed houses, and tilled the soil. Their confidence in their achievements and their self-esteem as women and Israelis were echoed in the words of Beba Idelson (long-time member of Parliament and chairperson of the Working Women's Council, Israel's most powerful women's organization) who in 1973 proclaimed that the achievements of Israel's women have become an axiom around the world. In that same year, Shulamit Aloni (member of Parliament and leading feminist politician) observed: Our tragedy is that too many women are pleased to be deprived of their rights. (Both quotes from Hazleton, 1977, p. 15.) However, during the last 15 years, a more critical appraisal of the reality and a new consciousness raised by feminist activities have gradually eroded the myth of the liberation of the Israeli woman.

The status of women in Israel is fraught with contradictions. Women are educated in the spirit of modern achievement-oriented values which emphasize the right of the individual to develop her unique potential and to select a life course in keeping with her unique abilities and preferences. Social norms, furthermore, reward the woman for her own achievements independent of those of her husband. At the same time, there is no recognized social role for single women, especially never-marrieds without children (Bar-Yosef, Bloom, & Levy, 1978). Widely held traditional values endorse a patriarchal system of social relations which ascribes roles on the basis of gender and emphasizes the centrality of the patriarchal family with its sex division of labor. The normatively prescribed model for successful family life still requires that the husband be the major breadwinner and head of his household, and the wife, the primary caretaker of home and children. Her employment is defined as less important for the family. Nevertheless, there is a small, but growing number of women whose income and social status are equal to or even surpass those of their spouse. While Israeli society has opened new opportunities for women to participate in the public sphere, it has not adapted family roles or developed the services necessary to make career success possible without considerable strain (Izraeli, 1988).

This chapter underlines the tension between the perception of "woman as person" entitled to equal opportunities and of "woman as wife and mother" in a patriarchal system of relations; between the intellectual commitment to women's liberation and the emotional commitment to the traditional role of women as a mother and mainstay of the family.

WOMEN'S STATUS IN SOCIETY AS A SOCIAL PROBLEM

We can trace the beginnings of women's status as a social problem and the organized attempts to improve it to the beginning of the twentieth century and the period of the pre-state Jewish community in Palestine, known as the *yishuv* (Izraeli, 1981). The emergence of the modern Zionist Movement at the end of the nineteenth century coincided with that of other revolutionary movements and particularly women's liberation movements in Europe and United States of America, which were bringing about important changes in the status of women in society. Within the Zionist Movement, women were officially granted electoral equality at the third Zionist Congress held in Basel, 1899, at a time when no other country in the world, except for New Zealand and a few individual states of the United States of America, formally recognized women's right to participate in the political process.

The young and mostly single Zionists from Eastern Europe who had been influenced by the ideals of equality and social justice prevalent in the revolutionary socialist movements of the time, settled in Palestine where they formed *kvutzot* (collective living/working groups which were the forerunners of the *kibbutzim*) and later kibbutzim (communes in which all property is jointly owned; each adult is a member and wives are therefore not economically dependant on their husbands, nor the children on their fathers). In the early days, because of physical and economic hardships and the small proportion of women among the pioneering groups, family formation and privatization were discouraged. When the first children were born in the kvutzot, collective childrearing was established as a means for enabling women to continue their full involvement in the work of the collective.

The ideals of social equality as well as the new fellowship that developed between men and women during this period, however, did not lead to the rejection of traditional perceptions of women's work. In the kvutzot and the kibbutzim, women were automatically relegated to the domestic chores, which were defined as nonproductive work and hence as having less inherent value than the productive agricultural work performed by men. Only women were assigned to work in the children's houses and the expanding service areas. It is generally accepted today that this arrangement is responsible for the sex stereotyping of job roles on the contemporary kibbutz (Safir, 1990).

In response to their exclusion from the more valued physical labor of the kvutza, a group of women pioneers formed the Working Women's Movement in 1914. Its goal was to make women more equal partners in the process of national reconstruction. The Working Women's Council, the organizational arm of the movement, established in 1922, fought for employment opportunities for women in highly valued nontraditional work, such as building construction and floor tiling.

The Council's activities from the early 1930s reflected a shift away from experimentation and toward serving the needs of women in their traditional roles as wives and mothers. Among services established was a network of childcare centers, and occupational training for girls. The women's organizations, established prior to the establishment of the State (1948), continue to play an important role in contemporary Israel. They operate childcare centers, occupational training schools for girls, and legal aid services for women. They have played and continue to play an important political role initiating legislation on women's issues and providing a platform for women leaders.

BETWEEN TRADITION AND MODERNITY

Israel is located on the southeastern coast of the Mediterranean—the land bridge between Africa and Asia. Although a small country (10,840 square miles), [Israel Information Center, 1990], it is a country of wide geographical contrasts—snow- capped mountains in the north, the fertile central plains, the desert in the south. Even greater diversity is found within the population of 4.53 million, almost 90 percent* of whom live in urban areas. The four major religious groups—Jews (82 percent of the population), Muslims (13.8 percent), Christians (2.3 percent), and Druze (1.7 percent), each incorporating the gamut from secular to born-again sects—live together and yet separately within Israel. As a result of the constraints of space, the focus of this chapter will be on the Jewish majority. (For a more comprehensive review of the status of women in Israel, see Swirsky and Safir, 1990).

---

*Unless otherwise specified, all statistical data are taken from the official publications of the Central Bureau of Statistics. Those most frequently used in this chapter are the *Statistical Abstract of Israel* and *Labor Force Survey* for the relevant year.

The legal status of women in Israel is determined by one of the most modern and one of the most ancient legal systems in the world (Radai, 1983). The former, secular law, is based on the principle of one law for both men and women, while recognizing that a relevant distinction is not discrimination. The latter, Jewish (religious) law, views man and woman as different and not equal. It imposes a different legal status on each and assigns to each a different set of rights and obligations. Religious courts have sole jurisdiction over matters of marriage and divorce. Only men may sue for divorce. Women, children, and the mentally impaired cannot serve as witnesses in the religious courts. Jewish religious political parties, although relatively small in their parliamentary representation, have gained considerable political clout through their participation in government coalitions. For example, in the 1977 elections, as their price for joining the coalition, the right-wing orthodox party demanded (and brought about) the deliberalization of the abortion law. About 20 percent of the population defines itself as religiously orthodox, but the more right-wing sects compose only 3-4 percent of the population.

The major ethnic cleavage within Jewish society is between Westerners—immigrants from Western industrialized democracies, including Europe and the Americas—and Easterners—immigrants from the non-industrialized Islamic countries of the Middle East and North Africa. The latter imported a traditional orientation and more patriarchal family life-style. The distinction today, however, is more one of class than of cultural orientation. Relative to their proportion in the labor force, the Easterners have fewer resources than Westerners and are underrepresented in the higher-status education-based occupations. The women are doubly disadvantaged as both Easterners and women. Over half the Jews in Israel are first or second generation Easterners; the socioeconomic gap between the ethnic groups is greater in the second generation than among the immigrant parents.

A third source of conflicting pulls for women is between the collectivistic and the individualistic orientations of Israeli society. Collectivism emphasizes the individual's loyalties to the collective—whether nation or family—and his or her prior obligations to its needs and welfare. Individualism emphasizes the individual's obligations to his or her personal needs and welfare. Israeli society puts great value on the collective, although it has become more individualistic in recent years. Two survival issues of the Jewish collective are the defense of its borders from its enemies and what is called the demographic problem, the higher birth rate of Israel's Arab citizens. While both men and women do compulsory military service, only the man serves the collective through frontline duty and reserve army service throughout his adult life. The woman serves the collective by having (more) children and linking her well-being with that of her family, to which she is expected to give first priority. While individual occupational achievement has become an increasingly important channel for status attainment among women (as well as for men), public policy is directed more to promoting fertility than to disseminating information on birth control.

THE FAMILY CONTEXT AND THE LIFE CYCLE

Israeli society is a family-oriented society in which family stability is the rule. The question of whether to have children or to pursue a career is not part of the repertoire of options. Marrying and having children are cultural imperatives. Only 2 percent of women never marry; only 1 percent of all women who give birth are unmarried. Only one out of six marriages ends in divorce and only 5 percent of all households are single-parent households (85 percent of these are headed by the mother). Median age for first marriage is 22.5 for women and 26.0 for men. A childless couple, however, is not considered a family and children are considered as essential for a happy marriage. This may explain why *in vitro* experimentation and services are so developed in Israel. (The number of centers for every million people in Israel/United States of America is 4:1.) All treatments for infertility are covered by health insurance.

PREGNANCY, DELIVERY AND INFANCY

The fertility rate in 1987—the average number of children a woman may bear in her lifetime—was 3.05. During the last 30 years the fertility rate has dropped dramatically: among first-generation Eastern Jews, from 5.4 to 3.1; among Muslims from 8.1 to 4.6; Christians, from 4.6 to 2.6; Druze, 7.2 to 4.2. Among Israeli-born and first generation Westerners, it has remained stable (2.7 and 2.8 respectively) while among kibbutz members it has increased to an average of four. Among Jews, regardless of education, fertility varies with religiousness. Among the more extreme orthodox groups, six plus is the norm. Decrease in fertility is correlated to women's increasing levels of education and age of marriage.

Almost all babies are born in the maternity ward of a general hospital and are delivered by nurse-midwives. The average hospital stay for mother and child is four days. Infants are cared for by over 900 Well Baby clinics run by the Ministry of Health throughout the country. First contact with the clinic is made during pregnancy when women come for check-ups and can attend a prenatal class with their husbands. Husbands' participation is a relatively new phenomenon and varies with the couple's education and social class—the higher it is, the more likely both will participate and that the husband will be present during the delivery.

When the new mother returns home, a nurse from the Well Baby Clinic makes a home visit for the first child, to answer questions and instruct on feeding, bathing, and general infant care. The child's development is followed by these clinics until he or she begins first grade. All inoculations are administered at the clinics. Further inoculations, eye and teeth examinations are performed at school.

Jews traditionally have a preference for male children and especially that the first child be a male. Only the male is obligated to mourn by daily prayer for one year the passing of a parent. All male infants are circumcised a week after birth. On that occasion a large party is held, often catered in a hired hall, to which a large number of guests are invited. The event symbolizes the entry of the male infant into the covenant between God and the people of Israel. Although the circumcision is a religious ritual, it is observed also by those who are nonreligious. There is no equivalent ceremony for girls, although younger couples have begun holding parties to celebrate the birth of a daughter.

FROM INFANCY TO EARLY CHILDHOOD

Social life revolves around the children. Small children often accompany their parents to family and social events. Childcare, however, continues to be the primary responsibility of the mother. Early innovative labor laws were based on the perception that women are the natural caretakers of children and need to be protected in their roles as mothers from exploitation by employers. Employers may not fire women on grounds of pregnancy, provided she has worked for the employer at least five months before becoming pregnant. Women are obligated to take 12 weeks maternity leave with 70 percent pay covered by social security, and may take up to one year's leave without pay. During the first year after the birth, a nursing mother may take off an hour a day at the employer's expense. Labor agreements permit women with small children to work one hour less a day at the employer's expense, to take sick leave to care for family members. During the late 1980s some of these privileges were given to fathers as well.

Visitors are impressed with the freedom of the Israeli child, who spends a great deal of time playing out in the open. Because of the mild weather between March and November, most youngsters play outdoors and active play is common for both sexes. Cooperative play appears much earlier than in the United States of America because of early interaction in neighborhoods and early attendance in preschool programs. Children begin pre-kindergarten classes at age two. These classes are usually four hours a day. In addition, there are daycare centers for working mothers for which payment is subsidized by the Ministry of Labor and Social Welfare on a graded scale according to family income. These centers, open from 7:30 a.m. to 4:00 p.m., accept children from six months and are viewed as a positive solution for working women. There are not enough places, however, to meet the demand and if there is not a willing grandmother, then a childcare worker (metapelet) is hired for homecare. At three the child usually moves into pre-kindergarten sponsored by the Ministry of Education. In 1988, 67 percent of two-year-olds, 92 percent of three-year-olds, and 99 percent of four-year-olds were in some preschool setting. Children begin kindergarten during the year of their fifth birthday. School attendance is compulsory for both sexes through age 15 and free through the end of high school at age 18. From the pre-kindergarten stage right through primary school, however, there is a short schoolday which ends around noon or shortly after, following which children come home for the main meal.

The kibbutz family is much more egalitarian than its city counterpart, and childrearing in the kibbutz is very different from the traditional urban pattern. Until the late 1950s, children in all kibbutzim lived in separate age-graded mixed-sex children's houses. Over the last three decades there has been a move toward children sleeping in their parents' home and only the more ideologically committed kibbutzim today still maintain separate sleeping quarters. Nonetheless, children are communally reared. The child enters the infant's house at six weeks. She or he becomes part of a peer group that lives together until age 12-14, when the children leave the kibbutz for a regional kibbutz boarding school. The child's mother visits the infant house during work hours to nurse the child and the child spends late afternoon and early evening with its parents before it is returned to the infant house. In addition to strong peer ties, these children experience multiple mothering as the metapelet (the woman who is responsible for the child's care within the infant house) and her helpers are women. The role of the biological parents is basically expressive (loving), as training and discipline are taken over by the metapelet and later the class teacher/educator, who spends more time with the child on a daily basis than do the parents. Suzanne Keller (1983), who summarized the positive effects of multiple mothering, stated that the reduction of the role of the biological mother has not resulted in maternal deprivation, but in increased mothering from several figures. The biological family is thus less complex a system for the kibbutz child than for children generally, since the mother and father roles are relatively undifferentiated in their emphasis on affection, permissiveness, and nurturance toward the child. Nonetheless, research (Safir, 1983) indicates that these boys and girls are more sex-stereotyped and more conforming than their city cohorts, probably a result of the significantly greater sex-typing in the division of labor in the kibbutz compared with the city.

ADOLESCENCE

The peer group is a very important socializing influence in Israeli society. Birthdays are celebrated in primary school with the whole class. By third or fourth grade, the class meets for a weekly class night party at the home of one of the children. The youth movement (including scouts), while more significant in the past, becomes another activity that both boys and girls join with their classmates in fourth grade and continue to meet through the end of high school, twice a week. Many same-sex and cross-sex adult friendships are begun during this pre-adolescent period.

Primary school is followed by junior high school. In an attempt to enhance ethnic integration and close the educational gap between Easterners and Westerners, comprehensive regional junior and senior high schools were established in the 1970s to which children were bussed from a variety of neighborhoods. The extent of success of this project is still an issue of debate among educators.

As the boy infant is singled out at birth by ritual circumcision, at 13 he participates in a Bar Mitzva ceremony signifying his passage from childhood to manhood and his assumption of religious duties. The ceremony takes place during prayer services in the synagogue. In addition, a large party, usually catered in a hired hall, is held. It is not unusual for 200-500 guests to be invited to the party. The Bar Mitzva is again celebrated by both religious and secular families. Again there is no equivalent rite of passage for girls, except in the as yet small, non-orthodox religious movements.

At the end of ninth grade, children are channeled into either an academic or a vocational high school on the basis of their grades and ability tests. Weaker students transfer to vocational high schools. Pupil population at these schools is comprised of 55 percent boys and 45 percent girls. Graduates of the majority of these schools are ineligible to sit for matriculation examinations. All students in academic high schools follow the same program of studies in grade ten. They can then choose between different specializations during the last two years including humanities, social sciences, oriental studies, biology, economics, and mathematics/physics. Girls are most underrepresented in the math/physics and economic specialties.

DATING

Dating patterns vary and begin earlier among the non-religious elements of the population. Children in grammar school speak of having a girl/boy friend but pairing usually occurs within the peer social group; the couple does not go off on a date by itself until mid- to late adolescence. Platonic friendships are common. Casual dating is not the norm and once a couple forms, they continue to date for a minimum of several months. Girls often initiate these early relationships. A girl who dates a boy once or twice and then dates a new boy and switches again is considered flighty even if there has been no sexual relationship. It is not uncommon for couples formed at 14 to ultimately marry, but a large majority meet during army service or during university studies. The couple often participate as a couple in family functions, but their families don't formally meet until they decide to marry. There is no official period of engagement. Couples usually announce their decision to marry two to three months before the wedding date. In recent years pre-marital cohabitation has become more common and more normatively acceptable. This trend is also reflected in the relatively later marital age among non-religious educated girls.

Religious schools have separate classes for boys and girls and a large proportion of boys go to all-male religious boarding high schools where they come home every second or third weekend. The clubs of the religious youth movements are similarly segregated by sex. Dating is viewed as preparation for marriage and relationships not likely to lead to marriage are discouraged and short-lived. Religious girls marry earlier and among the ultra-orthodox, match-making is still the norm.

Kibbutz members virtually never marry a member of their own peer group with whom they have grown up. Joseph Shepher, who studied the phenomenon, claimed that the sibling-like relationship that develops among peers mitigates against sexual attraction or creates incest taboos. As a result marriage partners are chosen from younger or older groups, peers who joined as adults, members of other kibbutzim, or nonmembers. Since kibbutz life is organized around family, there is no role for the single person. Singles feel isolated and are more likely to leave, as are kibbutzniks who marry nonmembers. Consequently, the various kibbutzim run special programs, parties, and trips for singles, whose primary purpose is to provide opportunities for them to meet and marry kibbutzniks, increasing the probability of their remaining in a kibbutz.

WOMEN IN THE ARMY

Israel was the first and is still one of the few states to have universal compulsory military training for both men and women. Women serve two years, men three. Officer training obligates the recruit to sign up for an extra year during which he or she is paid as part of the professional army.

The nature of women's integration into the military became an issue following Independence. Should the defense forces be modelled after the Palmach (Jewish underground) where women were integrated into the various units, or after the Women's Auxiliary Corp of the British army where women were segregated in specialized units? Organizationally, these two plans were merged during the first two years of Statehood, making the Women's Corps (Chen) the responsible authority for training and judicial matters, while all work assignments became general army staffing decisions. Functionally, most army roles are segregated by sex, and from point of intake throughout army service, men and women follow separate career paths.

A second issue of contention related to the universality of conscription is that of marriage, pregnancy, motherhood, and religious conviction, which were defined as grounds for nonconscription of women. In 1953, the Knesset passed the Sherut Leumi (National Service) law which made two years of national service compulsory for those released on religious grounds. The law, however, was never implemented. In 1978, in accordance with the coalition agreement, the Knesset amended the military service law to facilitate the release of women on the basis of a declaration of religious conviction. The proportion of women released on the basis of a personal declaration of religious consciousness objection consequently increased from 18.5 percent to 25 percent, where it has remained since 1983. Approximately 65 percent of each cohort of women is drafted. Army service has been found to have a significant positive impact on women's self-esteem and occupational aspirations (Bloom & Bar-Yosef, 1985).

The two decades following Independence, when fighting units were consolidated but not greatly expanded, brought about a continuous restriction of women to more traditionally female (clerical) jobs and an increase in the sex segregation of occupations. The shortage in human (male) resources following the Six Day War (1967) precipitated a more extensive use of women in nontraditionally female jobs to increase the number of men for combat units. The critical self-examination in the aftermath of the Yom Kippur War (1973) and the intensification in the use of sophisticated technologies led the army to reevaluate its policies regarding the most efficient use of women (Izraeli, 1979).

In 1976, 210 out of 709 jobs (29.6 percent) were open to women, the majority of them clerical jobs. In 1978, the Commission on the Status of Women recommended that the number and type of jobs available to women be increased. By the end of 1980, 296 out of 775 jobs were open to women (38.2 percent). In mid-1981 the Army Chief of Personnel, with the encouragement of the Chief of Staff, ordered that all jobs be open to women except for direct combat jobs. Since 1984 the range of jobs filled by women has expanded greatly (60 percent by the end of 1985) and there is continued experimentation to break down the barriers to women's integration as far as possible. New technologies create new occupations for which the more educated women soldiers are well suited. However, the fact that women do not serve in combat units, their shorter period of service (two years compared to three for men), their disinclination to sign up for an additional period of army service, their release upon marriage, and their negligible availability for reserve duty were and remain major disincentives to intensifying the investments in women's training and to expanding the number of jobs available to them.

WOMEN IN COLLEGE AND UNIVERSITY

In the 25 years between 1959-60 and 1984-85 the number of students in Israeli universities grew sevenfold from 9,275 to 65,050, while the proportion of women among the student body more than doubled, from less than 25 percent to 50 percent. Since 1984 the major developments have been the growth in the proportion of women among graduate students and their movement into male dominated specializations. In 1987-88, women constituted 50.3 percent of the students for the first degree, 48.4 percent for the second degree and 40.7 percent for the third degree. Although they are still overrepresented in traditionally female academic niches, they are entering new fields in growing numbers. In the academic year 1987-88, women students represented 71 percent of those enrolled in the humanities, 54 percent in the social sciences, 43 percent in mathematics and the sciences, 42 percent in law, 37 percent in medicine, 31 percent in business and administration, but only 15 percent in engineering and architecture—most in architecture.

WOMEN AT WORK

There are over 620,000 women in the civilian labor force. Between 1954 and 1989 the proportion of women in the civilian labor force grew from 21 percent to 40 percent. Among Jewish women the figure reached almost 45 percent but among minority women it was 14.8 percent (up from 7.2 percent in 1970).

Women joined the labor force in response to the demand created for educated workers by the growth in public and community services (primarily education and health) as well as financial and business services from the end of the 1960s to the mid-1970s. At the same time, growing military and defense-related needs absorbed men from the civilian sector, shrinking the pool of those available for the civilian economy, a trend intensified by the growth in the number of students in the universities. In most cases the demand for labor came from occupations such as teaching, social work, and clerical work, where women already had a foothold. In others it came from occupations previously closed to women, such as bank tellers, where, unable to attract men in sufficient numbers, employers were compelled to hire women. In addition, new occupations which initially had no clear sex label, such as in the fields of computers and human resource management, were receptive to women. The demand for labor during the 1970s increased opportunities for older women who had previously encountered difficulty competing for jobs.

An analysis of the trend in the age distribution of the female labor force reveals a drop in participation rates among women aged 24 and under, due largely to the prolongation of school education and partly to an increase in the percentage of women inducted into the army. Peak participation by age in 1970 was 18-24; in 1975 it was 25-34 and since 1984 it is 35-44. This upward drift reflects an increase in the proportion of older women with higher education. The proportion of married women grew from 25.7 percent in 1968 to 45.5 percent (51.7 percent among Jewish women) in 1988. In addition, the presence of small children has become less of a deterrent to women's employment. In 1987, almost 60 percent of all Jewish women, with a youngest child aged 2-4, were in the labor force and among women with 13 and more years of schooling the figure was more than 75 percent. The age distribution for Muslim, Christian, and Druze women is very similar to that of Jewish women in 1970, with participation peaking at 18-24 and then declining. The majority of Arab women in the labor force work until marriage or the birth of the first child and then leave the labor market.

Ethnic differences, especially among younger cohorts, may be attributed primarily to differences in educational attainment. Women from Europe or the United States of America are on the average better educated. The impact of education on employment rates is revealed by the following: the more educated a woman is, the more likely she is to have a job. This applies to Arab women as well, although the effect of education is not as powerful as it is for Jewish women. The lower employment rates found for first and second generation women from Asian or African countries become negligible when we compare women with the same levels of education. Furthermore, among those with 16 or more years of education, the employment rates for women are the same as those for men. The female labor force is on the average more educated than the male labor force. The median years of schooling in 1987 was 12.5 years for women and 11.8 years for men.

Additional changes facilitated women with small children to work outside their homes. Early in the 1970s, the number of daycare centers tripled as part of government policy to encourage female labor force participation. There are today some 1,000 childcare centers, subsidized and supervised by the Ministry of Labor and Social Welfare for over 90,000 children aged up to three years. Furthermore, many of the new job openings permitted part-time employment, or were concentrated in the public sector where work schedules could be better synchronized with schoolday schedules. Half-time workers are entitled to a proportionate share of all benefits enjoyed by full-time workers, including tenure. The rising expectations for a more materially comfortable style of life created greater reliance of the family on a second income. These factors, as well as the availability of ever-increasing numbers of women with higher education, make it likely that the upward drift in the female labor force will continue. If employment opportunities begin to shrink, however, new women may be discouraged from entering but it is more likely that a larger proportion will be unemployed than in the past.

WORK AND FAMILY

The analysis of sex differences in the labor a market must be placed within the wider context of the relationship of the work system to the family system. While the family is valued by both sexes, it impacts differently on men's and women's occupational roles. In a study of men and women in middle level and high-ranking jobs, Gafni (1981) found no sex difference in relative importance attributed to career and family. However, reanalysis of her data revealed that for women there are highly significant negative correlations between the relative importance attributed to family and the following: (1) preference for a job that entails making decisions and exerting authority; (2) aspirations for a more senior managerial position to perceived chances for advancing to a more senior position; and (3) a belief that she is qualified for a senior managerial position. None of these correlations is significant for men. The greater importance women (but not men) attach to family life, the more likely they are to limit their investments in their career.

Husbands invest the same time in housework and childcare whether wives are employed or full-time homemakers (Peres & Katz, 1983). A study of 137 dual-career couples (Izraeli and Sillman, 1989) in which both husband and wife were physicians found that women did two-thirds of the total hours spent by the couple in family work but that wives' earnings affected husbands' participation. However, among those physician couples where women contributed 50 percent or more of the family income, husbands reported spending more time in childcare and errands but not in domestic work, than husbands whose wives contributed less than 50 percent of the family income. That men serve in the army reserves through age 50-55 for up to 45 days a year also intensifies the sex division of labor in the household.

Comparing a sample of Israeli career women at mid-life with a similar group of women from the United States of America, Lieblich (1990) observed that Israeli women were less resentful of their husbands' lack of participation in both childcare and housework and experienced less role conflict. She explains this difference by the lesser importance Israeli women attribute to their careers and the greater centrality of the mother/wife/helpmate roles to their identity.

MIDDLE AGE—THE CROWDED NEST

The induction of her son or daughter into the army (at 18 years) rarely leaves the woman with an empty nest. More often, the result is an intensification of mothering. The household revolves around the army leaves of the young soldier. He or she may return home one to three weekends a month, bringing the dirty laundry that needs washing and careful ironing. Favorite foods and cakes are prepared. When the soldier is not home for a long period, mother often bakes cakes to send him or her packages. The middle aged woman, even if she is employed, often helps her married children by babysitting for her grandchildren and providing other personal services.

A study of women and men working in technological professions (Etzion, 1988) found that moving into middle age affects men and women differently. Women tend to become more self-confident and to experience less role conflict and less burnout than similar younger women, while the opposite is true for men, who show signs of greater burnout, boredom, and dissatisfaction than younger men.

OLD AGE

Women generally welcome retirement more than men do and are better prepared for it. In a series of studies of couples over the life span, focusing on the elderly couple, Friedman (1987) found a shift in the power balance, with women feeling more powerful and less vulnerable in the relationship and men less so than in earlier periods. She argues that women make greater investments in establishing social ties and consequently enter old age with more supportive social networks of friends and kin than do men.

The centrality of family life includes concern for aging parents. Elderly parents tend to live in the same city and rarely more than an hour or two from one of their offspring. Among larger families living within the same city, care for elderly parents may be shared among the offspring. Most of the responsibility for care falls on the woman, whether she be daughter or daughter-in-law, although among Eastern Jews males traditionally play an active role in caring for parents and meeting their physical needs. With the growth in the number of elderly but the decline in number of children they have to care for them and women's entry into the labor market, care for the elderly is emerging as a serious social problem.

The number of elderly citizens over 65 years of age increased almost fivefold since 1955 and their proportion in the population grew from 3.9 percent to 9.7 percent. Women constitute 54 percent of all those 65 years and older. The elderly are also growing older, with 41 percent of the elderly over 75 years. Approximately 92 percent of the elderly live in private homes, that is, in noninstitutional settings. Of these approximately 44 percent live as couples, 38 percent live with other family members, and 19 percent live alone (75 percent women). Regardless of where they live, however, it is very likely that at some point they will require and expect to receive intensive attention from offspring and it is most likely to be from a daughter. A sizeable proportion of women consequently experience the middle-age squeeze— supporting children who are launching their careers, caring for grandchildren, and responsible for elderly parents. The availability of institutional alternatives lags far behind demand and most of those built in the last decade are geared to the wealthy and healthy among the aging population.

Almost all the more than 500 kibbutzim in Israel were established and initially populated by young people, often before marriage. Today the more established kibbutzim are more than 50 years old and have sizeable elderly populations. Furthermore, life expectancy for women in the kibbutz is three years more than for their urban counterparts, and for men in the kibbutz it is six years more. While the economic structure of the kibbutz relieves its members of financial insecurity, social norms encourage the older members, men and women, to continue working as long as they are able to. Kibbutz members attribute their longevity to these factors plus full employment of all adult members. As members age they may move into a less demanding job and work fewer hours. In a society where social status is greatly influenced by the individual's contribution to the collective, the problem the kibbutz faces is not only physical care for the aging, but finding meaningful social roles for them to play within the kibbutz community.

SUMMARY AND CONCLUSIONS

This review of the dominant themes in women's lives over the life course highlights the contradictory pulls between a tradition that is valued but is also problematic with regard to women's status. It focuses on the opportunities inherent in modernity which also entail new tensions and conflicts. Jewish tradition emphasizes the centrality of family life and motherhood to women's identity. The anti-family ethos of U. S. feminism of the 1970s made that movement less attractive to Israeli women who were determined to enter the labor market without sacrificing family life. Jewish tradition, however, also carved out a role for women that was separate and not equal.

Public policy in the form of collective labor agreements and legislation provided working mothers with protection, and women's organizations provided subsidized childcare. This enabled women to combine family and work but confined most married women to part-time jobs, while the short schoolday and the inadequacy of services for working mothers constrained women from making the heavy investments necessary to advance their careers.

The United Nations Decade for Women produced, in Israel as in most other countries, a dynamic that led to the reevaluation of gender equality in all stages and phases of the life course. The Ministry of Education reexamined textbooks for sexism; women's studies have been introduced in three out of five universities; some teacher training seminars included the study of gender stereotype in the curriculum; the army expanded the jobs open to women; each of the universities has a woman advisor on the status of women; protective legislation has been expanded to include both parents—these are some of the developments that reflect the change. Despite these and other initiatives, there is no clear and consistent anti-sexist policy in any sphere of public life. Neither are there efficient means of combating sexist policies when uncovered.

Women's growing commitment to the labor market and the increase in higher education among women are undoubtedly the most significant developments for women's status with both specific positive repercussions for their career opportunities and diffuse implications impacting on women's self-esteem, aspirations, and life-style. They are reflected, for example, in the trend toward delayed marriage: In 1961, 33 percent of women 20-24 years were not married, while in 1987 the figure was 55 percent. Women who marry later also generally attribute greater importance to the work role and to personal fulfillment. These subtle but profound shifts in women's value orientation may be expected to produce new opportunities but also new conflicts for women's lives in the decades to come.

REFERENCES

Bar-Yosef, R., Bloom, A. R., & Levy, T. (1978). *Role ideology of young Israeli women* (Research Report). Jerusalem: Hebrew University, Work and Welfare Research Institute.

Bloom, A. R., & Bar-Yosef, R. (1985). Israeli women and military experience: A socialization experience. In M. P. Safir, M. T. Mednick, D. N. Izraeli, & J. Bernard (Eds.). *Women's worlds: From the new scholarship* (pp. 260-269). New York: Praeger.

Etzion, D. (1988). Experience of burnout and work and non-work success in male and female engineers: A matched pairs comparison. *Human Resource Management, 27,* 163-179.

Friedman, A. (1987). Getting powerful with age: Changes in women over the life cycle. *Israel Social Science Research: A Multidisciplinary Journal,* (special issue on *Women in Israel,* D. N. Izraeli, guest editor), *5,* 76-86.

Gafni, Y. (1981). The readiness of women and men in Israel to accept top management positions. MA thesis, Bar-Ilan University, Israel.

Hazleton, L. (1977). *Israeli women: The reality behind the myths.* New York: Simon and Schuster.

Izraeli, D. N. (1979). The sex structure of occupations: The Israeli experience. *Journal of Work and Occupations, 15,* 404-429.

Izraeli, D. N. (1981). The Zionist women's movement in Palestine 1911-1927. *Signs: Journal of Women in Culture and Society, 7,* 87-114.

Izraeli, D. N. (1988). Women managers in Israel. In N. Adler & D. N. Izraeli (Eds.). *Women in management worldwide.* New York: M. E. Sharpe.

Izraeli, D., & Sillman, N. (1989). A comparison of dual career physician couples with equal and unequal earnings. Paper presented at GASAT 5: *Gender, Science, and Technology.* Technion Institute of Technology, Haifa, September 17-22.

Keller, S. (1983). The family in the kibbutz: What lessons for us? In M. Palgi, J. Blassi, M. Rosner, & M. P. Safir (Eds.). *Sexual equality: The Israeli kibbutz tests the theories.* Philadelphia: Norwood Press.

Lieblich, A. (1990). A comparison of successful Israeli and American career women at mid-life. In B. Swirsky & M. P. Safir (Eds.). *Calling the equality bluff: Women in Israel.* New York: Pergamon Press.

Peres, Y., & Katz, R. (1983). Stability and centrality: The nuclear family in modern Israel. *Social Forces, 59,* 687-704.

Radai, F. (1983). Equality of woman under Israeli law. *The Jerusalem Quarterly, 27,* 184.

Safir, M. P. (1983). Sex role education/socialization on the kibbutzim. In M. Palgi, J. Blassi, M. Rosner, & M. P. Safir (Eds.). *Sexual equality: The Israeli kibbutz tests the theories.* Philadelphia: Norwood Press.

Safir, M. P. (1990). How has the kibbutz experiment failed to create sex equality? In B. Swirsky & M. P. Safir (Eds.). *Calling the equality bluff: Women in Israel.* New York: Pergamon Press.

Swirsky, B., & Safir, M. P. (Eds.). (1990). *Calling the equality bluff: Women in Israel.* New York: Pergamon Press.

Students at Cairo University, Khartoum Branch

Photo credit: Dr. Ramadan A. Ahmed

9

Women in Egypt and the Sudan

Ramadan A. Ahmed

Egypt is a country occupying the northeastern corner of Africa and the
Sinai peninsula, which is usually regarded as part of Asia. Strategically
situated at the crossroads between Europe and the Orient and between
north Africa and southwest Asia, Egypt, which has Pharaonic ancestors
and Arab fathers, has an area of about 386,100 square miles, of which
only 3.6 percent is normally inhabited, the rest is desert. It has an
estimated population of 48 million, which includes 49.6 percent females.

The Sudan has an area of 2.5 million square miles. The population is
estimated at 21.5 million people, of which 49.22 percent are females.
The climate varies from a dry, hot desert in the north to a continuously
rainy, very hot equatorial temperature in the south. The inhabited rural
areas are limited to the cultivated stretch of land between the White and
Blue Niles near the capital Khartoum. The greater part of the land is
either a vast desert or a tropical forest. Modernization is manifest in the
capital, Khartoum, and a few other cities. Sudanese life, particularly in
the outlying rural areas, has a more communal life-style. The cities in
the Sudan give clear evidence of the metamorphosis from a rural to an
urban life. The traditional way of life still exists, but is gradually
diminishing.

Egypt and the Sudan share Arabic as a common language. They have
the same culture and are predominantly Muslim. In addition to
considerable natural wealth, each country has large reservoirs of oil and
numerous mineral resources. Both countries, suffer, however, from a
number of population problems. They differ in some ways, yet are
similar in others, such as a high rate of population growth (2.8 percent
annually for both countries); a young population; large families; a high
mortality rate (prenatal, maternal, and infant); a moderate life expectancy (in Egypt 57 years and in the Sudan only 47 years); and an uneven
distribution of wealth. Moreover, Egypt and the Sudan are linked by a
charter of economic and political integration, signed in 1982, as a move
toward unity.

Before one can discuss the status of women in both Egypt and the Sudan, one must examine first their historical role. A failure to provide this would lead to conclusions difficult to understand and superficial at best when compared and contrasted with the women in Western or developed societies.

AN OVERVIEW OF SIMILARITIES AND DIFFERENCES BETWEEN EGYPTIAN AND SUDANESE WOMEN

Similarities

The first similarity between Egyptian and Sudanese women is rooted in their joint history, during which women enjoyed a high status. In ancient Egypt, women were given rights and respect as human beings. They were not secluded but had a high status and could even participate actively in the social, economic, and political life of the state government. One example of this is Queen Matkara Hatshepsut of the eighteenth dynasty in the New Kingdom, who ruled from 1473 to 1458 B.C., with the full panoply of decision-making power. It was a period of expansion of trade and of exploration. She is referred to as the greatest queen in ancient Egyptian history.

Under Islam, women in both countries, as all women in the Muslim world, enjoyed a high status in all fields of the society's activities, particularly in the first period of Islam. Until the 1500s, Sudanese women enjoyed a favorable status and high prestige, especially in the eastern parts. There the Beja, the largest of the tribes, accorded women positions of power. Among the Dinka and the Nuir tribes of the southern area, women rose to attain the status of tribal chief or king (queen): that is, the system allowed the son of the king's daughter or the son of the king's sister to inherit the throne. Such a system was common in the old kingdoms.

In more recent time, women also had high status. For instance, among the Shaygiya the story was told of Miheria bint Abboud (*bint* means daughter), who encouraged and led the men into battle against the invasion of the Sudan by Turkish and Egyptian invaders in 1821. And then one hears reports of women who served in the Mahdist political and military movement against the colonization of the Sudan in the latter part of the nineteenth century, who acted as spies, message carriers, and intelligence agents. Currently, other similarities among Egyptian and Sudanese women include the problems they face and the interests they share. Both are very children-oriented. Each suffers from similar impediments toward improving their present situation such as illiteracy, old die-hard traditions which are difficult to eradicate (for example, relative neglect, especially during the prenubial years), problems of mother/childcare and housekeeping chores, the high divorce rates, as well as improvement and development of their social, economic, and political situations in urban and rural environment. In contrast, men concentrate their efforts on politics, religious, and business affairs, and social events. In the latter part of the twentieth century changes have occurred, namely with regard to the important role played by women in agriculture and/or cattle raising. Women's participation was estimated during 1976-83 to be at 23.3 percent in Egypt and at 50 to even 90 percent in the Sudan of the total labor force in these occupations. The marked increase of the number of women in these fields was due to the exodus of a large sector of the male labor force, in particular, to the Arab oil producing states. The number of emigrant workers was estimated for Egypt to be more than 2.5 million and for the Sudan to be more than half a million. Among the ranks of the emigrant workers and professionals were large contingents of farmers. In some regions of the Sudan, the migration of the male work force to urban areas in the Sudan, or beyond the border, reached 35 percent of the available males of working age, and precipitated a need for the incorporation of greater numbers of women in the labor pool while they retained their traditional duties.

Differences

Egyptian women have achieved more marked progress in education, work opportunities or career, family legislation, status, political rights, and decision-making. The feminist movement in Egypt began earlier and is more cohesive and more involved in social issues. Feminist institutions (such as associations, women's clubs, and women's projects) are more numerous in Egypt. However, the Sudanese woman is more strongly influenced by tradition with regard to marriage, life-style, appropriate clothing, and customs of socialization.

THE WOMEN'S MOVEMENT IN EGYPT: A HISTORICAL REVIEW

The first sympathizers for women's emancipation in Egypt appeared in the latter half of the nineteenth century. It was from Judge Amin Qasim (1865-1908), a well-known disciple of a religious scholar, and a pioneer feminist named Muhammed Abduh (1849-1905) that these ideas developed into a manifesto for women's liberation. Two of Amin's books, *Tahrir al-Mara* (The Emancipation of Women, 1899) and *Al-Mara al-Jadida* (The Modern Woman, 1900), are the first works known in Arabic on this topic and remain on every Arab feminist's reading list to the present day (Minai, 1981, p. 73ff).

Using as the touchstone of his argument the premise that women's freedom and emancipation are essential to the development of nations, Amin initially asserted that Islam, in its true form, recognizes complete sexual equality between spouses. Subsequently he argues, but this time in secular terms, that no society can be strong if it does not recognize women's right to freedom together with their basic, natural human rights. In his works, he espouses that:

1. Although women have no right to higher education, they must nevertheless be so trained as to be able to cope emotionally and economically with the tyranny of marriage.
2. The chador, or veil, demeans them, serves no purpose, does not prevent adultery, and in true and final analysis, acts as an obstacle to the blossoming of a healthy attitude of the sexes vis a vis one another.
3. Although Islam permits marital polygamy to those who can be fair and equitable to each of the spouses they take, he underscores the failure to do so by detailing searingly the agony of wives ill-treated.

Condemned initially as non-Islamic and non-Egyptian, his works nevertheless almost immediately goaded on to action the women of the upper class who effectively adopted his writings as their guide. Slowly, but slowly, the rights they vindicated were granted. Thus, in 1956 they got the right of suffrage and of running for office; and in 1979, they succeeded in getting the marriage and divorce laws so liberalized as to take them into consideration for the first time. In the forefront of their movement were the aristocratic and the university educated women who had entered the work force in droves and in such fields as to influence the public's attitude toward them (Minai, 1981, p. 73).

But for all their efforts, those of the aristocrats who left their harems to demonstrate, march, boycott, and strike against the British and those of the lower classes who toiled quietly to disrupt the British by sabotage and such means as they could find, encountered headstrong, ungrateful, and selfish opposition from their own men. Their reaction was to form the Feminist Union in March 1923 under the leadership of one of their own, Huda Sharawi (1879-1949).

On return from an international conference in Rome, Huda flung her veil overboard as she disembarked, causing great scandal, especially as the wife of a pasha. Other aristocratic women later followed suit, all in the feminist cause. A great admirer of the accomplishments of the women's movement in the United States of America, she plunged herself into the midst of things: she attended women's conferences, called on suffragettes, and founded their mouthpiece, the magazine *L'Egyptienne* in 1925. *L'Egyptienne* was published under the editorship of Ceza Nabrawi, who had attended the Rome conference with Huda and had joined her in casting off her veil. In order to achieve the reform, Huda had to encourage the aristocratic class, especially women, to join and support her efforts. Twelve years later, an Arabic version, *Al-Masria* (The Egyptian Woman) was published (Minai, 1981, p. 71).

(This movement gave priority to the marriage and divorce laws and improving education for girls. Its first major success was in 1923 when the marriage age was set at 16 for girls and 18 for boys. In 1927, three years after women had gained the right to equality of education, the first women entered the University of Cairo, but not without a damper being put on their newly won right as society reluctantly opened up careers to them, except, of course, in midwifery and teaching. Thus, for example, as law school graduates, they could not hold jobs other than those of writer or journalist for a long time. The balance of their agenda, including the abolition of polygamy, was postponed for decades. In reaction against the overriding social prejudice to their holding down virtually any kind of paying job, women increased their consciousness-raising campaign. They took it upon themselves to look after the social welfare of the state, nationally neglected till the 1960s, by setting up and running schools for girls of poor families and prostitute rehabilitation centers, clinics, orphanages, and childcare centers. Their moment came in 1947-48 when cholera ravaged the country and they were able to persuade villagers to submit to vaccinations. Of benefit to them all along had been the efforts of Huda Sharawi and her companions (Minai, 1981, p. 69ff).

In 1974, the Egyptian feminist movement witnessed the beginning of a new era. The Egyptian Women's Organization was abolished as a result of dissolving the Egyptian Socialist Union, thus allowing for the establishment of political parties. A governmental committee for women was formed under the auspices and supervision of the Ministry of Social Affairs.

By way of contrast to their Egyptian counterparts, the Sudanese women had to fight their way to emancipation against almost insurmountable obstacles. In contrast to the short-lived Anglo-French occupation, the Sudanese had to counter 60 years of colonialism, one of the longest and most arduous struggle for freedom in the Middle East and the Arab world. During these decades, not only did the Sudanese have to absorb massive infusions of English language and culture but also constantly to water the garden of the Arabic language and Sudanese culture, tradition, and history which the incumbent government was only too glad to see wither. In this state of affairs therefore, it befell the lot of the Sudanese womenfolk to erect a bastion of conservation. This they succeeded in doing by keeping their daughters at home in the Muslim tradition, uneducated, and not allowed out in public until a very late age. In the Sudan, there were no feminist leaders in the beginning of this century. The story of women's liberation begins with their fight for national independence at the beginning of the twentieth century, when they stepped out of their domestic roles. Once they had acquired a taste for the outside world they wanted to stay there, but serious obstacles stood in their way. Sexual segregation, which had limited women's educational and professional opportunities for centuries, could not be abolished as long as woman's virtue was measured by her compliance with this practice.

In spite of social barriers, women worked alongside men in several organizations to bring about an end to colonial rule. After World War I, Sudanese women progressed within the nationalist movement by organizing the "Graduates' Movement," which was a club for graduates of Sudanese schools. This was an idea that originated with the teachers of the Omdurman elementary school in 1914. However, its implementation was delayed because of the war, and the club was not inaugurated until the summer of 1918. The pioneers of the Graduates' Movement were interested in the education of girls. This made women realize all the more their need for such education and gave impetus to the progressive movement. There was strong opposition to this trend, and it grew stronger; religious leaders were frightened of the emancipation of women. The British administration also opposed it, sometimes secretly and sometimes openly, putting forward feeble excuses and taking advantage of the backwardness that plagued the country in 1920s. During this period women played a unique role from inside their homes, for the secrecy of the meetings, the movements of members of these societies, and the organizational encounters all depended entirely on these women. The graduates understood the women's question well and clearly; they perceived it as part of the problem of the nation as a whole.

Women began to make progress daily, though it slowed down or speeded up with the rise of the tide of nationalism. Then, with the advent of World War II in the early 1940s, the Graduates' Conference revealed its political face. This confrontation helped to bring pressure to bear on the government to increase the number of schools in general, and hence the number of girls' primary schools and training colleges for women teachers. In addition, the education of girls at the intermediate level was started. As the number of educated women increased, they began to think of their uneducated sisters. The result of this was the beginning of literacy work among women, and the beginning of studies to carry forth this task (H. K. Badri, 1984a; 1984b, p. 97).

However, the few women who held jobs received only about four-fifths of the wages earned by men, and the women in the south received even less. While women were allowed seven days' pregnancy leave, they were not granted any retirement pensions; when they got married, they had to resign their permanent work contracts for work on a month-to-month basis. These and other conditions gave rise to the women's movement which culminated in the first Union of Sudanese Women, formed in 1946. This was followed by women's professional organizations, as part of the national movement, which was striving for political independence.

In 1952, and after a period of stagnation, the Women's Union was revived with a membership open to all women, educated or uneducated, urban or rural. The Union's activities included the founding of the newspaper *Sawt al-Mara* (The Woman's Voice).

As a result of the participation of women in the October 1964 Revolution, women gradually gained the full right to vote, the right to nominate, and the right to membership in political parties.

In 1965, for the first time, a woman was elected to and served in the parliament of the government of Sudan. During 1965-69 women achieved equal pay for equal work, and in 1969 the government approved women's demands for abolition of the month-to-month work system, alimony reform, and extension of maternity leave to eight weeks.

The break between former president Nimeiri and the Left, following the 1971 Communist-backed coup attempt, led to the abolition of the Women's Union, because of its early association with the Left. In

November 23, 1971, however, a new Union was established. Its title was the Sudan's Women's Union (SWU), and it was run under the leadership of the Sudanese Socialist Union (SSU). The SWU concerned itself mostly with political issues and paid scant attention to women's issues. The effectiveness of the Union suffered from a rapid turnover in leadership. In April 1985, the government of Nimeiri was overthrown and the Union of Sudanese Women was abolished again. Instead, a new National Committee for Women was formed. At present, there exist sharp ideological differences between various factions represented in the Committee (*Al-Sahafaa*, April 30, 1985).

INFANCY AND EARLY CHILDHOOD

Although the Quran and Prophet Muhammed himself recognized the equality of the sexes 14 centuries ago, and even though about 70 years ago the first Muslim feminist reasserted the equality of the sexes, girls in both Egypt and the Sudan are still counted second-best.

Preference for Sons

Like many of their counterparts in the Western world, parents in Egypt and the Sudan prefer sons. It is said that a man with a son is immortal, whereas a girl is brought up to contribute to someone else's family tree.

There are many compelling economic reasons why parents would prefer a boy. At least 70 percent of Egypt and the Sudan are rural. Here, sons are indispensable as muscle power on the land. Without their continued presence on family land, parents would have to look forward to a miserable old age. Unlike girls, boys do not have to be supervised very closely, since their sexual behavior cannot dishonor the family or compromise their chances for marriage. If a girl survives infancy in the poverty-stricken areas of Egypt and the Sudan, she is saddled with work as soon as she can walk, and often she cannot even attend the cost-free primary education (Galal el-Din, 1984).

Women's nurturing duties begin early in life, such as helping with babycare and kitchen duties, and frequently working with real farm equipment and weaving tools. Although not always counted in government surveys, girls are, in rural areas especially, economic assets from the start. They constitute a large labor force of usually unpaid workers and helpers to their parents. If they were counted along with their brothers, who hire themselves out as farmhands, sweatshop assistants, or peddlers, the prevalence of child labor would be staggering.

The picture is quite grim. Enrollment figures for elementary school children are perhaps a better indication of how many girls help their families survive. Only about half of the girls of school age in Sudanese urban areas receive primary education, while over two-thirds of the boys of that age are allowed to attend school (Galal el-Din, 1984). In Egypt, the proportions reach about 70 percent for girls and 85 percent for boys

(Central Agency for Public Mobilization and Statistics, 1978). The picture is far worse in the rural areas in both countries; for example, in some Sudanese rural areas they reach only 10 percent or below (Galal el-Din, 1984).

So economically and socially advantageous and necessary is a son that men—even those well informed of the latest findings of genetics—will get divorced and take on wife after wife until one bears him a son (Minai, 1981, p. 84ff).

Throughout Egypt, and especially in the Sudan, women are viewed as subordinates to men, but vital for nurturing; yet there are several ways to mold little girls to that ideal.

With premarital and extramarital sex commonplace in spite of its being forbidden by the Quran itself, an awesome burden befalls the parents to safeguard their daughter's virginity while preparing her for her future role of mother. How this is effectuated varies from family to family according to its socioeconomic status (Minai, 1981, p. 85). Professionals and the well-to-do do not have to depend on their son's work in old age, and so their wives feel less threatened if their baby should turn out to be a girl rather than a boy. The daughter is likely to receive a good education. This makes her fear to divorce much less than her poorer sisters who remain without education and thus without marketable skills. N. Minai (1981, pp. 85-86) noted that:

Accordingly, the mother is not prone to transmit her own insecurity and resentment to the daughter who arrived in lieu of the much-hoped-for son. She may try again and again for a boy . . . and if she still fails to produce a son, her husband is not likely to insist that he have a son from another wife.

Early parental stereotyping of the behavior of their children, emphasizes masculinity for boys and femininity for girls. Such discrimination later results in the sexes having negative attitudes toward one another. At the same time, it was found that the primary school curriculum encouraged and fostered the traditional stereotyping of boys and girls. This stereotyping does not only occur during the childrearing period and in the school curriculum, but is also seen in the mass media and films. Minai (1981, p. 138), and also El-Abd (1983, pp. 91-95) pointed out:

Muna al-Hadeedy analyzed 410 Egyptian films shown between 1962 and 1972. She concluded that much more should be done to upgrade the image of portrayed women as beautiful but brainless, whose sole mission in life was to catch the most eligible bachelor . . . [but] as the hero stepped out of sight they pined away, fell into the hands of villains, or wandered into prostitution and belly dancing.

FEMALE CIRCUMCISION

It is appropriate here to discuss a problem that is related to the sex-stereotyping and socialization process for girls in both Egypt and the Sudan,
that is, the problem of female circumcision. Female circumcision has
affected about 84 million women in 30 countries in Asia and Africa,
among them Egypt and the Sudan (*Sudanow*, December 1984, p. 28ff).
The practice of female circumcision is inextricably linked to the position
of women in Egyptian and Sudanese societies.

Genital mutilation was medically accepted as a treatment of masturba-
tion and "nymphomania" in the West in the nineteenth and early
twentieth centuries (Minai, 1981, p. 96). In the Middle East today the
operation is performed in three main ways:

1. The simplest form is the Sunna circumcision, in which only the tip of
   the clitoris (prepuce) is sliced off,
2. The intermediate, more radical type, is a clitoridectomy, calling for
   the excision of the entire clitoris and leaving some parts of the labia
   minora intact, or the removal of the clitoris, the whole of the labia
   minora, and parts of the labia majora, and the stitching of the two
   sides together, leaving an opening,
3. Even more harrowing is the practice of infibulation (or Pharaonic or
   Sudanese circumcision). It involves the removal of or the sealing of
   the labia majora and the labia minora together after the entire clitoris
   has been removed, leaving the two raw edges to adhere, which
   produces a lengthwise scar. The most widespread genital mutilation
   in the Middle East, however, is clitoridectomy. Its practice among
   non-Muslims as well as Muslims suggests a non-Islamic origin
   (Minai, 1981, p. 96ff; *Sudanow*, December 1984, p. 29).

It was noted that the clitoridectomy existed also in the Upper Nile
Valley of Egypt during the Pharaonic period. The Quran does not
discuss the practice. It seems that the Prophet Muhammed himself could
not eradicate it. The practice is attested to by a tradition that holds that,
unable to prevent a clitoridectomy in progress, he enjoined that, at least,
no destruction be wrought on the organs. Prophet Muhammed said:
"Reduce, but don't destroy." Opinions as to the thrust of this injunction
vary: some claim it sanctions the practice, others the contrary. Among
those who consider it sanctioned, those who follow the Sunna procedure
cause the least damage. Yet, laws to the contrary notwithstanding, the
Egyptian and Sudanese hinterlands continue with the practice, persuaded
there can be no good marriage without it (Minai, 1981, p. 97ff;
UNICEF, 1983; UNICEF, 1984). Although facts and figures about
female circumcision are available for Egypt and for the northern areas
of the Sudan, little is known about the situation in the southern areas of
the Sudan (*Sudanow*, December 1984, p. 31).

The practice is deeply rooted in many traditional societies. Women
are circumcised in the name of religion, cleanliness, or morality. Some

women in Egypt, especially in the rural areas, and in the northern parts of the Sudan practice circumcision because it has been their custom from ancient times on. They find it difficult, but valuable because it is the tradition (*Sudanow*, December 1984, p. 28).

Female circumcision is one of many traditional practices that adversely affects the health of women and children as well. Circumcision can take place at any age from one week, up to before the birth of the woman's first child. Often it is part of an important puberty ceremony (UNICEF, 1983; UNICEF, 1984).

In different areas in both Egypt and the Sudan, and also in other countries in which the practice of circumcision is common, people in general support the practice, believing it to be part of their faith. But in fact neither the Quran nor the Bible claims that it is necessary. However, different groups believe that it is an aid to cleanliness and chaste behavior for women and girls, and that uncircumcised women are dirty and consumed by sexual desire. It is known that public opinion in the Sudan, and in Egypt to a lesser degree, is still against ending the circumcision of females. Therefore women suffer in this way for no reason except that they are females (*Sudanow*, December 1984). The type of female circumcision performed in Egypt is the clitoridectomy; it is less dangerous than the Pharaonic circumcision, which is common in the Sudan.

The medical problems that stem from female circumcision and infibulation are numerous. Some Sudanese gynecologists stated that 50 percent of the problems treated at women's clinics in the Sudan are the result of circumcision. The problems that can result from circumcision and infibulation are bleeding, infection, tissue scarring, anemia, tetanus, retention of urine, painful menstruation, difficulty in passing the menstrual flow, infertility, obstructed labor with the danger of causing harm to both mother and baby, and many more problems. Furthermore, young girls can suffer severe psychological trauma. They become scared of the adults who have subjected them to this torture (process) and wives tend to be reluctant to discuss their problems with their husbands. Some men find that they suffer from potency problems when they are unable to break through the artificial barrier created by infibulation. Far from being a test of fertility, it can be a test of the marriage. Sexual difficulties bring marital discord, sometimes divorce (*Sudanow*, December 1984, p. 29; A. E. Badri, 1984, p. 15ff; El-Mamoun, 1984; Houssain, 1984).

Just how is this operation carried out, especially in the rural areas of the Sudan? The local midwife lesions the inner surface of the labia majora by scraping them down with knives or razor blades and sutures them together with thorns of the dwarf acacia plant and bits of string. Then, through the tiny aperture left at the base, she inserts a matchstick or a piece of small bamboo twig for the passage of menses and urine. Next, the patient is put on a mat with her legs bound together right down to the ankles so to remain until she first urinates, the sign the operation is a success. A week later, the thorns are extracted, but the bonds on her legs will stay on until the lesioned flesh of the labia has grown closed together and healed up. If the girl survives any hemorrhaging or infections and gets married, then—and this without anesthesia, cauterization, or application of nettle—she will be cut open so as to be able to copulate and eventually give birth. After birth, her labia are resutured only to be cut open later when again necessary. A number of problems often set in, such as frigidity, urinary retention, incontinence, pelvic infections, and obstetric complications that could damage a future fetus. In some cases, the genitals are so scarred and maimed through such operations that the woman is no longer capable of normal intercourse and childbearing. And, no longer able to gratify her spouse's appetite, she is cast out for a younger and healthier wife. Yet, notwithstanding all this, infibulation continues to be practiced not only in the Sudan, but in Somalia, Djibouti, and Ethiopia, in neighboring countries such as Kenya and Egypt, and in remote places such as Nigeria, Mali, and the Arabian peninsula (Minai, 1981, p. 96ff).

Female Circumcision in Egypt

Egypt is a country that has already had some success in its campaigns to eradicate female circumcision. The change in public opinion in Egypt came as part of the modernization process. It was included in programs of family education, and general health care. Traditional healers, who had previously supported and performed circumcision, became agents of change within their own communities, explaining the dangers of the practice to their own people. Women had success in Egypt in changing public opinion because circumcision was not treated as an isolated issue. However, there are a few groups, mainly from Egyptian rural areas, who are almost stubborn in their persistence of the practice. Minai (1981, p. 98ff) wrote that:

> In more enlightened urban areas in Egypt, the crippling versions have given way to the Sunna circumcision, but this is no less psychologically traumatizing for the young victim, and may lead to sexual frigidity in adulthood. . . . Circumcision is declining among enlightened people in the larger cities in Egypt. But it does not mean that parents who refuse to mutilate their daughter care less about her chastity. They just use other ways when she reaches puberty.

Female Circumcision in the Sudan

When one looks at a map of the Sudan that shows the region and types of circumcision, almost all of those performed in the Sudan are of the Pharaonic type. Yet all the Sudanese Muslim women in the northern region are circumcised. In the southern region, there are no circumcisions indicated which means that, apart from perhaps very few instances, no circumcised women are to be found in this area. However, a survey carried out in 1983 by the Faculty of Medicine, University of Khartoum, showed that approximately 15 percent of the women were circumcised. Later follow-up interviews held by experts working in the field in the southern region of the Sudan gave support to findings of the Faculty of Medicine (UNICEF, 1983; UNICEF, 1984; *Sudanow*, December 1984). On the other hand, according to certain Sudanese gynecologists with whom I have discussed the matter, the practice of the Pharaonic or Sudanese circumcision is not found among Sudanese Christian women in the south (personal communication).

EDUCATION

Education in the Arab countries in general, and as in the Third World countries, has its cultural characteristics. Such characteristics have deeply influenced the current social sex-stereotyping of men and women. However, the educational system is more biased in rural areas.

It is a fact that Islam recognized the importance of education for each believer, man or woman, and that the Prophet Muhammed exhorted that education is the duty incumbent on every believer, since he said: "For all Muslims education is compulsory." But until recently, the figures for school enrollment in both Egypt and the Sudan, as in other Arab countries, showed in general that females remained seriously disadvantaged in education (*Sudanow*, December 1979, p. 37ff; UNICEF, 1984).

Girls' Education in Egypt

Egyptians, like other Islamic peoples, believed for a long time that education for girls was not formal (that is, not taught in schools), but rather was taught at home. This tradition was followed until the mid-nineteenth century. It was the favorite endeavor for upper-class families to educate their daughters. Some years later, girls' primary schools were opened all over the country (Soueif, 1975, p. 4ff). The idea of educating girls was opposed until some of the upper class families enrolled their daughters. But in the minds of the girls' fathers, women's education was not conceived as possibly leading to a career outside the home. They saw only in girls' education a mark of social class. Then, gradually, the belief in the need for girls' education became widespread. During the last 60 years a great increase occurred in the number of enrollments of girls at all educational levels. While in 1920 girls represented 24.5 percent of the total number of enrolled pupils in the primary schools, this number increased to 42.9 percent in 1983-84.

In the intermediate-school level, girls made up only 21 percent of the total number of the enrolled pupils at this level in 1920, yet this number rose to 39.9 percent in 1983-84. While at the secondary-school level, the percentage of girls in 1920 was only 0.85 percent, in 1983-84 girls were 37.9 percent of all enrolled students at this level of education

(El-Sayed, 1974, p. 25ff; Soueif, 1975, p. 2; The World Bank, 1981; Azzam, 1982, p. 296; El-Abd, 1983, p. 24ff; *Al-Ahram*, May 21, 1985). However, the percentage of girls who dropped out of primary schools was higher than for boys, especially in rural areas, where the ratio was two to one (*Al-Ahram*, September 9, 1982). On the other hand, this high rate of dropping out at the primary-school level can be seen as a certain source of illiteracy. In the case of illiteracy, the rate in 1981 was 52.9 percent in general (38 percent for males and 62 percent for females). This rate has been estimated at 35 percent in urban areas and 64 percent in rural areas (State Information Service, 1983a, p. 11; 1984, p. 107; *Al-Ahram*, February 19, 1985).

This progress in female education reaffirms the intellectual capacities of the Egyptian girls and young women in various educational stages. Yet it is still limited to only a small portion of them, namely those who are helped by their social, economic, and environmental conditions to become effectively influential in community development.

Concerning the attendance of girls in the universities and other higher institutions, the number of female college students increased from zero in 1920 to 31 percent of the total student body in 1976 (Soueif, 1975, p. 2; Azzam, 1982, p. 295ff). Statistics showed that the 1,389 female graduate students registered during the academic year 1983-84 in Egypt (or about 10 percent of the total number of graduate students) were classified as follows: 41 doctoral (Ph.D.) students, 644 Masters students, and 484 Diploma Students. During the previous academic year, 1982-83, 33.8 percent of all postgraduate students were women (*Al-Ahram*, March 9, 1985).

Since 1929 and for the first time in contemporary Egyptian history, young women started to join the faculties at Cairo University (established in 1908). They began with the faculties of medicine, sciences, and arts, although the faculties of agriculture and engineering accepted women only beginning in the academic year 1945-46.

Girls' Education in the Sudan

In 1907, significant progress in the field of education for girls was achieved with the founding and opening in the Blue Nile town of Rufaa of the first modern primary school for girls. This school still exists. It was opened as a result of the courageous efforts of the former-Mahdist soldier, educator, and champion of women's rights, Babiker Badri. But it was not until 1920 that serious efforts were made to establish primary schools for girls. Higher levels of education for girls progressed slowly. The first intermediate school for girls was established in 1939, and six years later the first secondary school for girls was opened. In 1946 girls entered the Gordon Memorial College (now Khartoum University) (H. K. Badri, 1984a; and H. K. Badri, 1984b).

A substantial increase in school enrollment during the period from 1956 to 1982-83 occurred for both females and males. The rate of increase, however, was greater for females than for males. This trend was true for all three educational levels.

As a result of the social and economic changes that took place in the Sudan during the last two decades, there was an increase in the enrollment of female pupils. However, statistics indicated that the education of girls in the Sudan still has not reached its ideal point. The statistics for the academic year 1981-82 showed that the number of Sudanese girls enrolled in the three levels of education (primary, intermediate, and secondary schools) is still less than the number of enrolled boys at every level. Girls represented 39.9 percent of the total of enrolled pupils in the primary school, and 40.3 percent and 36.9 percent of the total enrolled students at the intermediate and secondary school levels, respectively (Sudan Ministry of Education and Guidance, 1982, p. 31ff; UNICEF).

The data for 1982-83 school enrollment showed clearly that the status of women (and girls) was changing in the Sudan. Even in the rural areas the enrollment data indicated that education was seen as desirable for females. In urban areas, education for females appeared to be valued almost as much as education for males. The trend of the data pointed to further increases in female school enrollment which, at least in urban areas, could match rates for males in the near future.

Although women's education in the Sudan has developed relatively quickly and women are now a very productive and dynamic segment of the society in the nation's development, the educational opportunities in the Sudan in general still lag behind the rate of increase of the population for all levels of education. Consequently, it does not reach all urban, rural, and underdeveloped areas. Moreover, there are no incentives or mandatory measures for parents of school-aged children. For traditional and economic reasons, parents have no great interest in sending their daughters to school (Ahmed, 1984, p. 43ff). One of the reasons may be the high rate of illiteracy among parents, which is conservatively estimated at 68 percent. Approximately 45 percent of the men and only about 18 percent of the women of the Sudan are literate, although in the urban areas the corresponding percentages have increased to just over 65 for men and nearly 40 for women. In the rural areas in the Sudan the percentages for both men and women are much lower: about 38 percent of the men and only 12 percent of the women are literate. Moreover, there exist negative attitudes toward girls' education. These are due to the dominating tribal values and strong Sudanese traditions, as reflected by the following observation: the higher the stage of education, the lower the girls' attendance (Ahmed, 1984, p. 44).

Development of Higher Education for Girls in the Sudan

Until the 1950s, there were very few girls who could complete their higher education. The first female college student was admitted in 1945 at the Khartoum University, then called the Gordon Memorial College.

The number of female college students has gradually increased, but not in the same proportion as that of college men. Increases of enrollments in the Ahfad University for Women, the Higher Nursing College (started in 1956) and the Girls' College at Omdurman Islamic University have contributed much to the higher education for women in the Sudan (Mohammed & Habiballa, 1985, p. 4). As already mentioned, the two decades from 1965 to 1985 have witnessed a steady increase in women's enrollment in institutions of higher education. Twenty percent of the college students were women who attended, like their Egyptian counterparts, studies in economics, arts, and law faculties, although women made up only 5 percent of the total number of students in the faculties of engineering and agriculture.

MARRIAGE

Islamic societies, among them Egypt and the Sudan, have remained strictly marriage-oriented and conspire relentlessly to round up every bachelor into the matrimonial fold. Islam prohibits premarital relationships between a man and woman, but at the same time it encourages marriage. To begin, there is Prophet Muhammed's decree that marriage is the only road to virtue. Even an irreligious bachelor usually feels compelled to marry by his need for sons as security against old age, since most countries did not provide pensions until recently. Marriage is a Sunna (the Prophet's practices and teachings). Islam also prohibits celibacy. The Prophet said: "There is no celibacy in Islam" (Minai, 1981, p. 189; Shalaq, 1982, p. 20; Satti, 1985, p. 7).

Marriage customs in both Egypt and the Sudan are similar; of course, there are slight differences, but one can say that the marriage customs in both countries are traditional. Moreover, they seem to be deeply influenced by social and economic circumstances, such as the increasing migration of the labor force in Egypt and the Sudan to the oil producing countries. There are about 2 million Egyptian and more than 600,000 Sudanese workers employed now in some Gulf States (Mahmoud, 1983; Galal el-Din, 1985, p. 80ff).

Patterns of Mate Selection

It is useful to mention here that Prophet Muhammed advised his followers to choose their partners carefully because the family, from Islam's point of view, is the backbone of the society; Islam has clear instructions on establishing a family (Satti, 1985, p. 7). In both Egypt and the Sudan the patterns of mate selection, in general, are traditional in nature. However, as Minai points out (1984, p. 154ff):

the changes that are taking place in marriage customs today in Islamic countries, among them Egypt and the Sudan, aim to improve a woman's chances of choosing her own husband, by according her greater freedom to meet men and by easing the burden of dowry. It is believed that this amply takes care of the modern woman's sexual needs: as they may be fulfilled only within marriage, what could be better than allowing her to marry the man she desires ?

The average age of marriage in urban areas is higher than in rural areas. In Egypt it is between 25-35 years for men and 20-30 years for women in urban areas, while it is between 20-25 years for men and 16-18 years for women in rural areas. In the Sudan the ages were about the same.

Well-educated men in Egyptian urban areas prefer that their future wives have the following characteristics in this order: education, skills in housekeeping chores, and wealth. Men in rural areas have another order of the desirable characteristics: a good background, high moral standing, a good reputation, keeping active skills in performing housekeeping chores, beauty, and the best education (*Al-Ahram*, February 8, 1985 and June 4, 1985; cf. Khalifa, 1975, p. 63ff; United Nations, 1972; concerning the age of marriage in Egypt see also Central Agency for Public Mobilization and Statistics, 1978).

In the last 20 years, advertisements have appeared in Egyptian newspapers in which women and men seek husbands and wives that highlight the tenacity of traditional notions of masculinity and femininity, and which may have no survival value today. These women and men, who almost always are well educated, want husbands and wives in good circumstances. In particular, women want husbands with occupations that pay better than theirs for practical reasons; but they insist also on their future husbands being taller and older. Men invariably advertise for women who are younger, shorter, and less educated than they are (Minai, 1981, p. 160ff).

One can observe that many female university graduates in both Egypt and the Sudan are not married. In a recent survey (conducted by the present writer especially for this chapter) on the male and female university students in Khartoum, it was found that the chief reason for their life-style was that the male graduates tended to prefer that their future wives be less educated women, either from higher or lower secondary schools, or even primary schools, or possibly their illiterate village cousins (R. A. Ahmed, Cairo University, Khartoum Branch, unpublished research, December 1984). This problem was more acute in the Sudan than in Egypt. However, it should be widely discussed. It is discouraging for women's education when these graduates, who are supposed to set an example, either avoid their duty or cannot get married. Sudanese society should comply with the following slogan: "Educating girls may be one of the country's best investments toward future growth and progress" (*Sudanow*, March 1985, p. 7).

DIVORCE

Under Islamic law, a marriage can be dissolved in three ways: repudiation by the husband (*Talaq*), divorce by mutual consent (*Khula*), and judicial separation (*Tafriq*). Some Islamic countries permit only the first method. Others, including Egypt and the Sudan, permit a combination of some or all. N. Minai (1981, p. 174) wrote:

> Divorce is a particularly painful alternative to polygamy. The Prophet Muhammed's divorce laws were kinder to women. A man could not throw out his wife on a whim. He had to pronounce his intention to divorce her on three occasions. Prophet Muhammed further ordained that no one could remarry his divorced wife before she had been remarried and divorced by another man; he could not divorce her as warning or as a punishment and then remarry her when he had gotten his way. (See also: *Population Reports*, November 1984; Fyzee, 1955, p. 93ff; Shalaq, 1982, p. 25; El-Ghandour, 1985, p. 295ff.)

It has been suggested recently that in Egypt the promulgation of the law necessitated the services of a judge to get the permission for the divorce. Enumeration of the reasons was essential, as well as letting the wife present her point of view. Then the judge would try to reconcile the spouses or submit them to the arbitration of the Quran. If he did not succeed he would issue a court sentence of divorce with or without the wife's compensation according to what he thought of the husband's grounds for divorce. No matter what the amount of compensation for the wife, it is never quite adequate and undoubtedly, divorce is harmful to her children (Fahmy & Ramzi, 1976, p. 21). According to the Personal (Marital) Status Law no. 44, which passed by executive decree in 1979, the divorced wife was entitled to the house that she occupied while she was married, and to 40 percent of the husband's salary for three years. If she was married to the same husband for more than 15 years, she drew alimony for life or until she remarried. Unless she was proven an unfit mother, her daughters would stay with her until their marriage, and her sons until they were 15 years of age (Minai, 1981, p. 178). However, in Egypt there were great arguments and discussions about the effects of the supplemental law, which made divorce, as well as polygamy, more difficult for husbands; it also encouraged men to take much longer to choose wives. In March 1985, Egypt rescinded its 1979 Family Law, a modified Sharhia Law, on the basis that it was unconstitutional. Two months later, the Egyptian Parliament passed a new Marital Law, very similar to the 1979 law. According to the new law, a divorced woman can keep her children until the daughter reaches 11 years and until the son reaches the age of 9 years. However, in the Sudan a divorced woman can keep her son until he is 7 years old and her daughter is 9 years old. Yet the law has been modified to allow custody up to adulthood, if the mother asks for that; however, in this case she is not entitled to financial assistance (Satti, 1985, p. 10).

A relatively high proportion of all Sudanese married women reported dissolution of their first marriages (17.5 percent). Overall, 82.5 percent of the married women were still in their first marriage. Of the remaining 17.5 percent, 5.8 percent had their marriage dissolved by the husband's death, and 11.7 percent by divorce or separation (*Sudan Fertility Survey*, 1979, p. 45).

Polygamy

Polygamy was not introduced by Islam, although it was a common practice in many ancient societies because of certain social and humanitarian considerations, such as infertility and in regions where the female population outnumbered the male population (Shalaq, 1982, p. 20; Satti, 1985, p. 13; El-Ghandour, 1985, p. 138ff).

Polygamy is not prohibited either in Egypt or in the Sudan. In fact, the polygamy rate in both countries is very low (below two or three per thousand) due to economic reasons (A. Khalifa, 1973, pp. 17 and 42ff; 1975, p. 70f; El-Meligui, 1975, p. 209ff; *Sudan Fertility Survey*, 1979). The statistics show that the number of men who have more than one wife is constantly decreasing. The proportion in Egypt in 1970 was only three per thousand for well-educated couples and eight per thousand for uneducated couples (El-Meligui, 1975, p. 212). The data given by the *Sudan Fertility Survey* (1979) show that the proportion of women then (at the time of the survey) in a polygamous marriage was 16.8 percent of the total of the adult married Sudanese women. The data show also that the percentages of polygamous spouses differed according to the women's age categories. These were as follows: 11.1 percent of women under age 25; 16.6 percent of women aged 25-34, and 21.2 percent of women aged 35-50 (*Sudan Fertility Survey*, 1979, p. 48).

An alternative to banning polygamy is to enact some moderate change. In 1979 amendments to Egypt's Marital or Personal Status Law required the husband to inform his current wife of his intention to marry another woman and to inform the future wife of his current marital status. Since secrecy facilitated polygamy, this measure may have discouraged men from taking additional wives. The first wife was entitled to a court divorce and possibly monetary compensation within a year, if she found out that her husband had married again without informing her first.

PREGNANCY AND CHILDBIRTH

Attitudes and Practices

It is expected in both Egypt and the Sudan that every woman will become a mother after marriage. This expectation is deeply rooted in Islamic cultural tradition. Islam sets the mother at the highest level.

During the past periods of harem life, or because of ignorance and poverty, women had become little more than a sexual object and childbearing machine. Related to that, and to the male image of women as weak and second place, it appeared that pregnancy and childrearing became the only duty of a woman. That is a possible way for a married women to keep the relationship with her husband very strong, and to avoid divorce. It may explain, at least partly, the high rate of fertility in both Egypt and the Sudan, especially in rural areas, and particularly among uneducated married women. This high rate of fertility in both countries is a function of many factors, such as the universality of marriage; the early age of marriage, especially for women; the cultural correlation between femininity and fertility; lack of social security for women, especially in old age; the high rate of mortality among children (which has been estimated in Egypt at 53 per thousand, and in the Sudan at the 120 per thousand), especially in rural areas, which reached in some Sudanese rural areas 250 per thousand in the first year of life. The high rate of fertility is also due to the fact that parents prefer to have boys rather than girls for traditional, economic, and social reasons. As already mentioned, the cultural pattern encourages the belief that fathers who have boys are immortal. Rural women particularly consider that their value depends on their ability to bear children, especially boys. Children are traditionally a source of prestige to rich families, and of income to poor families (United Nations, 1972; Galal el-Din, 1977a; Minai, 1981, p. 91; The World Bank, 1981, p. 168ff; *Population Reports*, November 1984; *Al-Ahram*, October 10, 1985).

Studies in Egypt (A. Khalifa, 1973; summarized by Hamzawi, 1982) and in the Sudan (M. Khalifa, 1978; Galal el-Din, 1984) showed that education appeared to be universally related to fertility among Egyptian and Sudanese employed urban women. Hamzawi's study in 1982 confirmed that the relationship between female employment and fertility in urban areas persists when other variables that affect fertility (for example, the wife's and husband's level of education, age, family income, and length of residence in an urban area) are controlled. Hamzawi's study also indicated that even in urban areas, educated women working in well-paid and/or highly satisfying jobs are more likely to limit fertility to continue to work.

Concerning the relationship between women's work and fertility, it was found that employment outside the home gives women the freedom to move about in the community and interact with others; thus, we can consider the freedom as an important social factor in the use of contraceptive methods (A. Khalifa, 1973, p. 125ff; Hamzawi, 1982).

The *Sudan Fertility Survey* (1979; see also Galal el-Din, 1977a; The World Bank, 1981, p. 168ff; Saghayroun, 1985, p. 48ff), which investigated the relationship between fertility, education, and age, showed that well-educated and younger women (under 45) tended to have fewer children (two to five children), than the uneducated or less educated and older women, 45 and older (four to six children). On the other hand, it seems that women's employment opportunities may have affected their fertility. Fertility tended to be lower for better educated women, working women with high incomes, and women in larger cities. Some studies showed that fertility in both Egypt and the Sudan tended to be higher in rural areas because agricultural labor for women in rural areas seemed to encourage large families. Most studies showed that the type of economic activity in which women generally engaged, especially in rural areas, may have encouraged them to have more children. Women (and men also) who work in the fields may wish for children, especially sons, to lessen their burden (Hamzawi, 1982, p. 17).

In Egypt there are more than 2,000 centers for the health care of mothers and babies. These centers have helped more than 1.5 million mothers in 1984. The death rate of pregnant mothers decreased in 1984 to eight per thousand and this reflected the increase of the health care services in Egypt during the last few years (Al-Akhbar, March 23, 1985).

In both Egypt and the Sudan, as all over the world, pregnancy and delivery are connected with local customs and beliefs. Some of these are harmful, either to the mother or the infant or both. Some customs practiced during delivery, such as the use of a kitchen knife or an arrow in cutting the umbilical cord, also contribute to infectious diseases and a high rate of maternal and infant mortality, in the Sudan in particular.

One of the most important problems in the Sudan is delivery and its relation to the health of the mother and the child. There are two kinds of deliveries in the Sudan: traditional birth attendants and midwives.

Traditional birth attendants (TBA), who perform an estimated 80 percent of all deliveries in rural areas (communities), hold the key to maternal and child health in the Sudan. Moreover, they have an intimate knowledge of the mothers, who in turn give the TBA their full confidence. Mostly illiterate, the TBA is usually trained in an informal way by her mother or an older relative. She enjoys much respect in the community for her practical work experience. It was estimated that in Egypt in 1985, not less than 50 percent of all deliveries in the rural areas were performed by the traditional birth attendants (Al-Ahram, March 28, 1986).

The TBA midwife has received no training course at all, but also is crucial to maternal and child health care in the Sudan. The village or local midwife is trained in delivery techniques at a government school for 18 months. After completion of the training, the village midwife returns to her community, where the village council pays her a modest monthly salary.

According to a 1983 UNICEF report, more than 40,000 children die in the Sudan each year from malnutrition and infections. Child health and nutritional problems in the Sudan present a real challenge to the concerned authorities. The infant mortality rate has been estimated in 1984 at 120 to 140 per thousand, which is a sad reflection of the standard of health care that is available. Acute diarrhea and chest infections cause 60 percent of the deaths, while infectious diseases like measles, whooping cough, tuberculosis, diphtheria, and tetanus kill approximately 20 percent of the children under five years (Sudanow,

November 1984; Saghayroun & Rizkalla, 1984). Immunization programs are the only way to improve the situation; however, there persists a widespread ignorance of the importance of immunization.

Breastfeeding constitutes a heavy physical burden on women, who spend a good part of their lives giving birth to and breastfeeding their children. A recent Egyptian study reported that 97 percent of rural mothers nurse their babies by breastfeeding (natural feeding) (*Al-Ahram*, January 2, 1985). Breastfeeding on demand for up to two years of each of five to seven children adds up to a very large proportion of adult life spent under heavy nutritional and physical stress. At the same time, Egyptian and Sudanese women are working and are expected to contribute to the economic support of the household.

ADULT ACTIVITIES: CAREER OPPORTUNITIES

Women in both Egypt and the Sudan have always been working, but now with the increase of industrialization, for the first time they have the right to enter the labor force on their own, to undertake jobs outside the home, which they obtained without the help or permission of their men (Soliman, 1977, p. 3).

In Egypt, women started working outside their homes as a means of social security, that is, in order to be financially independent and to increase the family income. Women began working before society was able to prepare suitable conditions to help them organize their household chores, care for their children, and plan their families (Soliman, 1977, p. 4ff). Women's employment in Egypt is relatively recent, and was limited to those whose provider had lost the ability to work for one reason or another. However, the activities in this category for women were restricted to some industries and housekeeping services.

Egyptian labor law was modified in 1971 to stipulate that during the three months of the maternity leave (a postpartum leave), a woman was to receive her full salary as it was stated in the international agreements. However, a woman was not entitled to have more than three leaves during the period of her employment. This modification has also given the female worker who nursed her baby the right to get nursing breaks for one hour daily, for one year beginning after delivery. This additional daily one-hour break was included in the working hours and entailed no reduction in salary (Soliman, 1977, p. 9).

Women's participation in governmental work was concentrated in the age groups below 35 years, which represented 70 percent of the total female labor force (1966 census). This was the natural result of the large number of girls who started to go out to work during the last years after they had reached a certain level of education.

Women's contributions were concentrated mainly in the fields of education and health services. The educational services sector absorbed about 54 percent of the total female labor force and the health-care services sector nearly 22 percent of the same total. These two sectors absorbed 76 percent of the total female labor force working in the government in 1966.

The real problem that faced Egyptian working women (and also Sudanese), and limited the number of women who entered the labor force, was that of childcare. In Egypt, Decree no. 68 of 1961 stated that every employer who employed in one place 100 female employees or more should provide a day nursery for the female workers' children who were between the ages of three months and six years (Soliman, 1977, p. 10). Soliman (1977, p. 12) noted that:

> The problem of childcare leads to another problem; [namely] the problem of the sickness of children and the lack of opportunities for the working women to get vacations for this reason. So, even if the child was sick, the woman was obliged to take him or her to the kindergarten, which was dangerous for his or her own health and for the health of the other children. In this case the woman was forced either to take off from work or to leave her sick child in the kindergarten without the special care necessary for him or her, which caused anxiety and distress to the woman and consequently affected her productivity.

The effects of the work of mothers on their children's behavior were the topics of some Egyptian studies (Youssef, 1975, p. 25ff; Adam, 1981, p. 139ff; 1982, pp. 55ff and p. 81ff). The results showed that:

1. There were no differences between the children of working mothers and children of non-working mothers in terms of adjustment, emotional stability, and academic achievement.
2. The attitudes of girls toward the work of their mothers was more positive than those of the boys.
3. The working women, in general, and especially the young ones and those of low socioeconomic status, were found to be more rigid in personality than the non-working women.
4. The working woman faced a conflict as she performed her two roles as a mother and as an employee.

The results also showed that the working woman dealt with the conflict in a positive manner only when she had a positive self-concept, a high level of education, and less responsibility for her children, for example, when she had no pressing need to take care of her children herself.

Concerning the husband-wife relationship, the working woman still suffered from men's negative attitudes of women, which stemmed from false generalizations (Adam, 1981, p. 149ff). In this context, a survey done in Egypt (in Abd el-Fattah, 1984) found that about 58 percent of the husbands approved of the jobs of their wives. The survey also showed that from the husbands' point of view, the working wife was more mature, more stable, and more well-adjusted in marriage, and always successful.

AGING

As a result of the steady improvement that has taken place in the last few decades in both Egypt and the Sudan concerning health care services in the working environment and life in general, the number of the elderly has increased. The percentage of the elderly (65 years old and older) has been estimated in Egypt in 1976 at 3.6 percent of the total population. This percentage had risen to reach in 1985 6.5 percent (or 2.5 million elderly persons, of whom almost half were females) of the total Egyptian population. It was also found that in 1976, 61.5 percent of the total elderly population were living in rural areas, while the other 38.5 percent were living in the urban areas (Central Agency for Public Mobilization and Statistics, 1978; *Al-Ahram*, January 11, 1985). In the Sudan, the number of elderly people (65 years old and older) was estimated at 3.2 to 5 percent of the total population in 1973. It was expected that half of them were females (Galal el-Din, 1977b; Saghay-roun & Rizkalla, 1984).

The Egyptian government devoted special attention to the elderly people, male and female. A number of clubs and homes were estab-lished to provide the aged with health, social, and psychological care in compensation for what they had offered to their country in their active years. Private social associations working in Egypt were also helping to provide medical and social care and assistance to the elderly. The Ministry for Social Affairs in Egypt established 35 homes for elderly people, serving about 2,000 senior citizens in both Cairo and Alexandria, in addition to 18 clubs for the elderly, serving about 10,000 members. Elderly people could get a monthly pension, which was established in the 1970s through a presidential decree. More than a million elderly male and female residents enjoyed these benefits (State Information Service, 1983b, p. 14; 1985, p. 111).

CONCLUSIONS

As we have seen, despite many legal changes that have taken place with issues of sexual equality and equal status of women in both Egypt and the Sudan, there remains a wide gap between equality of law and equality in actuality. Generally speaking, Egyptian and Sudanese women still encounter obstacles that prevent them from achieving real progress and keep them from participating actively in the developmental process of their countries. Although women in both countries have achieved progress in many fields, such as education, work and professions, personal and family legislations, feminist movements, and so on, much work remains to change current beliefs about female circumcision, illiteracy, higher education, health care (for mothers and babies as well), job opportunities, and the participation of women in economic, social, and political activities. Such changes in the population's ideas will not lead to any progress in women's status, unless attitudes in Egypt and the

Sudan (men and women as well) toward women and their roles in the society change and become more positive.

To improve the status of Egyptian and Sudanese women and to equip them for undertaking their responsibilities and enjoying their rights, it is not enough just to discuss the Egyptian and Sudanese women's secondary role, although the factors affecting women's lives were taken into consideration in both countries. Rather, it is necessary to change their economic, social, and political circumstances. For that we have to go deeper into the causes and roots that have led to this inferior position of women, for example, social and economic situations resulting from the differences between men and women and their relation with work and production on one hand and the differences in quality of production itself (H. K. Badri, 1984a; H. K. Badri, 1984b).

REFERENCES

Abd el-Fattah, K. A. (1984). *The psychology of working woman* [in Arabic]. Beirut: Dar el-Nahada el-Arabia, 2nd ed.

Adam, M. S. (1981). Modern Egyptian woman: Sociological and psychological studies. In M. El-Gawhry (Ed.). *The Egyptian Yearbook of Sociology* [in Arabic], Vol. 2. Cairo: Dar el-Maaref. Pp. 119-160.

Adam, M. S. (1982). *Woman between home and work* [in Arabic]. Cairo: Dar el-Maaref.

Ahmed, R. A. (1984). The place of school psychology in Sudan at the turn of the century. *School Psychology International, 5*, 1, 43-46.

Al-Ahram. (1982, 1985, & 1986). Egyptian daily newspaper [in Arabic].

Al-Akhbar. (1985). Egyptian daily newspaper [in Arabic] Sat. March 23.

Al-Sahafaa. (1985). Sudanese daily newspaper [in Arabic] Tue. April 30.

Amin, O. (1899). *Tahrir al-Mara* (The emancipation of women). Cairo: Matbaa al-Maktabaa al-Sharaiya.

Amin, Q. (1900). *Al-Mara al-Jadida* (The modern woman). Cairo: Matbaa al Maaref.

Azzam, H. (1982). The Arabian woman and work: The participation of the Arabian woman in the labour force and her role in the development process. In Arab Union Studies Center (Ed.). *Woman and her role in the Arab Union Movement* [in Arabic]. Beirut: The Press of the Arab Union Studies Center, 265-301.

Badri, A. E. (1984). Female circumcision in the Sudan. *The Ahfad Journal* (Sudan), *1*, 1, 11-21.

Badri, H. K. (1984a). *The feminist's movement in the Sudan* [in Arabic]. Khartoum: Khartoum University Press.

Badri, H. K. (1984b). The history, development, organization and position of women's studies in the Sudan. In UNESCO (Ed.). *Social sciences research and women in the Arab World*. UNESCO, Paris: Frances Pinter. Pp. 94-112.

Central Agency for Public Mobilization and Statistics. (1978). *Detailed results of the 1976 general census in Egypt* [in Arabic]. Cairo.

El-Abd, A. A. (1983). *The rural woman* (Read series no. 484, in Arabic). Cairo: Dar El-Maaref.

El-Ghandour, A. (1985). *The personal status in the Islamic legislation*, 3rd ed. [in Arabic]. Kuwait: El-Falah Publishers.

El-Mamoun, N. A. (1984). Pharaonic circumcision [in Arabic]. Unpublished paper presented at Seminar on participation of women in local development. Khartoum.

El-Meligui, E. (1975). Women in personal status laws. *The National Review of Social Sciences* (Egypt), Special Issue on Women, *12*, 2-3, 201-224 [in Arabic].

El-Sayed, A. M. (1974). The development of girl's education in Egypt. In M. I. Soueif (Ed.). *The changing social position of women in the contemporary Egypt* [in Arabic]. Cairo: The National Center for Social and Criminological Research, 1-81.

Fahmy, N., & Ramzi, N. (1976). Woman's role in social development. *The National Review of Social Sciences* (Egypt), *13*, 2, 1-35 [in Arabic].

Fyzee, Asaf A. A. (1955). *Outline of Muhammadan Law*. 2nd ed. London: Oxford University Press.

Galal el-Din, M. E. (1977a). The factors affected the fertility, family planning and birth control in the Sudan. In A. M. Ahmed (Ed.). *Studies in the development issues in the Sudan* [in Arabic]. Khartoum: Khartoum University Press, 45-78.

Galal el-Din, M. E. (1977b). *Some issues of population and development in the Sudan and in the Third World* [in Arabic]. Khartoum: Khartoum University Press.

Galal el-Din, M. E. (1984). The discrimination between masculines and feminines and its reflection on woman's position and her role in the society. *Journal of the Social Sciences* (Kuwait), *12*, 3, 7-35 [in Arabic].

Galal el-Din, M. E. (1985). The foreign labour force coming to the Arab countries. *Al-Mustaqbal al-Arabi* [The Arab future], (Lebanon), *75*, 80-97 [in Arabic].

Hamzawi, R. A. (1982). The relationship between female employment and fertility. Unpublished Ph.D. dissertation, School of Applied Social Sciences, Case Western Reserve University.

Houssain, A. B. (1984). Delivery and circumcision in Sudanese women [in Arabic]. Unpublished paper presented at Seminar on women participation in the National Regional Development in Kordfan, El-Obied (Sudan).

Khalifa, A. A. (1973). *Status of women in relation to fertility and family planning in Egypt*. Cairo: The National Center for Social and Criminological Research.

Khalifa, A. A. (1975). Some demographic characteristics of Egyptian women. *The National Review of Social Sciences* (Egypt), Special Issue on Women, *12*, 2-3, 63-76 [in Arabic].

Khalifa, M. A. (1978). Some recent data on marriage in Khartoum. *Sudan Journal of Development Research* (Sudan), 2, 1, 1-20.

Mahmoud, M. E. (1983). Sudanese emigration to Saudi Arabia. *International Migration* (The Netherlands), *21*, *4*, 500-515.

Minai, N. (1981). *Women in Islam: Tradition and transition in the Middle East*. London: John Murray.

Mohammed, M. Y., & Habiballa, M. (1985). Enrollment of women in higher education in Sudan. *The Ahfad Journal* (Sudan), 2, 2, 3-8.

Population Reports. (1984, November). Law and policy: Laws and policies affecting fertility: A decade of change, E/7.

Saghayroun, A. A. (1985). Women's status and fertility in the Sudan. *The Ahfad Journal* (Sudan), 2, 1, 46-52.

Saghayroun, A. A., & Rizkalla, M. (1984). The Sudan's demographic position and its impact on the development process [in Arabic]. Unpublished paper presented at the Second National Economic Conference, Khartoum (Sudan).

Satti, Z. A. (1985). Women and family in Islam. *The Ahfad Journal* (Sudan), 2, 1, 3-14.

Shalaq, A. (1982). The historical development of the Arabian woman's positions. In Arab Union Studies Center (Ed.). *Woman and her role in the Arab Union Movement* [in Arabic]. Beirut: The Press of the Arab Union Studies Center, 15-41.

Soliman, N. H. (1977). An evolution of some services offered to women at work. *The National Review of Social Sciences* (Egypt), Special Issue on Women, *14*, 1-3, 3-16 [in Arabic].

Soueif, M. I. (1975). The changing role of women in contemporary Egypt. *The National Review of Social Sciences* (Egypt), Special Issue on Women, *12*, 2-3, 1-20 [in Arabic].

State Information Service, Ministry of Information, Arab Republic of Egypt. (1983a). *Social welfare in the Arab Republic of Egypt* [in Arabic]. Cairo: Ministry of Information.

State Information Service, Ministry of Information, the Arab Republic of Egypt. (1983b). *Highlights on the five-year plan for economic and social development in the Arab Republic of Egypt* [in Arabic]. Cairo: Ministry of Information.

State Information Service, Ministry of Information, the Arab Republic of Egypt. (1984). *A report* [in Arabic]. Cairo: Al-Ahram Press.

State Information Service, Ministry of Information, the Arab Republic of Egypt. (1985). *The Egyptian woman* [in Arabic]. Cairo: Al-Ahram Press.

Sudan Fertility Survey. (1979). Principal Report, Vol. 1. Khartoum: Department of Statistics, Sudan Ministry of National Planning.

Sudan Ministry of Education and Guidance. (1982). *Educational statistics for the academic year 1981-82*. Khartoum: The Press of the Ministry of Education and Guidance.

Sudanow. (1979, 1984, & 1985). Sudanese monthly magazine.

UNICEF. (1983). Women in the Sudan: Soba center for the training of girls under the auspices of the Department of Social Welfare. Information paper no. 7-10/83. UNICEF, Khartoum: Sudan Country Office.

UNICEF. (1984). Women in the Sudan: Female circumcision: Evaluation of a campaign against its practice. Information paper, no. 19-4/84. UNICEF, Khartoum: Sudan Country Office.

UNICEF. (1984). Women in the Sudan: Development programmes for and with women in Sudan. Information paper no. 20-10/84. UNICEF. Khartoum: Sudan Country Office.

United Nations. (1972). *Demographic yearbook*, 24th issue. Special topic population census II. New York: Department of Economic and Social Affairs, Statistical Office.

World Bank. (1981, August). *World Development Report*. World Development Indicators: National and International. Adjustment Annex.

Youssef, F. (1975). "Flexibility-rigidity" trait among working and non-working women. *The National Review of Social Sciences* (Egypt). Special Issue on Women, *12*, 2-3, 25-54 [in Arabic].

Nmutaka Agnes Oby Okafor

Among many southern Nigeria tribal groups, pregnant women avoid eating snails, particularly the great *Acatina margiriata,* lest the baby is afflicted with much flow of saliva. The Efiks and the Ibibios still practice the custom of unlocking all locks and untying all knots in the house of a woman who is about to have a child, because all such are believed to retard delivery. The Ibibio woman usually would not eat of a double yam or double plantain during her lifetime for fear she would give birth to twins. The reason for this was that the birth of twins meant death to mother and her babies until not very long ago. In subsequent years, the mother would give up her twins to be disposed of while she fled for safety in a town set apart for mothers of twins. She went through a period of purification for twelve moons (one moon is equal to 28 days) before she was permitted to socialize again with others. In fact, the birth of twins was seen as an unusual happening. Hence it was customary to get rid of the twins by killing them, and in some areas the mother too. The Yoruba people would allow the first of the twins to survive and the second was left to starve to death. The mother then made a doll to prevent the surviving twin from feeling lonely.

It is of utmost importance for a pregnant woman to make different preparations for delivery ahead of time. This is done according to the custom of her tribe. For example, the mother-to-be among the Hausas of northern Nigeria starts to gather firewood about the fifth month of her pregnancy, so that when she is put to bed, there will be a constant supply of hot water to bathe her often from the first day of delivery for a period of 100 days. She also gathers spices such as ginger and hot red pepper, then grinds and keeps them for cooking. A young wife pregnant for the first time will return to her parents' home around the eighth month of pregnancy for the delivery of her first child. The husband does not accompany her; neither is he expected to be present at the time of delivery. Female friends of the young mother wait on her during her labor with one or two old women who serve as midwives; also present is the girl's mother. The foremost duty of the midwife is to cut the umbilical cord.

V. C. Uchendu (1965) writes that among the Igbos of southeast Nigeria, a woman may deliver in her husband's or father's compound provided the actual delivery takes place in a woman's backyard, which often has a wall around it. The woman is attended by experienced women who themselves have been mothers, and a local midwife. Male assistants are rarely sought except in complicated cases. When a prolonged labor is imminent, the oldest male head of the family or of the compound pours a libation of water to the ancestors. The expectant mother is asked to examine her conscience in case she has broken the sex taboo by having sexual intercourse during the daytime. Traditionally, it is believed that daytime coitus delays the placenta. Another belief is that infidelity on the part of the woman could cause difficult delivery and even death during delivery. The woman must confess to her infidelity before she can deliver. If the baby does not scream at birth, the midwife must prick it slightly to make it whimper vigorously in order to be welcomed by women attendants, who applaud the cries loudly. The husband hears the cry and a woman brings him the good news. Women attendants look for the husband to give him a beating on the hips, a gesture V. C. Uchendu describes as signifying fruitful sexual activity.

The attending local midwife cuts the umbilical cord about six to eight inches from the base and the afterbirth (placenta) is buried at the site of the birth.

The baby is bathed in lukewarm water. The mother herself is given a thorough hot bath and helped into a scrupulously cleaned and tidied house where a fire has been made for her and her baby. It is customary for both to sleep on the same bed. This assures her love for her baby and respect for her duty as a mother.

The mother stays indoors with her baby and nurses the umbilical cord until it falls off. It is kept and not buried until after the baby is named. The mother chooses her most fruitful oil palm tree and buries the baby's umbilical cord at its foot. In later years the boy builds his house around the tree, evidence that he is a free-born.

A male child is circumcised eight days after his birth, and the mother can leave the compound for the first time when the wound heals. Usually the mother is not permitted to come out in public for a month. She must not cook or work in order to protect her and her baby from infection and fatigue. For the two years or so that she must nurse her baby, she is persuaded to eat the choicest food.

The disposal of the placenta has important and different meanings for different tribal groups. C. K. Meek (1969) tells us that the Hausas put the placenta in a pot and bury it at the back of the house. In so doing the child is ever afterwards drawn to the place of his birth. And the Jarawas believe that the failing reproductive powers of a young woman can be restored by returning to the spot where the placenta of her first-born was buried.

It is a very common custom among all tribes to massage the woman's abdomen with hot water after birth. This is done to rid the body of impure blood and to make the woman strong. Among the Hausas and Fulanis, the practice is performed two times a day for a period of 40 days, then reduced to once a day for a further period of 60 days. The mother is given a light porridge prepared with hot red pepper. She in turn feeds her baby on breast milk. The massaging of the abdomen, an Igbo custom, is often done by the woman's mother, who goes to stay with and help her daughter as soon as she puts to bed. She makes sure the new mother does not flinch from or skip the hot uncomfortable massage and bath for as long as it is required. She helps to nurse the baby's umbilical cord and the circumcised organ of a baby boy. She bathes the baby especially during the first few days when the mother is too weak to bathe her baby, and she cooks the right food suitable for the new mother's delicate stomach. The new mother takes porridge mixed with plenty of hot pepper and smoked fish, meat, and yams. A woman who puts on weight after delivery is admired and approved of. This is evidence to the outside world that the husband loves his wife and provided for her.

PURIFICATION RITES

It is a customary belief that pregnancy and childbearing induce a state of uncleanliness; therefore women should be cleansed after birth. Of some northern Nigerian tribes, C. K. Meek (1969) writes that the Berom woman is forbidden to do any work or cook for two months after birth. At the end of this period, purification rites are performed before she resumes her normal life. The Idoma husband does not eat food prepared by his wife until three months after the date of delivery. And the young Hausa wife, who went to her parents for the delivery of her first baby, does not return to the husband until 100 days have elapsed. In the same way, the Fulani tradition allows the young wife to return to her husband at the end of two years.

AN OUTING CEREMONY OR CHURCH-GOING AMONG THE IGBOS

The Igbo mother attends an outing ceremony several weeks after the birth of her baby. Traditionally, this took place at the village market square, but today the Christian mother attends church with her baby accompanied by relatives, numerous friends, and other members of the community. After the church service, a big party is held at the residence of the woman's husband. It is an occasion for feasting, dancing, and "showing off" her husband's wealth. Guests are served different types of prepared meat, biscuits, drinks, *jollof of rice* (rice pilaf), and *fufu* (yam dumplings) served with highly seasoned *okra* soup. The guests in return shower the mother and her baby generously with gifts of money or baby's clothes, for example, dresses. After this occasion the woman can resume her normal life.

In general, children are shown profound affection by their parents. The Igbo parents overprotect their toddler, however, when the next baby arrives the child turns to the paternal and maternal grandmothers for the fulfillment of attention. At the same time the child is expected to grow up into a responsible person without necessarily being taught to be one. As the child grows up, he or she helps to take care of the younger siblings when the mother is not available. Girls are trained by their mothers, while boys after early childhood have more to learn from their fathers than from their mothers.

Traditionally, the Igbo woman nursed her child for two and a half to three years. It is customary for a woman to abstain from sexual intercourse while she is nursing a baby. The belief is that getting pregnant before a baby is weaned makes it sick and could result in death.

When the mother's milk goes bad, and baby rejects it, a herbalist applies some herbs, in some cases mixed with hot alligator pepper, to the affected breast. The baby is not fed the breast milk until it is good again. When the baby is ready to be weaned, the mother rubs her breasts with bitter leaves and offers the baby mashed rice or yams mixed in red palm oil, and also fruits such as banana and papaya.

CLITORIDECTOMY

It was customary among many tribes for young girls to go through the ritual of a clitoridectomy. The Benin, Basa, Igbo, Ijaw, Mada, Kakanda, Shuwa, and the Yoruba all practice it. The age of the operation and all the rituals that go with it are not exactly the same among different tribes. C. K. Meek (1969) tells us that among some northern tribes, the Yorubas, and the Benins, the operation is performed on girls before the ages of seven and fifteen, usually by an old woman, as in the case of the Yorubas and Kakanda, and occasionally by the local barber; the rite is believed to be an aid to chastity. Butter, shea-butter, or another soapy substance is then applied to the wound to help it heal.

For some Igbo communities, it was traditional for the girl to wait until she reached maturity before her clitoridectomy took place. V. C. Uchendu writes that in some communities, the ceremony takes place during the girls' fattening seclusion called the *Mgbede*. However, while the *Mgbede* is popular, clitoridectomy does not always follow it in many communities. P. Ottenberg (1965) reports that among the Afikpo and Igbos, clitoridectomy, which is traditionally accompanied by cicatrization and sometimes tattooing of the arms and torso in decorative designs, is the traditional ritual equivalent of boys' initiation into the *ogo* society, which involves the elements of ordeal and preparation for social adulthood. It is compulsory for all girls and formally takes place shortly before marriage during a period of three months in which the girl is secluded in her future mother-in-law's house and the cicatrization and clitoridectomy are performed. This seclusion, *ulo ubu* or "the fattening house," never really involved great efforts to fatten the girls. Today cicatrization and "the fattening house" have disappeared, and the clitoridectomy is performed in early childhood.

MARRIAGE

Marriage rites and the ceremonies associated with it vary among the different tribes. Traditionally, polygamy is the preferred form of matrimony. In some places it is customary to propose marriage to a girl before she is born. For this type of marriage, the father of a young boy arranges with the pregnant wife of his friend that if her baby is born a girl, she shall be betrothed at birth to his son. In other instances, once a baby girl is born, she could be betrothed immediately to a young boy or a young man accepted by her family. The male waits for the girl to grow up. In such early marriages, it is customary for the boy's father to supply food to the girl's mother until the two young people reach marriageable age. This happens when the girl attains puberty. The Muslim Hausa father marries off his daughter at puberty when she is 13 or 14 years old to a man of his choice; preferably a close kin, especially first cousins. The boy may be about 20 years at his first marriage. The parents of the young couple arrange the first marriage. The groom's father pays the agreed amount of dowry to the bride's father. The bride is removed, veiled, and taken on horseback to her new home. She wails and struggles to escape. This customary ceremony transports the young people into adulthood by marriage. The girl has no right to oppose the parents' choice. In contrast, however, the Muslim Fulani parents do not force husbands on their daughters; the daughter chooses her own husband. However, the children of the father's brothers are given first preference.

The Yoruba parents are very much involved in their children's marriage, but childhood marriage has become less common. Parents must express their opinion and approve of the suitability of their would-be daughter-in-law's family health and her moral character. A young bride-to-be gets presents from her would-be husband. The young man must work on his future father-in-law's farm, help him build a house, and make contributions to important funerals of the future bride's close relatives.

Marriage takes place when the girl is about 16 to 18 years old, and the man is in his middle or late twenties. When the suitor pays a dowry to the girl's parents, he acquires the sole right to sexual access to her as his wife, the rights of all children born by her during their marriage, and the rights to her domestic labor.

The Yoruba wife is very overtly submissive to her husband, and at the same time is independent of him economically. For example, she must serve him food on bended knee but she is free to secure a divorce. The time of her marriage to the husband determines her seniority in his compound. She is customarily junior to all males born before her marriage, and she calls them "husband" when they are her husband's collateral, and calls them by their nickname if they are young. In return they call her "wife" or by the name of her children. It is common for two or more women to remain married to one man at the same time. Each wife has a room of her own within the big compound where she sleeps with her children. Traditionally, the wife and her husband do not eat together.

Today divorce is more frequent. One principle cause of divorce is childlessness in a young women, and the social stigma attached to it. When sterility is the issue, divorce is certain. The woman secretly moves to live with her male lover and subsequently sues her husband for divorce. When divorce is granted, the woman is made to pay back part or all of the money paid by the husband at the time she was married, including the cost of outstanding gifts he gave to her and various contributions he made to her parents.

A woman can bring her young children from her previous marriage to the new husband. She can keep them until they are seven years old, and then their natural father can claim them to live with him.

The death of a woman's husband does not end the marriage unless the woman so desires. When a man dies, his marital rights go to his junior brother, or to his son by another wife other than the woman's own son, who can take care of her and her children financially. But the woman has the choice to divorce the heir if she does not want him. In the case of older wives, who are past childbearing age, their own children take care of them and the heir's duties are merely nominal.

REFERENCES

Andreski, I. (1970). *Old wives tales*. New York: Schocken Books.
Lloyd, P. C. (1965). The Yoruba of Nigeria. In J. Gibbs, Jr. (Ed.). *Peoples of Africa*. New York: Holt, Rinehart and Winston.
Meek, C. K. (1969). *The northern tribes of Nigeria*. New York: Negro Universities Press.
Ojike, M. (1946). *My Africa*. New York: Von Rees Press.
Oppong, C. (Ed.). (1983). *Female and male in West Africa*. London: George Allen and Unwin.
Ottenberg, P. (1965). The Afikpo Ibo of Eastern Nigeria. In J. Gibbs, Jr. (Ed.). *Peoples of Africa*. New York: Holt, Rinehart and Winston.
Smith, M. C. (1965). The Hausa of Northern Nigeria. In J. Gibbs, Jr. (Ed.). *Peoples of Africa*. New York: Holt, Rinehart and Winston.
Uchendu, V. C. (1965). *The Igbo of Southeast Nigeria*. New York: Holt, Rinehart and Winston.

Indian Bride

Life Stages in the Development of the Hindu Woman in India

Usha Kumar

Any statement generalizing about the experience of the Indian woman, will immediately call for a serious modification to include the exceptional and the particular. Any assertion about her psychological development will of necessity be conditioned by a set of specific circumstances. In a country of wide diversity, where differences between the urban and the rural population, between the high and the low caste, between the educated and the uneducated individuals are immense, the range of observation has to be limited for a sharper focus. The powerful impact of some sociological variables, such as poverty or religion, depresses or masks the subtle psychological influences on the developmental pattern of the woman. Though proportionately small, the Hindu, urban, middle-class, educated women are fairly large in number (60 million) and certainly an emerging force to be reckoned with on the national scene.

An exploration of the psychological terrain of the Indian inner world must begin with a cluster of ideas, historically derived, selected and refined, through which Hindu culture has traditionally structured the beliefs and behaviours of its members. At the heart of this cluster of governing ideas is a coherent, consistent world image in which the goal of human existence, the ways to reach the goal, the errors to be avoided, and the obstacles to be expected along the way are all dramatically conveyed (Kakar, 1978, p. 15).

An essential core of these ideas structuring specific belief systems and daily practices comprises ideas of duty or life tasks *(dharma)*, ideas of destiny and time *(karma)*, and ideas of self-realization or salvation *(moksha)*. An intricate intertwining of these three major concepts provides a patterned way of screening and construing reality.

For instance, the ideas of destiny and time *(karma)* lead a woman to an easy acceptance of her secondary position in the family. She must have deserved to be born a woman because of her *karma* of the previous birth. For this reason, a female does not necessarily hold the family, or society at large, responsible for her plight. Furthermore, her future salvation *(moksha)* lies in conducting herself to observe the prescribed life-tasks *(dharma)* with sincerity.

THE WOMAN IN THE HINDU WORLD VIEW

Given the background of these widely held belief systems among Hindus, of import here are those constructs that are in use to interpret reality. Some of these readily available constructs provide meaningfulness to a woman's experience of self, others, and the world. These are mentioned below.

Reality Is Construed Through Bipolar Constructions

Hindu religion, in particular, presents reality as the existence of opposites. Whether depicted in the male-female principle or through fusion-separation or good-evil dimensions, it is polarities that map the life-space. Irrespective of the content of these polarities, the tensions, conflicts, ambivalences, and their resolutions become a part of the inner world. The existence of contradictory emotions and simultaneously experienced feelings are also accepted by the individual. Life is not a matter of either this or that; it is both. Therefore reality is complex, defying classification into neat logical categories.

An example of polarity is the theme of the woman being both passive and active. Both representations are correct. The female principle manifests itself as the primal power and activity. *Prakriti* (nature) is the feminine principle, all-pervading and dynamic, while *purusha* is the masculine principle, predominantly passive and instrumental. Belief in the mystical power of woman exists deep in the Indian psyche, and the male domination is conjectured to be an overreaction to their fear of this destructive power (Nandy, 1976). The woman has available to her the image of the self-sacrificing, chaste, submissive, singularly faithful woman along with that of the powerful, creative, life-giving force.

In a mythologically instructed community, the models to which the woman may aspire are condensed in the form of *Sita*. In the images of *Durga* and *Kali (Shakti)* are present the dynamic creator of good and destroyer of evil. It is because of this archetypal mother-image that women have been given, traditionally and at least in theory, so much reverence. If *Ramayana* portrays women like *Sita*, the passive sufferer, the *Mahabharata* depicts some magnificent, spirited, and vibrant women like *Draupadi* (Mukherjee, 1979). Thus the inner world of the female (and the male also) has to be understood in terms of those polarities where construction of reality see-saws between the emerged and the submerged ends of the pole (Kelly, 1955), and where distinctly opposite images of femalehood are available to the woman in these constructions.

THE WORLD OF THE FEMALE IS PERSONAL IN NATURE

In India, both sexes, and women particularly, define themselves through their relationship to others. She is daughter to her parents, wife to her husband, daughter-in-law to husband's parents, and mother to her sons (and daughters). "The feminine role in India crystallizes a woman's connections to others, her embeddedness in a multitude of familiar relationships" (Kakar, 1978, p. 62). In addition, the woman's closeness to nature is revealed through her observance of rituals, holy days, and festivals which are related to the changes in seasons and nature. Both the relatedness to people and closeness to nature characterize the world of the female as autocentric (Gutmann, 1970) in which the order of events is seen as related to the self. Impressionistic evidence suggests that somewhat fused boundaries exist in the definition of the self and others in the female. The prevailing theme of separation-fusion of *moksha* (self-realization) very neatly fits into the autocentric world which presents a seamless unity in the natural order. The personal world of the woman is prone to exist in a setting where the nature of relationships provide significant differentiations in the self-image.

The Organization of the World is Hierarchical and Objects Are Classified Along Male-Female Dimensions

Even in the Hindu pantheon, gods and goddesses have a very clearly defined place of authority and subordinacy. In a worldly setting, two factors determine this in the hierarchy—age and gender. It is the oldest male who reigns supreme in the household. Woman's place is inferior to that of man's even if she is older than he. However, the oldest female rules the younger females. The deeply rooted male-female categorization is evidenced in the nature of language also. Even though semanticists find no definitive principle in the classification of objects, the classification is not so arbitrary for lay people. As a rule, it appears that objects are classified as male or female depending on the size, power, and activity of the object. It turns out that the agentic objects are males and communion objects are females. To understand reality accurately, one can hardly overlook the primacy of the ever-present male-female principle.

With this brief overview an attempt will now be made to understand Hindu woman's experiences throughout the life span.

INFANCY AND EARLY CHILDHOOD

The birth of a female child, even in educated families, is received with subdued feelings. This depends, however, on the number of children already in the family, and the number of boys. If the newborn infant is the only female among the siblings or is the firstborn, her acceptance is very much heightened. But if not, she is perceived as an economic liability. It is not an unrelated fact that the incidence of postpartum depression in the mother is much higher after the birth of a daughter than that of a son (Kakar, 1978). The norms of the community, and not the legislation against dowry in marriage, act as sanctions of this behavior. The ineffectiveness of the legislation is reflected in the blatant advertisements by nationalized banks soliciting customers to save for their daughter's marriage (incidentally, it is to save for the son's education).

The general unacceptability of the female birth is revealed inadvertently in many diverse areas. Mothers do not count their daughters when their obstetric career is recorded for medical purposes. Family planning workers and nurses have to keep this in view to get accurate records. Professional managers working in multinationals frequently fail to mention their sisters as members of their family in the family history interview. In a WHO project in which midwives were trained to give postnatal care to the newborn and as a part of their training had to inform the nearest hospital about the birth of a child, they failed to notify the hospital when a female child was born. When they were told in no uncertain terms that information about *all* babies had to be recorded, they were surprised. Why would any government be interested to know about the birth of female baby? Even though midwives may not come under the classification of "middle class," these examples are representative of most adult females who themselves accept this position of inferiority as a given.

The greatest hazard the female infant has to undergo is that of survival. It is a known fact that female infant mortality is much higher than that of the male. Maternal neglect in some families frequently borders on female infanticide. Female babies are taken to the hospital only when the malady has reached a critical stage, while male infants are referred with the first onset of the illness. Mothers let female babies cry much longer before they will pick them up to nurse them. This is possibly to get them used to the experience of frustration through oral deprivation. The male child, by comparison, receives immediate attention with the first whimper. Of course, mothers would not admit that they neglect their daughters. It was a rare mother who disclosed to the author her conscious decision to let her sick female child die so that she could save her twin, the male who was also sick. Their limited financial resources made them choose the male, letting the other go. Many parents will deny that female babies are not discriminated against as babies, but this is understandably a defensive stance.

Even families that can afford to have a reasonably adequate diet tend to give a preferential treatment to the male by giving him extra food like butter, milk, and eggs. This is basically an extension of the same rationale for safeguarding the health of males over and above that of the female, especially if resources are limited. A little girl very quickly learns to leave a bigger and better share of food for her brother because she learns about her secondary position from the way her mother behaves. It is not that a girl is prohibited to take these foods. She is not expected to indulge herself. On the contrary, oral deprivation is fairly common among young girls who fast regularly. A girl never forgets or is allowed to forget that she is a girl and her place is second to her brother and other male members in the family.

Despite the inferior status accorded the female child, there is evidence of some rather tender mother-daughter contacts. One such contact is the ritual of oiling and massaging the girl's hair. The close physical contact and the concern expressed by the mother for her daughter is indeed therapeutic in assuaging other hurts experienced through her inferior status. Possibly out of her weakness in these contacts, the mother identifies closely with the daughter because it reactivates her feelings of separation from her own parents.

From early infancy, the preparation of the female child is for marriage and motherhood. The girl grows up with the idea that she has to align herself with another family. Attached as she may be to her mother, she perceives the transitoriness of her ties with the family of her birth. Her perception that the parents' home belongs to her brothers only, while she has the status of a guest, gives very deep-rooted feelings of fear of loss of loved ones and of abandonment. Separation anxiety is aroused on many occasions later in life.

What does it all mean to the little girl during the first few years of her life? Oral deprivation may not shake her faith in the trustworthiness of the world but it makes for diffidence in approaching the outside world. Unsure of herself, a strong anchor exists in the knowledge that parents know what is good for her and that they will do their best. But these ties with parents are not enduring in that she is reminded that she is to "attach" herself to another family later on. The security in the acceptance of the traditional role is readily available to her to grasp. It is in these early experiences of fear of loss of loved ones that we see the beginnings of a depressive personality structure, the incidence of which is possibly as high as that of hysteria and anxiety neurosis among women in India.

It is conjectured that if young girls were tested in their belief in a just world the results would be no different from those of boys who are given preferential treatment (Lerner, 1978). This may be an example of an unconscious ideology that allows a girl to stay within the traditional status. Again, the Hindu beliefs of *karma*, the idea of destiny and time, and *dharma*, duty, act as ameliorative influences to take the sting out of the secondary status.

This is not to suggest that all girls escape unscathed. What is far more damaging to the girl's sense of identity and her self-esteem is the victimization of and submission to it by her mother, at the hands of the mother's mother-in-law. This does not merely humiliate, but also damages the daughter who watches her mother for clues as to what it means to be a woman. It is here the vicious circle begins. The mother-victim fills her daughter with either rage or resignation, neither condition being much of a launching pad for an easy self-acceptance of femininity.

In no society, as J. B. Miller (1976) states, does the person, male or female, emerge fully grown. A necessary part of all experience is a recognition of one's weaknesses and limitation. That most valuable of human qualities, the ability to grow psychologically, is necessarily an ongoing process involving repeated feelings of vulnerability all through life. Miller goes on to elaborate that women are better able than men to admit consciously to feelings of weakness or vulnerability. Obvious as it may be, women are truly much more able to tolerate these feelings which life in general generates in everybody. It becomes a basis of her positive strength. In this sense, it may be stated that the growing female child both superficially and deeply is more closely in touch with basic life experience and with reality (Miller 1976).

SCHOOL YEARS

Despite the keenness of middle-class families to educate both sons and daughters, education for the daughter is still perceived as functional to the objective of her getting married. (There has been a marked change in the matrimonial ads in the papers which now emphasize educated and beautiful girls instead of only beautiful ones.) Educated girls hold a better prospect of finding a "good" husband with whom parents can negotiate for a smaller dowry. Nevertheless, it is a very important factor in opening up avenues of new experiences to girls, not hitherto available despite the fact that there are no contradictions in the value systems of the home and school over the female role. Both institutions instill values of obedience, duty, and compromise (Cormack, 1961). This was confirmed in a study in which the 500 boys and 360 girls between ages of 9-22 years chose *Sita* as the ideal woman. From a list of 24 names of gods, goddesses, heroes, and heroines of history these subjects selected *Sita* by an overwhelming majority with no differences related to age or sex (Pratap, 1960). It is likely that this choice may still hold good more than two decades later.

However, this exposure to the world outside the home has the potential to challenge values promoted at home. However weak or subtle the challenge may be, this aspect is potentially instrumental in making the girl aware of models that defy the traditional role and it is this aspect that parents are apprehensive about when they send their daughters to school. Parents accede to the girl's education as a functional necessity in the modern age. But the girl should not develop critical faculties of her own to make independent judgments or discuss issues. Frequently, a girl who presents her views or even holds her own in a discussion is open to criticism.

Living the projections of the male anima, the girl is systematically trained in two salient spheres: the household arts and the social skills. Achievement and mastery in household arts and in social skills are two areas in which the girl is tutored from the beginning. Most of the learning is acquired by imitation, with mother as the model. The mother sets up clear standards of performance in these areas, gives quick feedback, and is vocal in her criticism. It is not uncommon to have young daughters express feelings of resentment and hostility against their mothers.

The above conditions of clear standards of performance, feedback, and mild rejection by the mother have been identified as conditions conducive to the learning of achievement orientation (Stein & Bailey, 1973). Even though the girl may feel herself to be in a "double-bind" in terms of scholastic achievement, there is clear support for achieving behavior in these two areas. A fact frequently overlooked is that an Indian girl does develop a strong achievement motivation by the training given to her to make her independent in specific areas.

Having suffered rejection and deprecation earlier, the learning of skills is restorative for her self-image and her self-esteem. Not only does she have clearly delineated areas in which to excel, she gets considerable approval for her performance. She is now in command of keeping her "narcissistic supplies" coming to her through her own achievement and through conformity to the expectations of those around her. It is this cultivation of competence that brings relief to the girl.

What impact does this have on her experience or herself? In Eriksonian terms, she develops a strong sense of industry which is ameliorative of earlier negative feelings of self and the stigma of being a girl. Being capable of an active role in managing her own rewards further reduces the helplessness cultivated through the traditional sex-role learning. This period is possibly the most significant in the development of ego-strength in the girl—her ability to use her skills to bring changes in the environment.

Also little understood is the managerial world of the female where, for instance, the mere act of preparing food for the family requires skills unknown and unpracticed by Western women. Everything is prepared from scratch. Combined with the vagaries of economic supplies, a future orientation calls for skills in budgeting, decision-making, and resourcefulness. Without elaborating further, one cannot fail to be impressed by the ingenuity of the female in her skilled management of the household.

ADOLESCENCE

The adolescent experiences of a girl in India present the same inner turbulence and upheavals as they do to a Western girl but the expression of these is controlled if not suppressed. Even if she is aware of the process of menstruation at puberty, her understanding of the physiological changes underlying it are grossly distorted. The girl is made to perceive herself as one who has lost her purity with the beginning of menstruation. She is expected not to cook food, touch pickles, or participate in religious ceremonies during her menstrual period. The idea of "pollution" and "dirtiness" is conveyed to her. In some middle-class families the girl may have to cease activity and spend time alone in the room. (This practice of isolation continues even after marriage and comes as a blessing in disguise. The girl is relieved of physical labor and earns rest which she badly needs.) There are no reliable sources available to her where she can get correct information or elementary sex education.

With the onset of puberty, parents' concern for a daughter's marriage is expressed in the seriousness with which they view their parental obligations. Her status as a young woman gives her a standing in the family but also restricts her movements. Unless in a group, interacting freely with boys of her age is prohibited. Male cousins and their friends may or may not be given access to the house. The sexual impulses aroused are accompanied by feelings of guilt, of having stepped out of one's role of chastity and purity. Refuge in fasting or observing the ritual of tying a cord around the wrist of the young man and proclaiming him as an "adopted" brother are some traditional ways of coping with the sexual feelings. The cultural stance on matters of sex ostensibly continues to be repressive even though the sharing of sex experiences among same sexed friends is not uncommon. Discussion of sex-related matters between spouses is hesitantly done in the first few years of marriage.

MARRIAGE

The adolescent girl would certainly enjoy her femaleness more than she does were it not accompanied by the guilt that she has become a burden on her family. For the parents, her unfolding physical attractiveness (or lack of it) becomes a matter of paramount concern. If the girl is dark-skinned or otherwise low on physical attractiveness, the family anticipates difficulties in arranging a match for her. The submerged feelings of inferiority and rejection surface again, heightening the dilemmas of adolescent experiences. Unless the matter is handled very sensitively by the parents who ordinarily arrange marriages of their children, a couple of rejections in negotiation for a matrimonial match can leave the girl's self-image devastated. The social comparison process is sometimes a matter of public evaluation rather than an individual activity. Parents unknowingly assign value or worth to their daughter and on this basis look for a husband of equivalent worth. Matching on the basis of temperament and habits is sometimes considered in these decisions.

A recent campus survey conducted by Parul Dave (personal communication) on college students regarding their views on marriage revealed interesting views of female students. Female students tended to express the desirability of a spouse who was older, more intelligent, and of a higher status and educational level than themselves. An overall superiority of the husband was perceived as necessary for establishing companionship in marriage. Furthermore, the female respondent allocated to the wife the responsibility of making her marriage work, ignoring the critical role of the husband in the marital dyad. Female students unequivocally opted for marriage as the preferred life-style over staying single or cohabiting. Among this sample, one-third admitted to having indulged in premarital sex. More girls than boys were regularly attending classes on sex education on the same campus.

Parents also tend to look for older and more educated spouses for their daughters, which has led to the practice of girls marrying early. This arrangement is thought to facilitate the woman's adjustment to the husband and his family. Thus the views of female students were representative of current social trends. Psychologically, it is likely that the deep-seated feelings of inferiority in the female find compensation in the perceived superiority of the male. A husband's achievement could be vicariously satisfying to the woman. However, the situation gives some legitimacy to the exercise of male superiority/authority in the house.

The tradition of divorce did not exist in Hindu families some decade ago. The couple preferred to live together unhappily or live separately, giving socially desirable reasons for the arrangement rather than face the opprobrium of divorce. The pattern has changed now due to several factors. The divorce laws have been revised to make it easier for the woman to get a divorce. Also, the education and economic independence among women are on the rise. Young adults' freedom to contract a "love marriage" also leads to the acceptance of their decision to dissolve the relationship. However, the proportion of divorces is still very low even though numbers have gone up. Marriage continues to be a lifetime relationship for overwhelmingly large number of couples.

The thought of marriage is pleasing to the girl. She has been mentally prepared for her identity as a wife and a mother. Parents provide security in that they will find her a husband, despite the accompanying disturbing thought of separation from them. The percentage of single women among Hindus is almost nil. When betrothed, her status rises among her friends (those who get married are desirable girls) and she enjoys the temporary attention and care given to her. Marriage is possibly the only elaborate ritual for a girl during her life. Clothes and jewelry are fascinating for any eighteen-year-old—the average age for marriage. These are some compensation for her during this period, despite her feelings of some poignant emotions.

When beset by the anxiety of approaching separation from the parents, the girl takes the uncertainty of her future stoically. More aware of her inner feelings, less expressive of her dark apprehensions, she gets ready for marriage. Even when she may not be happy about whom she is marrying, she is content that she is marrying because it pleases her parents.

Marriage has its compensations, most of all in the security and status it provides to the female. She wants to get through with it so that she can start the life for which she has been prepared. Vulnerable as she is in her traditional role, her social skills and training are her biggest assets. She anticipates that through her skills she will be able to win over her husband and her in-laws. Marriage firmly confers on her the socially acceptable identity of femaleness. This is clearly seen even in women with professional ambition who also prefer "arranged" marriage. Though feelings of insecurity in the professional role could be one of the underlying reasons, the factor of expediency cannot be overlooked. Remaining single presents women with more obstacles in the way of becoming a professional than being married. Using marriage as a means of social acceptability, women display an understanding of their social system which allows them to pursue their career only after the first obligation of marriage is met.

The practice of young, newly married wives continuing their education after marriage is on the increase. A new trend is also evidenced in the increased worth of a professionally trained working woman in the marriage market. Unlaudable as the underlying motives sometimes are, such as economic exploitation of the working girl by the husband and her family, it has inadvertently given impetus to vocational orientation in women's education. The working woman tends to enjoy a greater leverage in the husband's home and added feelings of self-esteem.

RELATIONSHIP WITH THE FAMILY

A bride's entry into her husband's family is at best anxiety provoking and at worst humiliating. The sense of being an outsider, coupled with the awkwardness of her relationship with the husband, leads to intense feelings of isolation and nostalgia for the parents' home. Not fully accepted in the husband's family and not completely released of her emotional ties with her parents' family, she feels a confusion of identity. Overwhelmed by her loneliness, she may be given to moodiness, frequently somatatizing some of her internal conflicts. Her coping behavior lies in seeking recourse to "playing" the daughter-in-law role and keeping her real feelings to herself. It is not that the young woman loses touch with what she feels, as one may want to conclude from watching some interactions. Taking the mother-in-law's indignities, which often border on physical injury, without any reciprocal offensive makes one wonder about the young wife's need to do so. It is here that J. C. Alhanassiades' (1977) study has relevance for the Indian woman. He tested the assumption that through the process of socialization, sex-stereotypes are internalized, becoming "second nature" for women. His investigation examined the self-concept, public behavior, and perceptions of female stereotypes and found significant differences between the self-concept of women, and their public selves, and their perception of the female sex-role. He questioned the reality of internalization of the sex-norms with regard to women. It is likely that women indeed do not internalize their sex-roles; rather, because of existing social structure, women "act" their sex-stereotyped roles against their "natural" inclinations. Obviously, under such circumstances, women's behavior is calculated and deliberate and one would expect considerable differences between their covert and overt behavior. Thus a young wife behaves subserviently not necessarily because she perceives herself as a submissive person or incapable of behaving assertively. She is capable of maintaining a consistent and stable image of self despite playing a variety of roles across different situations. Working within sex-role stereotypes is an expedient course with a strong likelihood that underlying it is an unwilling compliance. Alternatively, the female sex-stereotyping could be viewed as external constraints imposed on the woman.

This conception of "acting" the role is very similar to J. B. Miller's (1976) formulation of conflict between the male and the female. According to Miller, the degree to which the woman does or does not accept the man's conception about herself determines the nature of conflict. There is a minimal conflict when a woman accepts the man's dominant image of her. However, those women tend to be most effective who are conscious to a large degree of what they are doing and in so doing are really moving out of this model, while keeping up the pretense that they are not. They cater to the image of the superior importance of men. At the same time, they have developed enough sense of their own rights and abilities. The Indian woman, like many who have played the subordinate role, learns to manipulate the more powerful man in a manner that is subtle and frequently not observed by those who are being manipulated.

However, some of the knots in the relationship with the in-laws start to untangle themselves as soon as the woman becomes pregnant. Her earlier female identity of a daughter and a wife are merely a prelude to her identity as a mother—a final recognition of her fulfilled destiny. The earlier two roles are devalued, if not debased, unless followed by the third. And it is the birth of a male child that finally gives the wife her acceptance in the family. It is in this mother-son relationship that the profound influence of woman's quest for identity has to be understood.

According to A. Nandy (1976), the "mother-son relationship is the basic nexus and the ultimate paradigm of human social relationships. Motherhood is a compensatory mechanism that controls a woman to take on her motherly identity whenever cornered and to a man by forcing him to take on the son's role whenever in crisis" (p. 5).

S. Kakar (1978) observed that an unrelinquished umbilical tie with a mother who is perceived by the son as intense, seductive, and unsatisfied characterized the mother-son axis. The father is psychologically absent. The normal boundaries of the mother-son relationship are abridged, resulting in a kind of matching between the unconscious erotic fantasies of both the mother and son. This matching is detrimental to the son's capacity to form stable ego boundaries between himself and any agent that is emotionally important to him.

M. S. Gore (1961) arrived at very interesting findings in investigating husband-wife and mother-son relationships. In responding to three simple questions (namely, to whom did they feel closer, wife, mother, or both equally) 56 percent of males described themselves as being closer to their mothers than to their wives while only 20 percent felt closer to their wives. The percentage of respondents who said they were equally close to their mother and wife was not higher in the nuclear than in the joint families. The urban population tended to regard their relationship to their mother and wife as equally close.

Thus it is in the dynamics of the husband-wife-mother-in-law nexus that the experiences of the woman at this stage have to be understood. This mother-son relationship has a long past, starting from the birth of the son. What is very striking is the overvaluation of a male child in the Indian family. The omnipotence attributed to the male child by the mother, whose identity his birth confirmed, and by the father, whose salvation he assured, is unconsciously, if not consciously, conveyed to him. So little is expected of him in learning the developmental tasks that in the first few years, his narcissistic orientation finds no underpinning of skills permitting a mastery of the environment or competence to mobilize it.

RELATIONSHIP WITH THE INFANT

The young male infant's ego boundaries remain fused with the mother, who does little to help the child to separate himself. Continuous close physical contact with the mother adds sexual overtones to the existing symbiotic union. This aspect undergoes a traumatic change when reality demands that the boy go to school. Ill-equipped to cope with the world at large, there is a longing to return to the mother, who not only enjoys his helplessness but playfully and teasingly encourages the son to continue. Later, bereft of warmth and faced with austere and controlling male authority, feelings of inadequacy and weakness in the male are sharpened. His initial sense of omnipotence, amply supported by the social norms, now becomes a defense against these uncomfortable feelings of weakness in males.

Even though the middle-class woman would readily fuse herself with her husband's identity and allow herself to be completed by him, the personality structure of the male does not make this a comfortable process. His own narcissistic make-up, nurtured by the indulgence and care given beyond many years of his need, is searching for a symbiotic union himself. The wife can share her husband's identity only if there is a reciprocity or mutuality of fit. A husband's dependency on his mother cannot take the weight of another depending upon him.

Thus women find themselves let down by their husbands in their own search for selfhood. Devoid of emotional support and unprotected by the husband against the indignities suffered at the hand of the mother-in-law the woman turns to her children, especially the sons. Ironically, in her relation to her own son, a woman repeats the cycle of mother-child history.

Besides turning to her son, the young wife has varied reactions to the husband-mother-in-law axis. One is of hysterical rage against the husband and his family, which validates the male belief about the destructive power of women. Another reaction, possibly of a more independent woman, is to provide props for her husband's dependency. Through affiliative-nurturant modes these women feel very satisfied and "successful" in taking care of their husbands. Instead of being engulfed by the caring other, such a woman binds the husband and child by her own caring.

WORK ACTIVITIES

The compulsions of urban living and rising standards of living have compelled many urban women to take up work outside the home. It must be recognized that women display varying readiness for work. Some women find self-expression in work and prepare themselves during their education for a career. They have sufficient support from the family and husband to pursue their interest. These women have a well-developed sense of identity. The professional, career-oriented women from somewhat privileged backgrounds are classified in this group.

Then there is a large group of women who work because their survival depends on their day-to-day earnings. They are usually found in the unorganized economic sector and perform very hard physical labor such as carrying bricks, coir-making, working in quarries, and so on. Leela Gulhati's book *Profiles in Poverty* (1981) provides an in-depth profile of them. The most characteristic aspect of these women is that they work without an iota of self-pity, having begun work as children and continued with it after marriage. Despite long exposure to work, they were found to be fairly gender-typed women in their value system (Kumar, 1986).

The women who go to work in the service sector as teachers, telephone operators, clerks in banks and post offices, and so on are usually the "pin-money" earners. Work is perceived as either equivalent to what women do at home or as something that can be dropped when pressures from the domestic front so demand. Their work identity is subsumed under a much larger gender identity.

Finally there are those women who do not perceive work as a part of their gender identity. Whether suitably skilled or not, these women confine themselves to the domestic sphere entirely. If pushed to work, they find it painful to meet the demands of the marketplace as well as home simultaneously.

MIDDLE AGE AND AGING

The concern for children's welfare becomes the arena for the development of intimacy between husband and wife. Children act as facilitators in improving their parents' poorly established modes of communication (Kumar, 1978). They also act as a buffer between the mother and aggression directed to her by the father's family. Further, the mother-in-law, mellowed with age and possibly physically or economically dependent on her daughter-in-law, is now only a distant threat. The daughter-in-law-mother-in-law power balance starts to equalize, if not reverse. The daughter-in-law having raised children, especially sons, now feels relatively secure to exert her wishes in the family.

At least in the middle-class families, the restlessness experienced by a middle-aged educated woman is possibly no different from that of her Western counterpart. She feels considerable self-confidence, having established herself in the family and in social groups. Constructive channeling of newly released energies, however, is not always easy. But it is not unusual at all to find women devoting themselves to small business enterprises during this period. The achievement orientations cultivated in childhood find expression at this stage. Women giving lessons in cooking, opening textile printing shops, teaching in nursery schools, making garments on a mass scale are all activities related to their gender-based skills. A taste of economic freedom accompanied by reassuring confidence in herself through her achievements makes many women eager to take up challenges.

If a woman does not seek expression in economically gainful activity she may continue to become a powerful figure in her family and family affairs. The newly acquired independence in the husband's family is asserted initially in separating her family from the joint family set-up to a nuclear family unit. Those women who have sons indulge in match-making exercises. Finding husbands for daughters is time-consuming, even though the final decisions may be left to the males.

This period is possibly the most favorable of all the developmental stages for the Indian woman. Assertion, achievement, and independence are finally given expression in day-to-day activities. One is struck by the "pushiness" of women at this stage.

By acquiring the status of a mother-in-law, even relatively young women in their early forties change their previous roles of wife and daughter-in-law to incorporate the new one from which they obviously draw considerable satisfaction. The ironic aspect of this status is that the same woman who a couple of decades earlier had suffered the tyranny of her mother-in-law in quiet solitude, now does no better in that role. The identification with the aggressor is complete and the circle of psychological history repeats itself.

Despite strong emotional bonds with the son, the mother, who is likely to survive longer than her husband, fears economic dependence on the son. One of the reasons to keep the son's affection to herself, at the expense of alienating his wife, is to establish psychological control over him. Her ill-treatment of the daughter-in-law, to put it sympathetically, is a way of obtaining veneration which is otherwise given cursorily or denied to her. Having arrived at this stage of her life is indeed a testimony to her ability to survive—possibly survival of the fittest (Verghese, 1979). She has managed to survive several childbirths, she has taken physical insults and psychological maiming of her self-image, and she has managed to live through it all. Now is her grand moment to receive physical comfort and respect. She makes sure she gets it, even if she has to extract it.

There are also many women like the heroine of an almost unknown story written by Rabinadrath Tagore in 1914. Here a sensitive woman who has spent her life in the stifling rigid social system grows up with more intelligence than was necessary for performing the daily chores. After several years of drudgery she goes on a pilgrimage with an elderly female relative and sends a letter home. She writes to her husband saying that after standing today by the sea, she realized that she was not just a wife/daughter-in-law in his house-hold: "I have some independent relationship with the world and its Creator." She decides not to return to 27 M. B. Lane, her prison. Many a woman seek detachment from their earlier ties to seek their true identity in relationship with God.

Possibly there is something universal in the existential quality of life that compels people at the end to make some final attempt to come to terms with their own experiences—to seek a final integration of self. Whether or not the woman leaves her house physically to make this final attempt in quest of her identity, she certainly seeks detachment—a state for which she finds ample support in her religion and her family.

HINDU WOMEN TODAY: TRADITION AND CHANGE

The constitutional guarantees of freedom and equality, the political and legal platforms that signal recognition of these facts, and the growing awareness that women have to stand up for their own cause are some of the critical factors supportive of a move toward a radical change in the status of women. The present environment is as facilitative as it will ever be for women's entry into the twenty-first century. What is still a stumbling block is the inner insecurity of the women to recast themselves in a different role. The impatience of the younger and the acceptance of older generations have a mutually equilibrating effect on both generations. It is in the formal education of young girls that both young and old place their faith to herald the change. The Indian temperament is not inclined toward revolution but rather toward gradual long-term transitions, and this process is possibly already initiated. Indian women of the twenty-first century are poised for a change but it will require a keen observer to detect these changes in the inner world of the Hindu woman.

REFERENCES

Alhanassiades, J. C. (1977). The internalization of female stereotypes by college women. *Human Relations*, *30*, 187-199.

Bem, S. L., & Bem, D. J.(1970). Nonconscious ideology: How women are taught their place in society. In D. J. Bem (Ed.). *Beliefs, attitude and human affairs*. Belmont, CA: Brooks/Cole.

Carlson, R. (1971). Sex differences in ego functioning. *Journal of Consulting and Clinical Psychology*, *37*, 267-277.

Cormack, M. (1961). *The Hindu woman*. Bombay: Asia Publishing House.

Gore, M. S. (1961). The husband-wife and mother-son relationship. *Sociological Bulletin, 11*, 91-102.

Gulhati, L. (1981). *Profiles in poverty*. Delhi: Hindustan Publishing.

Gutmann, D. (1970). Female ego styles and generational conflict. *Feminine Personality and Conflict*. Belmont, CA: Brooks/Cole.

Kakar, S. (1978). *The inner world: A psychoanalytical study of childhood and society in India*. Delhi: Oxford University Press.

Kelly, G. A. (1955). *A psychology of personality construct*. New York: W. W. Norton.

Kumar, U. (1978). The functional and the dysfunctional role of inter-personal communication pattern in the Hindu joint family in India. *International Journal of Group Tensions, 8*(1 and 2), 120-129.

Kumar, U. (1986). Indian women and work: A paradigm for research. *Psychological Studies. 31* (2), 147-160.

Lerner, M. J. (1978). The just world research and the attribution process: Looking back and ahead. *Psychological Bulletin, 85*, 1030-1051.

McClelland, D. C. (1975). *Power: The inner experience*. New York: Irvington Publishers.

Miller, J. B. (1976). *Toward a new psychology of women*. New York: Penguin Books.

Mukherjee, M. (1979). Deadweight of tradition. The Sati Savitri ideal. *Manushi: A Journal About Women and Society, 2*, 10-11.

Nandy, A. (1976). Woman vs. womanliness. *Psychoanalytic Review, 63*, 301-315.

Ornstein, R. E. (1972). *The psychology of consciousness*. San Francisco: W. H. Freeman.

Pratap, P. (1960). The development of ego ideal in Indian children. Unpublished Ph.D. dissertation, Benaras Hindu University.

Stein, A. H., & Bailey, M. M. (1973). Socialization of achievement orientation in females. *Psychological Bulletin, 80*, 345-366.

Verghese, J. (1979). *Her body and her gold*. Delhi: Vikas Publication.

Dr. Uma Singhal with three Tharu Women

12

Tribal Women of India: The Tharu Women

Uma Singhal and Nihar R. Mrinal

India (Bharat) is the most populous and the seventh largest country in the world. According to the "World Population Data Sheet 1987," the Indian population reached the 800 million mark during the middle of 1987. It measures a total land area of 3,280,483 sq. km. It has a land frontier of 15,200 km. and a coastline of 6,083 km. Lying entirely in the northern hemisphere, the mainland extends between latitudes 8°4' and 37°6' north and longitudes 68°7' and 97°25' east. It is bounded on the southwest by the Arabian Sea and on the southeast by the Bay of Bengal. To the north, northeast and northwest lie the Himalayan mountain ranges. The southern tip, Cape Comorin (Kanyakumari), is bordered by three oceans, the Indian Ocean, the Arabian Sea, and the Bay of Bengal. India is adjoined in the north by China, Nepal, and Bhutan. A series of mountain ranges in the east separate India from Burma. In the east Bangladesh and in the northwest Afghanistan and Pakistan border on India. The Gulf of Mannar and the Palk Straight separate India from Sri Lanka in the south.

India has one of the largest concentrations of tribal populations in the world. The tribal communities comprise about 7 percent of the total population of India. Their major concentration is in the belt in middle India extending from Daman and Thana in Maharashtra on the western coast to the west of Ganga in West Bengal passing through the border regions of Maharashtra, Madhya Pradesh, Bihar, and Orissa. This belt joins the Himalayan tribal belt near Darjiling to the east. On the western end of the central belt, the tribal concentration can be further traced in the northern direction.

There are 212 scheduled tribes in India (Singh, 1985). They are widely different in size and culture. At one extreme are the Gonds, who are made up of nearly 5 million people; at the other end are the Onges, numbering only 112 individuals, and the Great Andamanese, whose number is hardly 31 persons (Sinha, 1989). While some of the communities are homogeneous, others, like the Gonds, are comprised of a number of smaller subgroups, some of which, for all practical purposes, may be very distinct except for their generic name. More than 200 tribal dialects are spoken by different communities in different states.

THE THARUS

The Tharus are spread from Nainital (India) to Janakpur (Nepal). They are largely found in the districts of Lakhimpur-Kheri, Gonda, Behraich, and Nainital in Uttar Pradesh and in the district of Champaran in Bihar. A good number of Tharus are also settled in Nepal where there is social intercommunication between the Tharus of India and Nepal. They were declared a scheduled tribe in 1967. The Tharu tract consists of 45 inhabited villages. The three main clans found among Tharus are the Rana, Dangora, and Kathariya. According to the latest survey in the Lakhimpur-Kheri district, on the periphery of Dudhwa National Park the total census of Tharus is 20,177 (Integrated Tribal Development Program Survey (ITDP), 1989). They are neither half-starved, half-naked, nor wild. They are well-fed, well-organized, and friendly people. Their only drawback is illiteracy. No Tharu is without land. The people have a sense of participation in deciding social disputes in the village affairs as almost everybody has a say in the day-to-day administration.

THE THARU WOMEN

Verrier Elvin (1976) makes no distinction between a tribal and non-tribal woman. She has the same passions, loves and fears, the same devotion to home, to husband and children, the same faults, and the same virtues; even her functions are the same. But when she is compared with a Hindu woman in India, she is certainly not the same. The Hindu woman is generally known as pure virgin, voluptuous temptress, obedient wife, honored mother, dreaded widow, and impure menstruating woman. The tribal woman is free from such reservations.

In Hindus as well as in a few other tribes, many restrictions related to maternity, motherhood, and menstruation are prevalent but they are not found in Tharu tribes. There is no dread associated with menstruation. A Hindu woman during the time of menstruation cannot enter the kitchen, cannot worship, and cannot take part in any religious ceremony. For three to four days she is treated as an untouchable, while a Tharu woman is allowed to go on with her routine engagements. Some time back, the *panchayat* (the bench of five tribal judges), tried to impose fines on menstruating women if they entered the kitchen, but they failed miserably. Tharu women wield considerable influence on their menfolk. They are beautiful and industrious while the men are generally sluggish and unwilling. The Tharu women have greater responsibility in domestic life.

The belief held widely by non-Tharus of Terai is that the Tharu women control witches and spirits, and know strong spells and counter-spells. They are dreaded and shunned by all caste people for this reason. The way the menfolk are treated by the Tharu women is openly discussed in non-Tharu homes. It is believed that the cause of loyalty of Tharu husbands is the magic of their wives. According to some people every Tharu man and woman has the power to cause harm or disease to others; hence they avoid passing Tharu villages. But the Tharus deny that they have any knowledge of black magic.

Because of the dominance of Tharu women, chastity may not be a virtue and the Tharu men do not worry much on this account. They may quarrel with each other, but the women always have the last word. Ill treatment of husbands by their wives is not uncommon; when it becomes intolerable the man approaches the *bharra* (the magician) and uses charms and amulets. When the mediation of the *bharra* is proved useless the man can approach the village chief, but again the woman has the final say. The men are used to the behavior of their women and they are generally yielding.

Finally, the Tharu women are very fair. They are good-looking in both the face and figure. They wear heavy silver armlets, bracelets, anklets, necklaces, nose-rings, and many colored shells. They have long black hair coiled into a long curl or twisted in back. However, since they have worked too long in water during the rice-sowing season and while catching fish, their toenails and fingernails are disfigured.

INFANCY AND CHILDHOOD

The Parent-Child Relationship

The birth of a female child raises the status of a Tharu father, although it does not do so in the case of a Hindu father. The Tharu father earns the blessings of his kith and kin and the virtue of *kanyadan* (donating the virgin). Male and female children are treated equally. The birth of a daughter in an old traditional Hindu family is still an unpleasant event.

The mother is the custodian of the child since birth. She takes care of all of the child's hygiene. If she goes to work, whether indoors or outdoors, she carries the child on her back. The mother wakes him or her up early in the morning. Weaning takes place only when another child arrives. Children of up to five years of age are seen nursing at the breast of the mother. When the child learns to walk the mother does not carry him or her on her back. If mother is not alive the child is reared by the grandmother or the closest female relative of the family. The father has no role in childrearing. During infancy the children sleep with their mothers, who sing a lullaby to lull them to sleep.

When the child is three or four years old the major role is played by grandmothers; but when the child falls ill the mother will attend the child until he or she gets well. To cure the child, sorcery or magic is used by the Tharu women. When they fail they call the *bharra* (the magic man). Most of the children get well in this process. However, nowadays some families have started to call on doctors.

Sex-Typing and Socialization

A few years back the dress for girls was a long skirt *(lehanga)* and backless blouse *(angia)*, while the boys and men wore only a loincloth *(langoti)*. Sometimes they used sleeveless shirts. Now there has been a change in the dress for both: Girls have started to wear *shalwar* and *kurta*, which are generally the dresses for all Hindu girls in the north. The boys have started wearing pants and shirts. Since the area is very close to Nepal, and there is free access to Nepal, most of the educated boys have started to wear imported jeans. Elderly persons have started to wear pajamas and shirts in place of loincloths.

The women are independent and dominating, while the men have inferior positions. This serves as a model for the activities, such as ropemaking, carpentry, and bringing in food from the jungle. The girls assist their mothers in the work of embroidery, in making baskets, and stitching *lehanga* and *angia*. They also assist in preparing the clay pots and coating thatched houses with a paste of mud mixed with water and cow dung. Some girls go to the jungles with the domestic animals, while the old women keep smoking and the young girls watch goats and other grazing animals.

The children learn to cooperate in the family affairs. Each member of the family is assigned a different task on Sankranti Day. All the members of the joint family eat together. The male members take their meal first. Generally the oldest man is the head of the family, whose prime responsibility is to take care of the health and discipline of the members of the family. Each member learns to work with efficiency. Quarreling and aggression is discouraged. If somebody falls ill the other members will share his responsibility. But if a person is not sick and has not completed his job due to carelessness or other unexplainable reasons, no one will raise any objection at that time. The complaints are made and settled annually on Sankranti Day (in January) when all the members of the family sit together and assess the annual performance of the family. Next year's work is also distributed on this day.

Cooperation among the members of the family is the chief characteristic of the Tharus; this trait extends to their community as a whole. They treat the village as a unit. On Deewali Festival, all the village people, males and females, young and old, gather at one place and repair the roads. During their rainy season the animals are all kept together outside the village so that the roads are not spoiled and cleanliness is maintained.

Tharu bathing is not very different from the Hindu custom. The menfolk take baths in the open while the women bathe in a corner of the house. Generally the mother wash the children's bodies from the water stored in tree trunks; soap is not applied. The hair is cleaned with a special fine clay. The females use a kind of broom to comb their hair. When the children grow, the daughters bathe with their mothers and the sons with their fathers, if there is a river nearby the females go to take a bath around noontime, while all males take their baths early before going to the fields.

The Tharu culture is matriarchal. Marked personality differences are observed as the children grow up. The females are clever, very active, and assertive while the males are humble, mild, accommodating, and submissive. The Tharu females are found to be happy-go-lucky, impulsive, lively, cheerful, and free, while the males are serious, conservative, and taciturn (Hasan, 1971; Srivastava, Kapoor, & Sakesna, 1977).

THE SCHOOL YEARS

The Educational System

There are only six primary schools for 45 Tharu villages with a population of 20,000. When a child reaches five or six years he or she is sent to one of these schools. Most of the children resist going to school as it is one of the most distressing days for a Tharu child to leave home to go to school. They are scared of the teachers. Often the children are beaten and sent to school forcibly. The rate of dropouts from these schools is very high. The total number of boys and girls in these six primary schools is 715 and 243 respectively (Integrated Tribal Development Program Survey, 1989). To check the high incidence of dropouts the Government of India has started *ashrams* (boarding schools). All the cost of lodging, boarding, and schooling is borne by the Government. However, such arrangements have not yet been made by the Government of Uttar Pradesh for girls.

These *ashram* schools are open to scheduled tribes and scheduled castes. (In India's caste system, the castes at the lowest rung of the ladder are termed "scheduled castes." They are also known as *harijans*, or Untouchables.) There are fourteen *ashram* schools in Uttar Pradesh (U.P.). Currently, in these *ashram* schools the number of Tharu boys receiving education in primary classes, in junior high school, and in high school is 20, 25, and 25, respectively. After passing high school a scholarship is provided by the provincial government for further studies. In Lakhimpur-Kheri, the number of girls in junior high school and high school is only eleven and ten, respectively. There are no female students beyond high school. The number of boys in graduate and postgraduate classes are fourteen and two, respectively. Tharus have been able to produce only one M.B.B.S., a doctor practicing at Gonda, in Uttar Pradesh.

Socialization

The Tharus believe in a joint family system. When the child is grown up the mother leaves the child at home and goes out to work. When the children are six or seven years old they are sent to school, but a large number of children either do not go to school or drop out. They only play around in dust. At present Tharu mothers are aware of the benefits of education and are determined to send their sons and daughters to school.

Values and Interests

Tharu children are taught to be obedient and honest. The Tharu houses do not have locks or boundary walls. The boys and girls who are studying in various classes have high ambitions and optimism. Many of them have passed their high school and intermediate school with very good grades. Some of the students have selected their vocations in advance. The illiterate and semiliterate know what occupation they have to adopt. They lack a wide variety of interests. The students are interested in movies (if they live in a city) or in hit songs. Television has not yet reached their homes or community houses.

MARRIAGE

Patterns of Mate Selection

During the 1940s and before the Tharus practiced adult marriages (Majumdar, 1944); but now child marriages are prevalent. This may be the influence of local Hindus. Generally the age range of marriage is 12 to 14 years. Marriage partners may be of equal age; sometimes the bride may be older than the groom. The main idea is that the girl should marry before menarche or immediately after it.

Wedding Arrangements

Pod-Pucca (betrothal). Usually *pod-pucca* (betrothal) takes place during childhood. It is arranged by a matchmaker *(mazpatia)*, who is an influential person generally known to both families. The proposal is initiated by the girl's family. After getting information about the boy the *mazpatia* will proceed to the village of the boy to assess the status and the position of the boy and his family. After some days the *tika* ceremony takes place in which a vermilion mark is put on the forehead of the boy. On this occasion the boy's parents and relatives visit the place of the girl with some sweets. Each of them is given one rupee each as a token of affection. The night is spent drinking, eating, and singing and when there is no distance between the villages the boy's party comes back in the evening. At the time of departure they are seen off by the girl's party. On this occasion drums are beaten.

Puchachu (confirmation). When the boy and the girl are grown up, the boy's parents and a few relatives visit the girl's village to fix the date of wedding ceremony. This ceremony is known as *puchachu* (confirmation). When they go for confirmation they take with them the bride price, as settled by mutual agreement. This may include some pulses, rice, and some fresh fish. The wedding ceremony takes place eight days after this *puchachu* ceremony.

Byah or *shadi* (the meaning is the same: marriage or wedding ceremony). Suitable months for *byah* or *shadi* (the wedding ceremony) are *Paush* and *Magh* (somewhere between December and February). Hindu marriages are also solemnized during these months. The marriage party goes in bullock carts, while the bridegroom is seated on the horse. When the groom's party is away to the bride, the women of the groom's family go to a nearby pond in procession, singing, with jaggery (a type of brown rock sugar), rice, and burning embers of fire on cowdung cakes. They worship the pond with folded hands. Some clay is taken home to make an open hearth *(chulha)* on which food is cooked for the members of the marriage party after their arrival.

The marriage party *(barat)* may include both men and women, friends, relatives, and neighbors from the village. Generally the marriage party reaches the bride's place in the afternoon and are received by the bride's people. The parents of the groom pay the remaining bride price *(dola)*, which may include some metal vessels, a domestic animal, some clothes for the bride, and a cloth sheet to cover her head. This is followed by drinking and dancing. The custom of paying the bride price, however, is not frequently followed these days.

Late in the evening after this ceremony, in an open space outside the bride's house, the oil *(tel)* and turmeric paste *(haldi)* is applied to the bride and groom by their sisters. This is done on two wooden boards placed side by side. The dress of the bride is made of red cloth and has a long skirt *(lehanga)*, a white backless blouse *(angia)*, a white scarf *(unia)*, and bangles. These clothes are brought by her affinal kin (relatives by marriage, such as a brother-in-law). The groom is dressed in a loose upper garment made of thin white cloth, pajama pants, a white turban, a cloth belt *(peta)*, a big kerchief *(alga)*, shoes and socks, a small sword, a tobacco pouch, a necklace *(harwa)*, a neck ring *(hasuli)*, and black thread around his neck *(phulwa)*.

After the application of turmeric and oil the sister of the groom and her husband announce loudly that the bride and groom are now married and have become husband and wife *(dheengra* and *dheengri)*. The village magician-medicine man *(bharra)* chants some incantations to bless the couple to keep the deities happy, and bad spirits away. After this procedure both husband and wife take seven rounds of the wooden board. In some families a Hindu pundit is invited to solemnize the marriage.

In the night or late in the evening the dinner is served to the groom's party. The females of the bride's side sing songs full of abusive language, ridiculing the groom's party; the women make vulgar sounds also with singing.

The night is spent drinking, dancing, and singing. The next day the groom's party returns to their own village. Everybody uses bullock carts, but the bride comes in a palanquin. While returning, the *bharra* keeps on chanting mantras to protect the party and the couple.

After one day the bride goes back to her house with her parents and relatives. There she remains for a few days or a few months, and if she is too young she stays for a few years.

Gauna (consummation). After a period of days, months or even years, depending on the wishes of the parents and relatives, the bride is brought to her husband's house. There she is asked to bring some water from the well and prepare a meal with it. For a few nights she has no chance to sleep with her husband as she is surrounded all the time by the ladies of the house. The couple may have intercourse when everybody is out of the house, and they are alone. This whole process is known as *gauna* (consummation).

Families

Tharus have a joint family system, and sometimes nearly 70 members live in a house. Grandparents, parents, and children live together. The boys do not separate even after their marriage. The task of the head of the family is to provide accommodations for each married member. The external appearance of the house is like a big hut, but there are many apartments inside the house. One room and one cot is provided for each couple. When couples go out they leave their children in the custody of elderly family members. Most of the houses are damp-proof and double-storied. The houses as well as the cattle yards are kept very clean. Since care for the animals is the responsibility of the women, they have devised unique methods of providing fodder to the animals to maintain cleanliness. The fodder is hung on the wall and the animals use it to graze by pulling the leaves. The elderly women have to take care of the provisions in the house, whether it be fodder, grains, fish, or water. The food stock is always kept on the first floor of the house, as the ground floor gets swampy.

Due to the structure and function of the joint family, the Tharus have economic stability. Each member contributes to the general fund of the family. There is a continuation of cultural elements in the family because the traditions, customs, and behavior are transmitted from one generation to the next one.

DIVORCE AND REMARRIAGE

There is no restriction on widow marriages among Tharus, unless the woman is very old and has grown children. The Tharu women have also the right to divorce their husbands.

When a Tharu woman finds her husband to be impotent, too young, weak, lazy, poor, bad tempered, retarded, insane, or if her husband has been imprisoned or has lost his social position, she may desert him and elope with the person of her choice *(urairi)*. This elopement becomes the talk of the locality. A *panchayat* (a bench of five judges) is called and she is asked to clarify her action. Since the Tharu women are vocal and more powerful they receive a favorable judgment at the *panchayat*. The *panchayat* fixes some amount to be paid to the former husband by the lover of the woman. In this case, the husband wants more and more money while the lover wants to pay the minimum as a fine. When this is settled, the marriage ceremony takes place. In place of the wooden boards they have to circle an earthen lamp placed in a winnowing fan. A widow is married by circling round an iron spike which is erected in the yard outside the house.

A man can divorce his wife if she is sterile, or if her children do not survive, if she is known to have had intimacy with some other person, or if she is suspected to be a witch. Since the Tharus are a polygamous society, he need not divorce a sterile woman but only brings a second wife.

PREGNANCY AND CHILDBIRTH

Attitudes and Practices

After the marriage ceremony has taken place each couple desires children as soon as possible. Sons and daughters are given equal status, but it is essential to have boys in the family. Earlier, some past generation back, the sex of the first child made no difference, but with the impact of Hindu culture, couples now prefer a male child.

There are not many pregnancy practices among Tharus. If the woman has a history of miscarriages or stillbirths she is given an amulet or charm tied on her arm by the *bharra*. She promises to offer a sacrifice. There are no taboos connected with pregnancy. Tharu women are good midwives who help the women during their delivery and the postnatal period. There is a low mortality rate of infants, as well as of the women of reproductive age.

After the delivery of a child the Tharu mother is not allowed to eat anything for two days. On the third day she is provided liquor made of fermented rice. She can drink as much as she wants. On the first day the child is immersed in water and the oldest man in the family chants auspicious words. After immersion the child is fumigated with fire and smoke in a traditional procedure. A bunch of long grass *(kans or kusa)* is dug out along with the roots. The head of a snake and the stinger of a scorpion are placed inside the tuft which is set on fire, holding the flames as close as possible to the child. This protects the child against the attacks of all kinds of secret enemies throughout his or her life. To protect the child from evil eye, an iron tool is kept in the room where the child sleeps. On the sixth day, all the relatives and friends are invited to attend the ceremony for blessings. The child is kept wrapped in a cloth, but no clothing is prepared for him or her. On the first day of *dussera*, the *mundan* festival (head-shaving ceremony) takes place, which is done by the maternal uncle of the child. (The Tharus do not use the services of barbers; they do it themselves.) The hair, with some rice, is immersed in the river or a nearby pond.

On this day a name is given to the child. Among Hindus the name is finalized by a Brahmin priest, who is also an expert in astrology. The priest decides the first letter of the names after considering the position of the planets at the time of birth. In Tharu society there is no set rule for giving a name to the child. If the child is born on Wednesday *(Budhwar)*, the male child may be named *buddha* and the female *buddhia*. Out of various names suggested by relatives a name is selected and announced by the oldest person of the family before a gathering of relatives and friends. Nowadays their names resemble the Hindu names, generally named for gods and deities. After this ceremony the mother may start her outdoor as well as her indoor activities.

Preparation for Childrearing

In fact no preparation is made in Tharu families for childrearing. When families are very large, the birth of a baby is a routine affair to them. Tharu women are good in herbal medicine. The elderly women take full care of a child after its birth; hence young couples do not worry much about the health of their child.

Mother-Infant Bonding

The mother-infant bonding is strong in Tharus. After the sixth day of a baby's birth, the mother can go out and work, carrying the child on her back. Nursing continues until the next child arrives. Fathers generally do not carry children, as this is the task of womenfolk. When the child starts walking he does not need any help, as there are many children around to play with him. The child learns many things from the older children. There is nothing to give them as rewards except cow's or goat's milk, which is very much liked by the children. During festival time mothers give them toys, such as parrots, carts, and toys with a whistle. The mothers sing lullabies to lull their infants to sleep, but when the children are older the mothers tell them stories. The main themes of the stories are honesty, simplicity, and, and so on. Weaning is delayed until the next child arrives.

ADULT ACTIVITIES

Most of the Tharus own their property. Not a single adult, whether male or female, is found without work. The work assignments are determined annually. Most of the Tharus are agriculturists, and they have the highest percentage of an economically active population among the agriculturists. Their main crops are rice, wheat, and pulses. The rice and pulses are not sold in the market but stored for personal use, while the wheat is sold to get money. They do not have any traditional or caste occupations, which are found among the Hindus. The non-agricultural Tharus earn their living by carrying loads on bullock carts for payment. Tharu communities have the reputation of being better cultivators than other communities. A decade ago some Tharus became landless when their lands were grabbed for farming by some businessmen from the Punjab and other States. Now the Government has put a ban on these kinds of land transfers.

Tharu women have a dominant position in their society. Unlike Hindu women, they move freely in the marketplace. They do not allow their men to enter the kitchen. Men cannot touch the drinking pots. The major outdoor economic activity is done solely by women. They go fishing and do the buying and selling. Earlier they were seen smoking and drinking in markets, but this has become somewhat rare now. Drinking is done only in their homes.

The superiority of Tharu women can also be marked in their behavior, which is completely different from that of the caste women of their neighborhood. The caste women go to the fields early in the morning. After working hard, they take their meal in the fields and work until late in the evening. The Tharu women go to the fields after having had a very hearty breakfast (similar to the American brunch); they work hard in the fields until afternoon and come back early in the evening to manage their household affairs.

One of the daily routines of Tharu women is to go fishing in stagnant pools, tanks, and shallow depressions. Generally the men accompany them when fishing in the big rivers. The women are experts in catching big fish, even if these weigh more than 50 kg. However, they do not kill crocodiles, because they believe that crocodiles are the kings of the water—and a king should be killed by a king and not by an ordinary person.

Whenever fishing provides a large catch, the women from the village will hold the net on both sides of the river. The fish that are caught are later distributed according to the number of persons in each family. Fish are never sold in the market; if too many fish are caught, they are dried and preserved.

Another example of the superiority of Tharu women is that one cannot find them working as laborers. If they want to carry a heavy load, they will not carry it on their heads. If their menfolk are not around, they will hire some laborer to do the task. The non-Tharu women will carry it on their heads and save the money. Many Tharu families crossed to Nepal when local landlords forced Tharu females to work as laborers after the independence of India.

Traditionally there has been an understanding between Tharu men and women about the sharing of property and belongings. Bird traps, plows, oil presses, field products, and earnings are owned by the men. Domestic pets, cattle, and poultry are owned by the Tharu women. Again, the woman is at an advantage because she can dispose of any property without asking her menfolk. However, the same kind of freedom is not enjoyed by the man; he has to ask permission from his wife.

Tharu women are experts in making useful articles such as earthen pots, earthen toys, baskets, mats, and hand fans. To provide the raw materials is the responsibility of their menfolk. These things can be sold in markets to make money. The toys, such as mats and baskets, scenes depicting animals such as elephants or horses, or men with bows and arrows are skillfully painted. Sometimes there are hunting scenes. Tharu men construct and repair their houses, make instruments, weapons, ropes, and do carpentry apart from agriculture. Tharu women do weeding, harvesting, winnowing, and thrashing. Sowing is done by the men, but they cannot do any weeding because it requires precision and persistence. Crop guarding is done by the males as it requires keeping awake during the night and sleeping out in the fields.

AGING

Individuals over 55 years are considered old people among the Tharus. Most of the aged are not able to tell their age correctly. Their age can be estimated by the age of their sons and grandsons. Usually the older women wear the *lehanga* and *angia*, while the males generally wear only a *langoti* (loincloth). Otherwise the whole body is naked. Both aged males and females are respected by their juniors. The younger generations always obey the elderly. Since families are large cooperative organizations, and since there are common social and religious obligations, there is always a need for elderly people in the society. The Tharu families are a productive unit and all the members of the family work together. The aged are no burden on the family. Generally the old people's task is to guard the families against disease and animal injuries. The aged are experts in herbal medicine. They successfully treat a variety of ailments.

An elderly man sleeps at the main gate of the house with a pipe in his hand. He guards the house against wild animals. In Tharu society, the oldest members have special rights, which are not enjoyed by other members. The elderly prefer somewhat easier tasks, like making rope and cots and drying fish and grain. Suicide among the elderly never occurs. Suicide is rare, but whenever it occurs, it is among youngsters who have failed in a love affair.

DEATH

The dead among the Tharus are either cremated or buried. Nainital Tharus prefer burial to cremation; Lakhimpur Tharus practice either according to the last wish of the individual. People dying of cholera, smallpox, or other epidemics are cremated, but those who die of snake bites are exposed on mounds outside the village. For three days they wait for the person to become alive, after which he or she is buried or burned. The body of the dead person is removed on the cot on which he or she was lying. A number of agricultural implements—sickle, spade, axe, and so on—are also taken to the burial place and placed at the side of the deceased. One leg of the cot is broken. If the corpse is buried, the body of the woman is lowered face upward, but face downward if it is the body of a man. A pot full of water is kept by the side of the deceased.

The pollution in the deceased family is removed by sprinkling water, which is purified by putting gold in it. After 24 hours a feast is organized in which a special plate is kept separate; it is taken to the place of burial or cremation along with water, *hukka* (smoking pipe), earthen utensils, and winnowing basket. When the food is placed before the soul, the relations and friends who bring it are not allowed to look back. All disappear under cover of darkness without making any noise on the way. They will keep together, take a deep breath, and walk as fast as they can. Running is considered an insult to the departed, while fear of spirits makes them run quickly. But they all stay together so their steps are automatically regulated. During the *Deewali* festival there is a joint mourning of all the deaths in the village.

CONCLUSIONS

Tharu women have a unique place in their society. They are superior to the menfolk in every aspect of life. They are fair and intelligent. They are in charge of family affairs. The notoriety that they have earned for their alleged black magic and sorcery has subjected them to a suspicion that prevents free social interaction with others. It is the dominant position of the women among Tharus that has received much attention. Because of the unusual predominance of women in their society, Tharu men do not seem to have learned to think independently. They have great reliance on their womenfolk.

REFERENCES

Elvin, V. (1976). Tribal women. In Devki Jain (Ed.). *Indian women*. New Delhi: Publication Division, Government of India.

Hasan, A. (1971). *A bunch of wild flowers and other articles*. Ethnographic and Folk Culture Society, U.P. Lucknow: Department of Anthropology, Lucknow University.

Integrated Tribal Development Program Survey. (1989). (Unpublished). Department of Social Welfare, Government of Uttar Pradesh.

Majumdar, D. N. (1944). *Races and cultures of India*. Lucknow: University Publishers.

Nesfield, J. C. (1888). Description of the manners, industries and religion of the Tharu and Boga tribes of Upper India. *Calcutta Review, 30*, 1.

Singh, A. K. (1985). *Tribal development of India.* Delhi: Amar Prakashan.

Sinha, S. (1989). Vanishing stock of Andamanese. *Times of India,* May 30, p. 2.

Srivastava, R. K., Kapoor, K. D., & Sakesna, V. (1977). Personality differences between male and female Tharus. *Indian Journal Personality Development 1*, 37-41.

Wedding Ceremony of Dr. Harry Gardiner and Ormsin Sornmoonpin Gardiner with C. Ratanaphaisal and Theers Karot

Phulporn Saenpbangpla and Ormsin Sornmoonpin Gardiner in Bangkok

13

Women in Thailand

Harry W. Gardiner
and Ormsin Sornmoonpin Gardiner

Thailand, known for centuries as Siam, is approximately the size of France, with a 1989 population of 55,017,000 and an annual growth rate of 2 percent. It is bordered on the south by Malaysia, on the west by Burma, on the northeast by Laos, and on the east by Cambodia (Kampuchea).

The name Thailand (Muang Thai), adopted in 1939, means "Land of the Free" and refers to the fact that it is the only Southeast Asian country never to have been under Western colonial domination. This independence, combined with a lack of religious, racial, or gender prejudice, and aided by a fondness for eclectically adopting ideas and values and making them unmistakably "Thai," has resulted in a distinctive blend of beliefs and attitudes. Ethnically, the population is 75 percent Thai and 14 percent Chinese, with 11 percent scattered among other groups. Ninety-five percent are Buddhists, 4 percent Muslims, and 1 percent hold a variety of other religious beliefs.

While a small number of Thais work as government employees, traders, and bankers, the majority are associated with agriculture. Among the 25 million workers in the 1989 work force, 59 percent were engaged in agriculture, 26 percent in industry or commerce, 9 percent in services, and 6 percent in government positions. Women comprised nearly half (46 percent) of the total labor force, compared with 35 percent in the Philippines, 32 percent in Malaysia, 27 percent in Taiwan, and 21 percent in India.

Abundant land and the fact that nearly 90 percent of farmers own their own land has made possible the development of a spirit of individualism which is reflected in many aspects of the culture. Fortunately, Thailand has been spared one of Asia's most pressing problems—overpopulation. It is one of the few countries in the region that could, if necessary, support a large population at an even higher standard of living. In 1985, the gross national product amounted to $42 billion. The major agricultural crops are rice, sugar, corn, and rubber. The country's major industries consist of agricultural processing, textiles, wood and wood products, and cement.

Four structures—family, village, temple, and nation—provide the Thai people with direction and define their social world.

The female life-cycle provides a compatible approach with which to examine the activities and relationships that are basic to women's lives. As Hammond and Jablow (1976) have stated,

> In societies throughout the world and throughout recorded history, women's primary roles have been family-oriented. . . . [T]heir outside activities tend to be extensions of their familial roles. . . . [T]he study of the familial roles (daughter, wife, mother, and sister) is thus fundamental to the understanding of women and their place in society.

Girls begin life as the little daughter or sister within a family, to be raised and prepared for future roles. A major change occurs with puberty and shortly thereafter with marriage. As a wife and a mother a woman will carry out, as those before her, the nurturing and training role. She will spend a large part of her life engaged in some type of work, occupation, or career. Each stage in the life-cycle provides a specific role to be performed.

INFANCY AND EARLY CHILDHOOD

What is life like for a female infant or child growing up in Thailand? Much depends on whether one is looking at rural Thais, who make up 85 percent of the population, or those raised in Bangkok or in one of the smaller urban areas of the country.

To begin, Thai parents generally do not express any consistent preference for a son or daughter, reflecting the equality so often said to characterize the relationship between the sexes in this country (Ward, 1963). Since neither sex is viewed as weaker or stronger than the other, Thai parents look forward to having children of both sexes.

Another sign of equality is illustrated by the following statement by Hanks and Hanks (1963) in their chapter from Barbara Ward's book on *Women in the New Asia*:

> As children, boys and girls play the same games, and both look after their younger sisters and brothers. Boys know how to cook a meal. Girls can cut grass, tend animals and work in the fields, for all children perform the same tasks restricted only by their physical strength. . . . Nor is esteem or privilege accorded to one rather than the other. Regardless of sex the same ceremonial procedures occur at birth. Male as well as female midwives assist the delivery. Childhood names differ little. Both sons and daughters grow sickness-preventing top-knots of hair which are cut ceremoniously before puberty. Nor are there special privileges within the family. Girls and boys

sleep together as children; priority of eating or receiving gifts is determined by age rather than sex. Achievements in school are applauded equally, and permission to continue education to a higher level is granted to daughters as well as to sons. (p. 436)

Childrearing in Rural Thailand

Most babies in rural areas are born at home. The first step and first word are noted but without much comment. Nursing is always done by the mother on demand, with no attempt at scheduling, and continues until the child is two or three years old, or until another child is expected. Other foods, such as rice, soup, or bananas, are added to the child's diet after the first year.

Following weaning, children are frequently placed in the care of an older sister whose main task is to see that no harm comes to the child. Due to the hot climate, most children do not wear clothes until they are three or four years old and toilet-training occurs later than in most countries. However, unlike Western children, Thai children are left to learn this behavior with little encouragement or punishment.

Life during the first four or five years is quite pleasant for most rural children, who have no responsibilities, are not held accountable for their actions (since punishment for misbehavior usually falls on the older child in charge), and whose every wish is usually satisfied immediately in order to maintain an atmosphere of peace and quiet. However, after this age, a child is often expected to serve not only all those in his or her own family but other relatives as well. As L. Tratnik (1969) has pointed out,

Any older relative has the right to demand personal service from a younger relative, as well as the right to criticize . . . conduct and to interfere in . . . affairs. This loose but demanding relationship . . . has its compensations. Within it a child can wander safely and come to no harm, can be sure of finding food and drink, a place to sleep, and relatives who support and console in times of stress. (p. 33)

Childrearing in Urban Thailand

Urban living, particularly in Bangkok, differs little from that in most Western cities. Following childbirth, Thai mothers remain with and nurse their newborn for about a month, after which they return to work, leaving children in the care of relatives or servants, who are inexpensive and relatively easy to hire.

However, class differences are clearly observable. Raising children among the lower classes of Bangkok is frequently more difficult than in other regions of the country. In addition to financial problems and a lack of parenting knowledge and skills, many mothers leave their children in overcrowded and poorly run nurseries where they become exposed to malnutrition and such infectious diseases as diphtheria, polio, and pertussis (Pantipan, 1980).

The situation is much different in middle- and upper-class urban families where each child generally receives a great deal of individual attention from hired servants. It is not surprising that many of these children become overprotected and overindulged. Servants take care of simple tasks as bathing, dressing, and keeping toys and other items in place long after a child is capable of doing these things for herself or himself.

D. Ryback (1974) indicated that Thai children were strongly discouraged from expressing aggression. This is consistent with findings reported by H. W. Gardiner (1968a; 1976). One study drew attention to the "considerable social and psychological strain produced in Thais as a result of an early emphasis upon the desirability of harmonious relationships and prohibitions against extreme emotional expression, particularly hostility and aggression" (Gardiner, 1969). Both Ryback (1974) and Gardiner (1972; 1974; 1985) have shown that a typical response to a social conflict is a smile—perhaps not so surprising in a country widely known as "the land of smiles."

THE SCHOOL YEARS

The Educational System

Higher education provides women with increased social status within their community and facilitates movement into higher status occupations. As a result women gain greater access to legal, political, economic, social, and cultural resources.

The 1937 Thai census showed literacy rates of 15 percent for women and 47 percent for men. Recent figures show 75 percent of all Thai women are literate, making them second only to Filipino women (82 percent) among the five Southeast Asian nations (Shah, 1985).

Until the twentieth century, education in Thailand was primarily provided only for male members of royalty or for monks. Princes needed to be literate in order to efficiently govern their provinces and communicate with officials in Bangkok. Monks needed to be able to read the religious texts from which they preached to the people. Since the remainder of society was largely made up of farmers, and village lore was transmitted orally, there was little need for more than basic skills.

The long-standing tradition that every male should spend at least a short period of time in the temple, either as a novice or monk, meant that a large number of boys were at least exposed to the rudiments of reading and writing in Thai, as well as in Pali (the language of Buddhist scriptures), and learned some arithmetic. But not all boys, and certainly no girls, benefitted from this type of instruction.

The government's concern for educating the population was first shown during the reign of King Chulalongkorn (1868-1910). He decreed that every temple should offer instruction to children—boys and girls— in its locality. In 1921, compulsory education for all children became the law and has been enforced throughout the country since 1935.

The present century brought a new importance for education for at least two reasons. First, the establishment of a widespread bureaucracy required educated women and men to staff it. Second, farmers were being confronted with new technology—much of it in written form— requiring technical skills beyond those offered by the traditional temple schools. At the same time, there was a need for new institutions that could teach specialized skills needed by those entering medicine, nursing, computer technology, engineering, and industry. In 1989, more than ten million students were enrolled in government primary and secondary schools. At the post-secondary level, there are 29 universities and other higher institutes of learning. Three-quarters of these have been established since 1960. Several of these have been built in the provinces and placed on equal status with those in Bangkok.

A number of years ago, the following pattern of enrollment reflected Thai female university students' career choices: 43 percent in humanities, education, and fine arts, 34 percent in law and social sciences, 18 percent in engineering, medicine, and agriculture, and 5 percent in the natural sciences (UNESCO, 1972). Today, at Chulalongkorn University in Bangkok, women outnumber men in the arts faculty and are found in equal numbers in the science faculty. Between a quarter and a half of the country's teachers are women. Increasing numbers are also entering the traditional profession of the educated—the civil service.

Adolescence and Young Adulthood

In an earlier section of this chapter it was noted that girls and boys are treated similarly during the early years of childhood. The situation changes with the advent of adolescence. For boys, puberty generally passes without much notice. They are expected to help the family with fishing, boat repairs, farming, and other activities, but these can be flexibly scheduled, leaving plenty of time for visiting with peers.

As for girls, Thais, unlike many societies around the world, place only minimal attention on first menstruation, which generally occurs around 13 or 14 years of age. A popular expression at this time is—"Now you are a complete woman." As such, a girl is advised to avoid certain foods, remain at home, and abstain from heavy work.

MARRIAGE

Marriage has traditionally been, and continues to be, an important event for adult females in most countries of Asia, with only a very small percentage of women never marrying. In Thailand, the minimum legal age at marriage for both females and males is 17. If we look at census figures representing the marital status of all Thai women over the age of 13, we find that approximately 31 percent are single, 56 percent married, 9 percent widowed, and 3 percent divorced or separated. Comparable figures for men are 40 percent single, 57 percent married, 2 percent widowed, and 1 percent divorced or separated.

As these figures indicate, the current marital distribution in Thailand, as well as in other parts of the world, depends not only on age at marriage and the proportion marrying, but also on marriage dissolution through either divorce or death of one of the partners. While separation and divorce apply to only a small proportion of women (as well as men) in Thailand, the number of widows is more than four times that of widowers.

Becoming a Wife in Rural Thailand

While attitudes toward mate selection and marriage practices have changed as a result of urban modernization, traditional patterns survive virtually intact in rural villages, where old ceremonies continue to retain their importance (Potter, 1977; Keyes, 1987).)

The Western concept of dating has been virtually absent in rural Thailand, even though the practice is increasing among "Westernized" residents of Bangkok and among those who imitate any behavior coming from the capital. Pairing off by individual couples is still the exception rather than the rule. However, a variety of social functions act as substitutes such as groups inviting each other to parties and to other activities. These groups frequently play a significant role in offering advice to a couple as individual relationships develop. However, because of this group interest, individuals sometimes find it difficult to break up since members often try to patch up difficult situations when they arise.

While self-selection of marriage partners is gradually replacing the tradition of arranged marriages, Thais still do not plunge recklessly into romantic love relationships. Practical and rational, rather than emotional, considerations remain paramount.

Becoming a Wife in Urban Thailand

In Bangkok and other cities, women tend to marry later as they continue their education and become established in careers. While young people frequently reject arranged marriages in favor of making their own choices, they still observe the traditional ceremonies associated with marriage, including the morning blessing and chanting by monks, the pouring of lustral water, and a large evening reception for friends and relatives.

Many of the changes that have occurred have resulted in a movement away from a traditional male-dominant or conservative attitude to a newly emergent feminine-egalitarian or liberal approach within marriage. This was first noted by Gardiner (1968b) and later by Gardiner, Singh, and D'Orazio (1974) in a series of studies focusing on marital-role attitudes. They reported that college women in Thailand were significantly more egalitarian in their marriage preferences (stress on shared decision-making and female independence) than comparable groups of college women in India and the United States of America. This finding was attributed to the greater degree of emancipation from traditional role expectations enjoyed by Thai women as well as even greater acceleration in equality, especially in education and the professions, resulting from contemporary social change. For example, Thai women feel more strongly than the other two groups that they should work if they so desire and disagree with the idea that marriage is the best career or that it should be a full-time job for a wife. A recent follow-up study reconfirms these earlier findings (Gardiner, 1989, personal communication).

Dissolution of Marriage

Laws regarding both marriage and divorce are important to understanding a woman's position in the Thai social system, especially her position within the family and her role as a wife and a mother.

Marriage can be dissolved in two ways: by mutual consent or by judicial decree sought by either party. If by mutual consent, the divorce must be made in writing and registered at a district office. Grounds for divorce are the same, with one exception: while adultery by the wife is accepted as grounds for divorce, adultery by the husband is not (Chung & Meng, 1977). Not surprisingly, women are attempting to change this situation.

When divorce is by mutual consent, partners must agree as to who will have parental authority over any children. Without such an agreement, parental authority automatically belongs to the father. In the case of divorce by judicial decree, parental authority generally belongs to the innocent party unless the court gives parental authority to the other party or appoints a new guardian. The guilty party may be ordered to pay maintenance to the innocent spouse if the latter either has insufficient income or no means of support at all. This right to maintenance ceases upon remarriage which, in Thailand, is not permitted until 310 days after the divorce or unless a woman has, in the meantime, given birth to a child (Chung & Meng, 1977). The reason for this waiting period is to prevent any confusion concerning the paternity of a child.

PREGNANCY AND CHILDBIRTH

As indicated earlier, Thai parents do not express a strong preference for one sex or the other and children of both sexes are treated equally during infancy and early childhood.

As N. M. Shah (1985) points out, in countries where age at marriage and contraceptive use are low and childbearing begins shortly after marriage, a large proportion of total fertility is likely to be contributed by younger women.   In Thailand, nearly one-third (32 percent) of childbearing takes place among women under age 25, 44 percent among women 25 to 34, and 24 percent at age 35 or over.   A recent study indicated that the median age at first marriage for Thai women is 18.5 years, with the median age at first birth 20.3 years (Hirschman & Rindfuss, 1982).

Another important indication of the status of women can be found in differentials in male and female mortality rates.   Since boys generally have a higher mortality than girls during the first year of life, primarily as a result of biological factors, subsequent gender differences in mortality and morbidity may be, in large part, a result of differential nutrition, health care, and sociopsychological attention given to one sex or the other.   This differential is particularly striking in Thailand, where infant mortality rates for girls and boys are 69 and 92 per 1,000 live births, respectively (Shah, 1985).

Pregnancy

In a study of four Asian countries (Malaysia, South Korea, Thailand, and Taiwan), Hirschman and Rindfuss (1982) reported that the incidence of premarital conceptions was very low with the exception of Thailand. The figures were 17.1 percent in Thailand, 9.8 percent among Chinese Malays, 9.1 percent in Taiwan, 7.9 percent in South Korea, and 5.7 percent among Malaysian Malays.

While misreporting of marriage dates is a common occurrence, and may provide a possible explanation for some of these figures, it is also possible that these data represent an actual behavioral difference since anthropological studies of village life confirm courtship patterns that have resulted in premarital pregnancies (Potter, 1977; Yoddumnern, 1981).

During the past two decades, a number of organizations, including the Thai government and the United Nations, have been encouraging greater use of birth control methods.   In 1971 contraceptive use was quite low, especially in rural areas, where only 11 percent of married rural women aged 15 to 44 were using any form of contraception.   Two years later, birth control use had risen to 23 percent among this group.   In contrast, contraception use among urban women during the same period rose from 33 percent to 45 percent.   By 1984, 65 percent of married women 15-44 were practicing contraception (Knodel, Chamratrithirong, & Debavalya, 1987).

Birth and Childrearing Practices

Birth practices in Bangkok and other large metropolitan areas differ in only minor ways from those found in most large cities, Western and non-Western. For example, the movement from an agricultural setting to a metropolitan setting has resulted in smaller families. This has sometimes brought with it certain dangers in exchange for the potential of better economic opportunities. As J. K. Kallgren (1980) has pointed out:

So long as the nuclear family remains healthy, the children are reasonably spaced, and resources for support are adequate, city life may indeed be exciting and richer in opportunities; but if illness strikes, or if the children occur too closely, or if regular income fails, the social costs for all family members may be great. They will be particularly acute for the women. (pp. 20-21)

What follows is a description of the situation as it generally applies to those living in rural villages who make up the majority of the population in Thailand. As indicated earlier, a couple typically has a child within the first two years of marriage. When a woman becomes pregnant, she does not change her behavior in any significant way and generally carries on with her household chores until the time of birth—even, in some cases, up to the last few minutes before delivery. Rural children are usually born at home with the mother resting on a mat or mattress on the floor assisted by a non-medically trained midwife and older female relatives or neighbors.

Shortly after the newborn's arrival, the umbilical cord is tied closely to the body and cut. The placenta, which is regarded as unclean, is buried and the baby's birth hair is often shaved. The baby is sponged, wrapped in swaddling clothes, and placed in a shallow basket made of bamboo where he or she spends much of the first month. The infant later is moved to a wooden or bamboo-slat cradle, suspended from the ceiling by ropes, where he or she is frequently swung by the mother or a younger sister or brother.

Thai babies are held and played with a great deal by their mothers, fathers, grandparents, and others. At around nine months of age, a baby is carried everywhere, usually straddled on the hip of an older (six- or seven-year-old) sister or brother. All of this attention, fondling, and carrying helps to strengthen leg and back muscles to such a degree that it is not unusual to see Thai infants standing with partial support at six or seven months, taking their first steps a month or two later, and walking without help by their twelfth or fourteenth month.

Selecting a name for a child is considered an extremely important event. Based on lunar calculations and an intricate manipulation of combinations of vowels and consonants in the Thai alphabet, it is accomplished with the help of the abbot of the local temple when the child is several months old. Once done, he or she is registered in the local records and officially recognized as a member of the community.

Toilet-training is gradual and accomplished with little, if any, punishment. Diapers are not used since most infants either wear nothing or only a shirt. Any messes are cleaned up without a scolding and by the age of two most children are able to go to the toilet without help. It is also around this age that children learn to express respect for elders and to accept their place in the family hierarchy.

Children stay with the family, playing in the family compound, until three or four years of age when they begin to move around the village playing with other children their age. Childhood continues in this happy, carefree manner until it is time to enter school.

SOCIOECONOMIC ROLES OF THAI WOMEN

The opportunity to engage in employment outside the home and to earn an independent income have been among the major factors in the rapidly changing role of women in most parts of the world.

It was mentioned earlier that Thai women, comprising 46 percent of the labor force, make a particularly strong contribution to their country's economy. This is due, in part, to a substantial demand for female workers in such areas as commerce, manufacturing, and services as well as the Buddhist view that material rewards will come only through universal work. The loosely structured Thai social system and the widespread practices of matrilocality and matrilineality also appear to be important components in high female participation. The large female/ male differences in participation rates observed in many nations of the world, including parts of Southeast Asia, do not characterize the situation in Thailand. For example, 80 percent of all Thai women age 30 to 39 are economically active, as compared with 98 percent of all Thai men in the same age group.

Perhaps the question can be posed: do all these positive figures really indicate a favorable improvement in the socioeconomic status of this new generation of Thai women? The answer depends on two important factors—the types of jobs these women are accepting and their motivation for doing so.

N. M. Shah (1985) notes that "the activity of most Thai women is a response more to the social and economic situation of their families than a desire for earning an independent wage for themselves." Still, in comparison with most other developing countries, rural Thai women play extremely important economic roles, providing a sizable portion of the family income through their marketing activities and control of family finances.

Looking at the data of the occupational distribution of the female labor force in Thailand, one finds 76 percent engaged in agricultural work, 10 percent in sales, 7 percent in production, 4 percent in professional, administrative, and clerical work, and 3 percent in services. Figures for women's share in specific occupations in Thailand reveal the following distributions in each category: professional workers (39 percent), sales personnel (60 percent), services (44 percent), agriculture (49 percent), production work (30 percent), and other occupations (34 percent).

One might infer from these figures that the heavy concentration of Thai women in sales and service occupations indicates that there may be a certain degree of employment segregation. In fact, Smith and Crockett (1980) found such segregation to be particularly extreme among young single women, especially recent arrivals in cities, who are frequently consigned to a handful of jobs such as spinners, weavers, maids, and cooks. However, increasing numbers of women workers are being employed in the growing electronics industry and some of them are beginning to be organized into labor unions (Blake, 1984).

An understanding of the current occupational status of Thai women is difficult. This is due not only to rural-urban differences but also to an intricate combination of legal constraints and protective measures. For example, under the Constitution every person enjoys freedom of occupation. However, according to the Civil and Commercial Code of Thailand, a married woman cannot establish a trade or business or engage in a profession without her husband's consent unless the profession or business is one she engaged in prior to her marriage. Women are not permitted employment in certain kinds of work, including the manufacture of explosives, or work that requires the lifting of heavy loads. They may not work between midnight and six in the morning unless the work has to be carried out continuously or needs to be operated in shifts.

A pregnant woman is entitled to maternity leave consisting of 60 days with pay in addition to sick leave. Perhaps most importantly, under the current Labour Protection and Labour Relations Laws, women and men are entitled to equal pay for equal work.

THAI WOMEN TODAY

Female status is not a unidimensional concept. Thai women, like their sisters in other parts of the world, are a unique blend of traditional customs and contemporary attitudes and values. They live in a modernizing society, one in which technological and sociocultural changes are sometimes occurring with great rapidity, bringing with them changes in socially sanctioned roles.

There is no doubt that in relation to other Southeast Asian countries the status of Thai women is, and always has been, exceptional. Their role in agriculture and the rural economy has been particularly important. They have traditionally made their voices heard in village government affairs, provided a sizable portion of the family income, and usually handled the family finances. In the professions, education, business, and government service, Thai women have become increasingly active, often in senior-level positions as teachers, nurses, doctors, and administrators.

For many rural women, life is not significantly different from that experienced by their mothers and grandmothers. But for women living in the country's urban areas, especially Bangkok, life has meant a repatterning of occupational and sex roles.

As for the future, Thai women and their daughters—those living in cities as well as those living in villages—will find themselves, sometimes deliberately, and sometimes due to circumstances, experiencing even greater changes in their lives. Some of these changes they will look forward to and eagerly embrace; others they may not.

REFERENCES

Blake, M. (1984). Constraints on the organization of women industrial workers. In *women in the urban and industrial workforce: Southeast and East Asia.* Development Studies Centre Monograph no. 33. Canberra: The Australian National University.

Chung, B. J., & Meng, N. S. (1977). *The status of women in law: A comparison of four Asian countries.* Occasional Papers Series no. 49. Singapore: Institute of Southeast Asian Studies.

Gardiner, H. W. (1968a). Expression of anger among Thais: Some preliminary findings. *Psychologia, 11*, 211-228.

Gardiner, H. W. (1968b). Attitudes of Thai students toward marriage roles. *Journal of Social Psychology, 75*, 61-65.

Gardiner, H. W. (1969). A cross-cultural comparison of hostility in children's drawings. *Journal of Social Psychology, 79*, 261-263.

Gardiner, H. W. (1972). The use of human figure drawings to assess a cultural value: Smiling in Thailand. *Journal of Psychology, 80*, 203-204.

Gardiner, H. W. (1974). Human figure drawings as indicators of value development among Thai children. *Journal of Cross-Cultural Psychology, 5*, 124-130.

Gardiner, H. W. (1985). Children's drawings as measures of cultural values: Past and future directions. In E. E. Roskam (Ed.). *Measurement and personality assessment.* Amsterdam: North-Holland.

Gardiner, H. W., Singh, U. P., & D'Orazio, D. E. (1974). The liberated woman in three cultures: Marital-role preferences in Thailand, India, and the United States. *Human Organization, 33*, 413-415.

Gardiner, H. W., & Suttipan, C. (1976). Parental tolerance of aggression: A study of preadolescents in Thailand. *Adolescence, 11*, 44, 573-578.

Hammond, D., & Jablow, A. (1976). Women in the cultures of the world. Menlo Park, CA: Cummings.

Hanks, L. M., & Hanks, J. R. (1963). Thailand: Equality between the sexes. In B. Ward (Ed.). *Women in the new Asia.* Paris: UNESCO.

Hirschman, C., & Rindfuss, R. (1982). The sequence and timing of family formation events in Asia. *American Sociological Review, 47*, 660-680.

Kallgren, J. K. (1980). Women in Asian cities, their political and economic roles: Research problems and strategies. In S. A. Chipp & J. J. Green (Eds.). *Asian women in transition.* University Park: Pennsylvania State University Press.

Keyes, C. F. (1987). *Thailand: Buddhist kingdom as modern nation-state.* Boulder, CO: Westview Press.

Knodel, J., Chamratrithirong, A., & Debavalya, N. (1987). *Thailand's reproductive revolution.* Ann Arbor, MI: Population Studies Center, University of Michigan.

Knodel, J., & Prachuabmoh, V. (1976). Preferences for sex of children in Thailand: A comparison of husbands' and wives' attitudes. *Studies in Family Planning, 7,* 137-143.

Pantipan, S. R. (1980). Substitute care for children in greater Bangkok, Thailand: A personal (general) social service study. Unpublished doctoral dissertation, Columbia University.

Potter, S. H. (1977). *Family life in a northern Thai village: A study in the structural significance of women.* Berkeley: University of California Press.

Ryback, D. (1974). Child rearing and child care among the Sino-Thai population in Bangkok. *Journal of Social Psychology, 92,* 307-308.

Shah, N. M. (1985). *Women of the world: Asia and the Pacific.* Washington, DC: Bureau of the Census.

Smith, P. C., & Crockett, V. (1980). Some demographic dimensions of occupations: Research implications from an urban Thailand case study. Paper presented at the East-West Population Institute meeting on International Cities in Asia.

Tratnik, L. (1969). Childrearing practices in Thailand. *Pennsylvania Psychiatric Quarterly, 9,* 28-33.

UNESCO. (1986). *Education of girls in Asia and the Pacific.* Bangkok: UNESCO Regional Office.

UNESCO. (1985). *Women: Domains of decision.* Bangkok: UNESCO Regional Office.

UNESCO. (1972). *Bulletin of UNESCO Regional Office for Education in Asia,* Vol. 7, no. 1.

Ward, B. (Ed.). (1963). *Women in the new Asia.* Paris: UNESCO.

Yoddumnern, B. (1981). Premarital use of family planning: Effects on age at marriage. *IPSR Publication no. 48.* Bangkok: Institute of Population and Social Research, Mahidol University.

Chinese Beauty

14

Women in China

Lucy C. Yu and Lee Carpenter

The role Chinese women have played in traditional society has been a romanticized myth. Classical and contemporary Chinese literature describes the life of the Chinese woman as one of gracious leisure within the confines of her natal home before marriage, and in her husband's home after marriage. In reality, however, a very small percentage of Chinese women lived this way in the "old days."

More likely, with China being an agrarian society until recently, the majority of Chinese women in traditional society came from more modest circumstances. For women of the lower social classes, life was far from a life of leisure. Peasant women not only had to care for their in-laws and rear their children, but they also were expected to spend much time in such non-household tasks as planting rice, harvesting, caring for livestock, gathering firewood, sewing, and selling goods to increase family income. Any income they generated belonged to their husbands. The women's economic contributions were taken for granted and not acknowledged.

The issues surrounding the status of Chinese women vary as widely as the region's geography itself. The Chinese are composed of heterogeneous subgroups with different ethnic, cultural, and religious backgrounds. Chinese women in various subcultures play different roles and have been accorded a different status at different times in history. Archaeological finds suggest that before the Chou Dynasty (1100 B.C.-220 B.C.) a matrilineal society existed which accorded women a high status (Jen, 1935; Creel, 1954; Mou, 1966; Wilhelm, 1970). Later, a patriarchal system was instituted during the Chou Dynasty. As men gained power in subsequent centuries, women's position began to decline (Lang, 1946). Women's status was further eroded during the Han and Tang Dynasties (206 B.C.-907 A.D.) and women's position in the home continued to deteriorate in the Sung Dynasty (960 A.D.-1127 A.D.).

Although female infanticide and footbinding are cited as oppressive practices designed to keep women in their place, they did not become common practice until recent dynasties (Yao, 1983). Many scholars (Chen, 1975; Lang, 1946; Li, 1978; Pao, 1979) found that Chinese women were most oppressed during the Ching Dynasty (1644-1911). Near the end of the Ching Dynasty both foreign influences and the impending nationalist revolution stirred the intellectuals to examine the status of women. The revolutionary nationalistic atmosphere encouraged women to participate in the revolution to save the nation from the failing Manchurian Empress and from foreign domination. Although an indication of this new attitude was reflected in the abolition of footbinding, the revolutionaries paid only lip service to the idea of gender equality.

When addressing women's status in China it is difficult to separate Taiwan and the Mainland, as both shared the same history and culture. Therefore, this chapter will try to address women's status in both locations.

OVERVIEW

Historically, marriage was a woman's highest aspiration. However, before marriage, a woman was not regarded as a full member of her natal family; she became a full member in her husband's family only after she gave birth to male heirs. If she did not marry there were few options open to her. Without the support of her parents, she could become a nun, a prostitute, an entertainer, a beggar, or a servant. Married or not, she had no legal rights; divorce was a male prerogative that could be invoked by the husband for any number of reasons. The divorced woman was a disgrace to herself and to her natal family. Neither divorced nor widowed women could remarry because of the high value placed on women's chastity (Lang, 1946; Yang, 1959; Levy, 1963).

The establishment of the Republic of China in 1911 and the People's Republic of China in 1949 was supposed to provide women with equality. One can cite the May Fourth Movement, and name a number of influential Chinese women in both the Republic of China and the People's Republic of China, but these well-known women and the position(s) they occupy(ied) are the exceptions rather than the norm (Witke, 1974).

In Taiwan not only career but social options are limited for the middle-class, educated woman. Her interaction within social circles after graduation is still limited to a few high school or college friends. Visits to/from and support of kinsmen diminished with upward mobility. The higher her husband climbs on the ladder of success, the more isolated his wife becomes. In peasant and traditional business families, the wife knows her husband's associates and other women in the community because she works or interacts with them daily. In middle-class families the men's work environment is separate from his home. The husband socializes with his male colleagues at work, invites them to have dinner with him, and goes to nightclubs and weekend recreation spas with them (Yao, 1983). These outings rarely include the spouses. Middle-class working women may meet and make friends at work, but these other types of social outlets are not available to housewives. Despite their isolation, however, many women feel that their obligations are to their husbands and children. Employment after marriage is taken as a sign of financial need or is viewed as selfishness on the woman's part.

In the People's Republic of China, women are more inclined to blame China's trouble on poverty and the bondage inherent in the feudal family structure. Women quote Karl Marx: "Social progress can be measured exactly by the social position of the fair sex." Theoretically, in the People's Republic of China women enjoy equal rights with men in all spheres—political, economic, cultural, social, and domestic. The state protects marriage, the family, and mother and child. Although official government publications can cite a number of positions occupied by women, statistically, women occupy inferior positions and reach lower ranks at every level (Snow, 1967). Chinese women face not only a conflict of values, but also a conflict of roles today. They still are limited by the traditional value system imposed on them for centuries in both Taiwan and the Chinese mainland.

THE LIFE CYCLE AND CHINESE WOMEN

Sex-Typing and Socialization

If we were to explore life in a Taiwan village in the 1940s, one would find that the status of women in the family had not changed a great deal since feudal times. Women were subordinated not only to their fathers and husbands but also to their sons. The husband always took his parents' side against his wife. Estrangement between the sexes was common. A body of a woman who died in childbirth was considered so dangerous that it could not be buried in the family graveyard. It was taken to the public burial place near the Dog Market.

The two sexes were strictly segregated from an early age. Socialization of men and women differed from birth. In important families the son was often taken from the mother's control at the age of seven and began his formal education by male tutors. The mother was responsible for the daughter and had authority over her; however, the authority was delegated by the father. The whole social structure of the family revolved around the father-son relationship. In traditional China, the first and foremost element of the patriarchal system was the father-son identification. This identification was based on two general principles which govern the entire kinship structure: the first is known as patrilineage generational. The second element is what was called "estrangement between the sexes and sex inequality." Both steps were intended to subordinate the husband-wife relationship and enhance the father-son relationship. In traditional China the locus of power and responsibility was overwhelmingly in the hands of men. M. Levy (1963) found that women held power only as mothers-in-law (or widowed mothers) and were subject to a dual subordination to males and to other women in the family hierarchy.

The establishment of the People's Republic of China in 1949 opened new avenues for Chinese women who sought emancipation. Theoretically, men and women were equal, and had equal educational opportunities. Women workers received free pre- and post-natal care and a 56-day maternity leave with full pay (Foreign Languages Press, 1972). However, in a family where there is competition for resources, the male children are given priority. Women's economic status is better in the People's Republic of China than in Taiwan or in traditional China. They are said to receive equal pay for equal work, and they receive 50 to 70 percent of their wages when they retire. However, retirement for women is at age 50, while the retirement age for men is not until 60. The adoption of the Marriage Law in 1950 in the People's Republic of China made it possible for women to be free from a centuries-old system of bondage. The law stipulated the free choice of partner, monogamy, equal rights for both sexes, and the protection of the legitimate interests of women and children. The emancipation of women in China achieved another stage during the "Great Leap Forward" of 1958, when an upward surge in Chinese agricultural and industrial schools began to develop. Many housewives became a part of this new upsurge; women were trained to operate modern farm machinery, and served as technicians in water conservation, forestry, fishing, and meteorology. The formation of rural people's communes with diversified economies, projects, and industries opened much wider fields of employment to women (Foreign Languages Press, 1972).

EDUCATION

The School Years

Traditional Chinese education consisted of private tutors for the wealthy. In order to advance in this type of educational system, people took civil service examinations. Women did not receive a formal education in Old China. The first school for girls in China was supposed to have been founded by Catholics in 1800. Actually, it was not until the Sino-Japanese War of 1894 and the Reform Movement of 1898 that modern education and the mission schools began to develop. Native education for girls was not officially accepted until 1905, when the civil examinations were abolished and a new school system was installed. Girls were allowed to enter only the primary grades. The establishment of the People's Republic of China marked the beginning of real education for women although previously domestic training and limited study in

Chinese classics qualified some women to be primary school teachers in traditional Chinese society where segregation among the sexes was again the norm. In 1906, among 648,220 students enrolled in non-missionary schools, 306 (0.17 percent) were girls. By 1916, however, 172,724 girls (4.35 percent) were enrolled. In 1922, 471,820 (6.32 percent) of the 6,615,772 students were girls. By 1915, four colleges for women were open. They were Gin Ling, a Christian school in Nanking; Hwa Nan, a Methodist college in Foochow; the Women's Christian Medical College in Shanghai; and the Government Normal College for Women in Communist China, Tientsin. By 1923 there were 6,500,000 students in government schools, 500,000 in Protestant and Catholic Mission schools, and 3,000,000 in the old type of private school (Snow, 1967). In 1918 the Teachers' College for Women opened in Peking. In 1919, as a result of the May Fourth Movement, coeducation became accepted. This was revolutionary. According to the Chinese Ministry of Education (Snow, 1967), by 1932, 15 percent of the elementary school population and 19 percent of the secondary school population were girls; by 1935, 20 percent of the middle school students were girls, and 16 percent of those in colleges and technical high schools were girls. Statistics were difficult to obtain during the Sino-Japanese War of 1937-45. Then came the Civil War between Nationalist and Communist China. When the Communists took over the Chinese mainland from the Nationalists in 1949, the government took over private and Christian schools and financed education with federal and state funds. When the Nationalists moved the government to the Island of Taiwan, private as well as government-supported schools were created.

Today, students in Taiwan have mandatory education until the ninth grade. On the Chinese mainland, students are encouraged to attend elementary school; however, it is not mandatory. In the countryside, many women remain illiterate because of their families' needs for their labor. School is a last priority for a family that is struggling for survival, especially for a girl.

Achievement and Socialization

Traditionally, the only achievement that Chinese women hoped for was to be married to a good provider for herself, to bear male children for his family, and to hope that these male children and their children would be successful. In modern China, both in Taiwan and on the Mainland, women still play supportive roles to men. They are judged and valued first by the success of their husbands and then by the success of their children. In contemporary Taiwan, urban middle-class women usually receive high school and college educations. These women return to domestic roles for at least the first 12 to 15 years of their married lives. Their education is a status symbol rather than a preparation for earning a living. A modern Chinese woman has the freedom to choose her husband; she can expect romance to play an important role in her selection process, but she probably perceives her role as similar to that of Chinese women from past generations. Thirty percent of the work force are women and this percentage is increasing (Diamond, 1973). But most women work in low-skill industrial jobs and service occupations. A number of them work in nursing, or teach in primary or secondary schools. Few appear in high-prestige professions such as medicine, engineering, university teaching, and even fewer reach administrative or managerial levels. N. Diamond (1973) estimated that only about eight percent of the women population is in the work force. These women were older than their male counterparts; they were educationally qualified, and their higher occupational status was the exception rather than the norm for that society.

In the Republic of China women are given equal opportunities for education. However, there is still segregation of the sexes in different occupations. Theoretically, women's education and training prepare them for all kinds of jobs and occupations, and they receive equal pay for equal work (Foreign Languages Press, 1972). Although government publications cite women scientists, doctors, engineers, bridge builders, air force officers, and pilots, men still predominate in the higher-paying, higher-status, managerial positions. However, unlike their counterparts in Taiwan, women in China (Mainland) have to work. Government mandates decree that all people shall work, including women. Since women are for the first time expected to be employed and contribute to the family's economic well-being, the status of women in the People's Republic of China has improved dramatically over that of women in traditional China. Both sides, however, pay lip service to the equality of the sexes despite real-life evidence to the contrary. Both sides have male-dominated and male-controlled societies.

A cursory survey of Chinese foreign students from Taiwan who have studied in universities in the United States of America seem to indicate that women concentrated in dietetics, library science, education, and social work. Usually their education stopped after the master's degree. Men concentrated on the physical and social sciences in disciplines such as physics, engineering, mathematics, law, medicine, and political science. There were more Chinese men than women who went on to obtain their Ph.D. degrees and more men than women in the labor market. The People's Republic of China recently allowed scholars and students to study in the United States of America. Since 1980 the percentage of women and men disproportionately favored men. In one large Eastern land-grant university in 1983, the Chinese sent 200 men and one woman.

Segregation of the sexes is the norm in both Chinas. Most junior high and senior high school students are either all-male or all-female. Primary schools are coeducational but girls and boys are seated separately. Dating and courtship as they occur in the West are a very recent phenomena. Until a few years ago, young people were not allowed to have friends of the opposite sex. Those who were seen frequently in the company of the opposite sex were considered delinquent.

Until 1967 all junior high schools in Taiwan were segregated by sex. Senior high schools are still segregated. Dating is not allowed in high school; evidence of dating or an exchange of romantic letters may cause suspension or expulsion from school. Although many high school students may be 18 or 19 years old, society considers them too young to date. In principle, most colleges are coeducational, but because men and women are channelled into different disciplines (that is, the hard sciences for men, social sciences for women), and because there are no required general courses for all students to attend outside their major, a student often goes through years of classes without having more than a handful of friends of the opposite sex. Since many students want to go abroad for graduate training, they must maintain high grades. There is little time left for extracurricular activities that might provide opportunities to meet members of the opposite sex. From their teens through their college years, students' contact with opposite sex peers usually is limited to siblings and cousins. Most often a person's closest friends are friends of the same sex. The close emotional tie these young people have with same sex peers is strong and important, and usually these friendships are expected to last a lifetime.

If their financial resources are not adequate to send all their children to college or abroad, many families will choose to spend the resources on their sons rather than their daughters, even if academic records may indicate that the daughter may be a better student than her male sibling (Diamond, 1973).

In primary schools children of both sexes are given a comparable curriculum within the same school. By the time they enter junior high school, however, girls elect more "humanities or social science courses than hard sciences. A number of them choose to abandon the academic track and enter home economics programs or other less vigorous curricula" (Diamond, 1973: 231). The women who continue to college are usually assigned to less prestigious departments and to those that do not lead to high-status jobs. The elimination of girls from hard science curricula comes from the school system, which has an inherent bias against women students. Women students themselves choose not to pursue careers in mathematics or hard sciences. Thus, one would see very few women physics or mathematics majors and many majoring in foreign languages, especially English, since proficiency in a foreign language will enable the women students to compete for better-paying jobs in foreign companies and also will make it easier for them to go abroad (Diamond, 1973: 233).

MARRIAGE

Traditionally, women married at early ages through arranged marriages. In hard times poor families sold their daughters as small servants *(Ya Tou)* or gave them out as future daughters-in-law *(tung-yang-hsi)*, in both instances before they reached puberty. In the well-to-do families, girls were raised by their own families until they were married. Once women were married they were committed to their husbands' family for life. Their primary role from then on was to bear male children to perpetuate their husbands' line of descent. Women could become grandmothers at a relatively young age. After a grandchild was born it would be a disgrace for the grandmother to bear another child. At this time the "young grandmother" retired from sexual life. Her husband took a concubine to satisfy his sexual needs. Moreover, sexual relations in marriage were for the purpose of providing male heirs for the family. When this function was fulfilled there was no longer any reason for the continuation of such relations between husband and wife.

Divorce was rare and granted only on the initiative of the husband. Remarriage was not allowed except in cases where a widow's parents-in-law arranged a second marriage for her with a man who agreed to join their family to take the place of their deceased son. A man could take on second or third wives after the death of a mate, but a woman was married to one man for life. She remained a celibate widow after his death and continued to serve his family.

In traditional China genteel widows who were childless had little to look forward to. After marriage a woman belonged to her husband's family. The door of her natal home from then on was closed to her except for occasional visits. Her status as a newly married daughter-in-law in her husband's home was low. The only hope she had for the future was to become the mother of her in-laws' descendants. When she became a widow and was childless, that possibility ended. If she remarried it only could be to a man of lower status or to a man who already had a wife. Suicide was a socially acceptable option to a variety of problems that offered no other solution. In U.S. society suicide attempts result in expressions of concern and help from friends, relatives, and social agencies. In China suicide is more than a signal of personal despair; it is viewed as the ultimate rebellion in a society that requires total obedience to one's elders. For women, this means total obedience to her in-laws, her husband, and her sons when they are grown. Therefore, the husband's family will try to avoid this adverse publicity and whether the suicide is successful or not, they are not likely to feel very charitable toward the daughter-in-law who has caused them to lose face by attempting suicide. To the young woman revenge may be a motive for suicide. Her death not only brings an end to suffering, it also gives her a sense of power and a means to punish her tormentors, for her natal family will try to revenge her death. While these authors are not suggesting that women's low status causes them to commit suicide, their suppressed state probably is one of the contributing factors. Therefore, the suicide rate among young married women was exceptionally high (Levy, 1949; Wolf & Witke, 1975); a few unmarried women and widowed women chose to become Buddhist or Taoist nuns (Wolf & Witke, 1975: 89-110).

Types of Marriage

In traditional China, when a woman was of marrying age, she entered marriage through different types of arrangements. She entered as the major wife, as a secondary wife, or as a wife to a man who would care for her parents (usually if her family had no male heirs). If she were to be her husband's first wife, she would be removed from her parents' home as a young adult, become a member of her husband's family's household, and give her husband's family the right to decide the descent of her children. This is the type of marriage everyone would choose ideally. The secondary wife usually entered the husband's home as a young child. Her parents-in-law, rather than her parents, brought her up. She did not enter into a conjugal relationship with her husband until she reached maturity. Her legal rights were the same as the first wife's except that she was expected to love her parents-in-law as though she were their daughter.

In the third arrangement the rules of residence were reversed. The daughter and the man she married lived in her parents' home. Her husband had definite filial economic obligations to her parents. Many marriages of this kind gave the husband's line the right to decide the descent of his children. In some cases, however, the husband changed his surname and took on the obligations of a son with respect to his wife's family. In this case all children of their marriage took their descent from the maternal grandfather. Usually men in this kind of marriage came from poor families; this kind of arrangement was not what most men aspire to.

In Taiwan today women retain their family names after marriage. They are allowed to inherit property and may retain the property and income in their own name. But in order for a woman to gain ownership of any property, a special contract must be drawn up: if this contract is not drawn, all property acquired before and during the marriage will go to the husband. However, women are held responsible for their husbands' debts (Diamond, 1973: 215).

In the Republic of China in 1980, the Marriage Law was passed which abolished the feudal marriage system that deprived women of the right to choose their partners. This law installed a democratic marriage system that gave women free choice of partners, mandated monogamy, and equal rights for both sexes. It also protected the lawful interests of women and children and outlawed bigamy, concubinage, child betrothal, interference in a widow's remarrying, and the extraction of money or gifts in connection with marriage.

FAMILIES

China has had different types of families since early times: the large joint extended family, the stem family, and the conjugal family. In the past these family structures usually operated within the class system.

Among the poorer classes, the Confucian hierarchy could not prevail although people tried to comply whenever possible. Polygamy and concubinage cost a great deal in money and resources; therefore, the poor classes could not indulge in such practices. The joint family probably was common during the feudal period. These types of families were the mainstay of Confucianism and the reservoir of feudalism in China, but became less common in the twentieth century. In the Confucian family system, women were excluded from property rights, dowry, inheritance, and gainful occupations.

The prestige of the wife derived from the prestige of her father before marriage and that of her husband after marriage. However, the first wife of the patriarchal head of the family had authority, although this authority was delegated to her because of her husband's position, and not in her own right. Although the first wife had no equality with her husband, secondary wives and mothers were subordinate to her, too. Upon the death of the patriarch his first wife came into her own. She could then look forward to years of autocratic rule over her children's family as the tyrannical mother-in-law and grandmother.

The conjugal family followed the joint family into the twentieth century. The conjugal family was comprised of the husband, the wife, and their children. This is the normative pattern in China today. For Chinese women to establish a monogamous conjugal family in place of concubinage and paternal authoritarianism, they had to first break through the tradition of the tyrannical mother-in-law.

The mother-in-law was very powerful in traditional China. The origin of her power can be found in the endogamous tradition (Snow, 1967). The son was obliged to take his wife from his mother's clan and the wife insisted that secondary wives be chosen from among her own sisters, thus gaining power as elder sister over her husband's secondary wives, in the Confucian tradition of older over younger sisters and of maternal aunt over her daughter-in-law. As far back as the Chou Dynasty, exogamy has been customary; sons may not marry paternal cousins or anyone with the same family name; however, it was common practice for sons to marry their maternal cousins. This type of marriage was a form of feudal politics and guaranteed loyalty between the two clans for the purpose of common defense and the good of both families.

Divorce

Women's position in the family from the Sung Dynasty (960-1127 A.D.) to 1950 did not change drastically. For instance, Chinese women still had no property rights. They could not inherit or bequeath property if a single male of the family was alive. Anything they earned was controlled by the husband or the father (Lang, 1946). The bride had no rights to her dowry; land was not transferred by marriage. Wealthy brides brought their jewelry, clothing, household articles, and furniture, but in divorce, they had no rights to them. The bridegroom's family would return equal value to the bride's family. It was believed that they should pay for her upbringing. Among the poorer classes marriage took the form of a purchase. Money or goods had to be paid for a bride. Consequently, the poor frequently were unable to buy brides. A Chinese woman was valuable in her own right only as a hostage or as a source of domestic labor. As a mother she had no legal control over her own children. The primary wife had delegated rights over the children of concubines. Confucian rule referred to the primary wife as the children's mother (Lang, 1946).

The right to a divorce with economic support is fundamental to the position of women. After the Tang Dynasty (206 B.C.-907 A.D.) the legal code provided for a divorce by a husband for seven reasons: **(1)** disobedience to her husband's parents; **(2)** failure to bear children; **(3)** adultery; **(4)** jealousy; **(5)** loathsome disease; **(6)** garrulousness; and **(7)** theft. The wife was protected by three rules: A husband could not divorce his wife if she had mourned her husband's parents for three years, if the family had become wealthy, or if she had no family to receive her back.

In reality, a wife could not obtain a divorce on her own. She could only obtain a divorce by the mutual consent of both families who arranged and contracted the marriage. The right of divorce belonged exclusively to men. A divorced woman only had the right to return to her own family.

Since women had no opportunity to earn a living and remarriage for a divorced or widowed woman was unheard of, a divorced woman had to return to her own family. As divorce was a reflection of bad feelings, she was seldom welcomed back for her failure to please her husband's family. The divorce meant that her father did not bring her up correctly; this surely caused her own family to lose face.

Divorce by law was rare in China aside from a few modern cities. Statistics on divorce are difficult to find. H. F. Snow cited, in 1930, 853 divorces in the Chinese section of Shanghai out of a population of 1,500,000. Canton in 1930 registered 174 divorces (Snow, 1967).

CHILDREARING PRACTICES

In both Chinas, a woman's wish for a career is increasingly interpreted as selfish and destructive. The media and public opinion strongly advocate the constant presence of a mother in the home during the first 12 years of a child's life. In the past and to some extent still among the lower classes, children were cared for by members of the extended family. However, in the new middle class the mother often is the sole caretaker; housing arrangements and social conventions are different from those found in the United States of America. The walled-in housing prevents middle-class children from playing with other neighborhood children. Middle-class housewives encourage dependency. N. Diamond found that some middle-class housewives believed it necessary to bathe 10- or 11-year-old children and dress them (1973). The middle-class child's only responsibility is to study. They are not allowed to waste time on cleaning, cooking, and other household tasks. Children in poor households, because their mother often has to work, are less dependent and more capable of a variety of chores, including caring for younger brothers or sisters.

Public opinion strongly suggests that the mother's continuous presence and involvement in the home is necessary for optimal development of a child during the first 12 years of his or her life (Diamond, 1973: 222). This opinion is both perpetuated by the media and supported by textbooks which show the mother in domestic as well as nurturing roles in the home. Both girls and boys from middle-class families are excused from knowing how to cook, shop, or maintain a home. Although education is highly valued in Chinese society, poor children often have to give up school and help the family earn a living. For middle-class girls, education is a means of securing high-status husbands. For boys education is the means to go abroad to secure better jobs. With high school diplomas girls in Taiwan can marry students who return from studying abroad with a Master's or Ph.D. degree. Some families arrange for their daughters to marry Chinese who are overseas or in the United States of America. In these cases, the girls usually must have a college degree in order to obtain a student passport. Although many women come as students, young women going abroad are told to find suitable husbands rather than to complete their study.

For both sexes, competition for available spaces in better educational institutions is great. Stiff quota examinations for admissions begin in junior high school but preparation for these competitions sometimes begins in primary school. Parents who can afford to will hire tutors to prepare their children; those who cannot will tutor the children themselves from grade school on. The ultimate goal is to prepare these children so that when the time comes they can get into better schools. The rigorous entrance examinations allowed one in ten primary school children to graduate from senior high and one in a hundred to enter a university in the 1950s. However, by 1970 the number of high schools and colleges increased, making it possible for 20 percent to enter senior high school and 4 percent to enter college (Diamond, 1973: 225).

It is not uncommon for students to stay up every night for several months to prepare for entrance examinations. The tutoring role usually belongs to the mother, if she is educated, or to evening cram schools if she is not. Although fathers are usually better educated than mothers, they rarely tutor their children for primary and secondary education— tutoring is viewed as women's work. Thus Chinese society through newspapers, television, movies, and the school system sends a message that a woman's place in the world is to be a mother. Her most important accomplishment is the success of her children. Traditionally, a mother's love and self-sacrificing role are glorified in popular lore and literature. On Mother's Day superwomen are honored for their contribution to their children's growth, development, and eventual success in securing a high-status husband or high-status occupation (although the latter is rarer than the former).

CAREER OPPORTUNITIES

Women in the more affluent middle class in Taiwan probably choose their husbands. The husband probably has a professional or white-collar job with the government or in business. The family consists of husband, wife, and their children; no in-laws live with them. The wife, unlike her lower-income counterpart, is educated. She most likely would have had three or four fewer years of schooling than her husband. The wife is still expected to be a devoted wife and mother. If her husband can afford it, regardless of her educational background, she does not work outside the home. Those who do work outside the home apologize and lament the fact that their husbands cannot afford to keep them at home. The middle-class housewife or the middle-class "working housewife" may seem better than her forerunners in traditional China. For women in Mainland China, work is required, and therefore they do not have to justify their working outside the home in order to save face.

Although both the Nationalist and Communist governments officially established equality for Chinese women, Chinese women's educational, occupational, and economic status today is not equal to men's. Compared to a few hundred years ago in China, however, women's status in society has improved a great deal. In recent decades we have seen new opportunities and new roles for women. But as it is with other social issues, while change opens up new frontiers, it also creates new problems. For contemporary middle-class Chinese women marriage and motherhood are still highly valued. Although employment is available to these women, the traditional roles of wife and mother conflict with what is expected of women at work. Employment requires arranging for the children's daycare. In Taiwan there is a shortage of daycare centers; in the Mainland the government provides daycare centers for children. But this means that working mothers have less time for homemaking and mothering tasks.

A number of positions have been occupied by women in the People's Republic of China. The *New York Times* reported that in 1957 2,400 women taught in Peking's colleges and universities. Twelve percent of the deputies in the National People's Congress were women; many farm cooperatives include women on their management board. Furthermore, women occupy important positions in the government. Madame Sun Yat-Sen was one of six vice presidents until her death; H. F. Snow (1967) reports that at one time the "Minister of Health, the Minister of Justice, the Minister of Supervision, the Minister of Overseas Chinese Affairs, the Minister of the Textile Industry, and the head of the Foreign Ministry press section are all women" (p. 1).

Other positive developments include the right to vote, pay equal to that of men, and retirement for women at 50 with a pension of 50 to 70 percent of their former wages. Marriages are no longer arranged, women no longer have to submit themselves to the tyranny of the mother-in-law; and prostitution is outlawed.

According to N. Diamond (1973), "Women who were educated in an earlier generation, who were in their 50s and 60s, rarely retreated into marriage." When they were interviewed by Diamond, they had "almost unbroken career lines." Some of them had temporary interruptions because of health or employment problems. Most of them had been employed since graduation from high school or college. The household register showed very few educated women in their 50s and 60s who were not working. In that same interview Diamond found that "women in their 40s showed more disruption in their career patterns and the women in their 30s and late 20s in our sample were the least likely to have any interest in continuing work after marriage and most likely never to have had any work experience at all" (p. 233).

The issues of equal pay and equal hiring practices exist on paper only. Women receive less pay than men, and are hired to fill lower-rank positions even if their qualifications are similar to men's. Although there have been changes in laws and customs that represent a movement toward equality of the sexes, true equality does not exist.

REFERENCES

Chen, K. Y. (1975). *History of Chinese marriage.* Reprinted in Taipei, Taiwan: Commerce Publishing.
Creel, H. G. (1954). *The birth of China.* New York: John Day.
Diamond, N. (1973). The status of women in Taiwan: One step forward, two steps back. In M. B. Young (Ed.). *Women in China.* Ann Arbor: Center for Chinese Studies, University of Michigan.
Diamond, N. (1966). *K'un Shen: A Taiwan village.* New York: Holt, Rinehart, and Winston.
Foreign Language Press. (1972). *New women in new China.* Peking: Author.
Han, F.L.K. (1948). *Under the ancestor's shadow.* New York: Columbia University Press.
Jen, T. J. (1935). Archaeological search for matriarchy in Chinese antiquity. *East Magazine, 1,* (January), 23.
Lang, O. (1946). *Chinese family and society.* New Haven: Yale University Press.
Levy, M. (1949). *The family revolution in modern China.* Cambridge: Harvard University Press.
Levy, M. (1963). *The family revolution in modern China.* New York: Octagon Books.
Li, C. (1978). *Lives of ancient Chinese women.* Taipei, Taiwan: LiMin Publishing.
Mou, H. (1966). Kung Yang's evidence of matriarchy in the spring and autumn period. *Hsin Ya Hsueh* PO.I.1 (August).

Pao, C. L. (Ed.). (1979). *Readings in Chinese women's history*. Taipei, Taiwan: Hu Tung Publishing.

Snow, H. F. (1967). *Women in modern China*. Paris: Mouton and Co.

Wilhelm, R. (1970). *A short history of Chinese civilization*. New York: Kennikat Press.

Witke, R. (1974). *Transformation of attitudes toward women during the May Fourth era of modern China*. Ann Arbor: Ann Arbor University Microfilms.

Wolf, M., & R. Witke (Eds.). (1975). *Women in Chinese society*. Stanford: Stanford University Press.

Yang, C. K. (1959). *The Chinese family in the Communist Revolution*. Cambridge: MIT Technology Press.

Yang, M. C. (1945). *A Chinese village*. New York: Columbia University Press.

Yao, E.S.S. (1983). *Chinese women: Past and present*. Mesquite, TX: Ide House.

Young, M. (1973). *Women in China: Studies in social change and feminism*. Ann Arbor: University of Michigan Press.

Two Sisters, Mami and Rika Fukae in Tokyo . . . in
formal, ceremonial dresses

Photo credit: Machiko Fukae

. . . In modern, everyday jeans

Photo credit: Machiko Fukae

15

Women in Japan

Naohiko Fukada

Japan (Nippon) is a group of islands that lie off the east coast of Asia and include four major islands: Hokkaido, Honshu, Shikoku, and Kyushu. In addition there are many smaller islands. The total land area measures 145,809 square miles (377,644 sq. km.), that houses a population of 120,235,000 people (1985) of which 50.8 percent are women.

The land makes a long arc from north 45° to north 25°. To the west of Japan lies the Sea of Japan, and on the east coast Japan borders the Pacific Ocean. The northern areas are cold in the winter, while the southern parts are hot in the summer. This large area of land provides a wide variety of animal and plant life.

About 85 percent of the surface area is mountainous, where at present one can find at least 40 active volcanoes. Sometimes these erupt in fire and smoke. In addition, many small earthquakes shake the islands of Japan. There are also numerous hot springs that provide resources for health and leisure time. Japan is a small country; the many mountains divide the land into small regions of different social customs, different dialects, and a variety of foods and different cooking styles. Nevertheless, because of their long history, the Japanese people have developed and share the same cognitive patterns, attitudes and cultural habits. Although influenced by the Chinese and the Korean cultures, the Japanese culture differs from both. When Japan became industrialized recently, it combined both the old traditional and the new modern characteristics.

Although the origin of the Japanese people is not clear, influences from China and Korea, including Buddhism, have left their mark on every aspect of the Japanese culture, such as life-styles, rituals, languages, and religion. Originally, the women in Japan held the dominant status in the family. But with the prevalence of Buddhism, the characteristic changed and women were given a lower status in the family and in society.

After the Meiji reform in 1868, Japanese people were exposed to the Western culture and to its ethnic differences. Especially after World War II, the U.S. styles in food, clothes, as well as jazz and rock music became popular. Before World War II many scholars went to Germany to study; however, after the war most scholars went to the United States of America to study all disciplines of the sciences.

The Japanese people of today have complex patterns of life-styles. These include traditional styles originating with Confucius and Buddhist influences. In addition there are the original Japanese styles, influenced by Shinto. However, the most powerful new trends come from the modern industrialization. In general, Japanese people are sensitive to new trends. As in the past, whenever they found new things, Japanese people learned from them and adopted them immediately. This is why the people of Japan change their life-styles rapidly, a characteristic that is true even today. And the life-styles of women in Japan are changing now as well. They have developed complex styles with multiple aspects.

AN OVERVIEW: MODERN JAPANESE WOMEN

The Japanese people experienced many changes in their life-styles, including women's norms, after World War II the biggest changes in the history of Japan occurred during these years.

Life Expectancies

The life expectancies for Japanese people increased over the years. In 1936 the average expectancies were 49.63 years for females and 46.92 years for males. However, by 1980 these had expanded to 79.00 years for women and to 73.57 years for men. These increases brought about great burdens on the aged themselves as well as on their families, and on the government, which took on some of the responsibility for their physical and mental health, in addition to economic support for the elderly.

The Family

The number of nuclear families has increased. In 1920, 54.0 percent of all households were nuclear families, while in 1980 the number rose to 63.3 percent. The average household currently includes about three persons.

Education

The educational level of women has been raised. After high school, 32.4 percent of the girls and 27.7 percent of the boys go on to higher education. Most girls go to junior colleges or to various kinds of vocational training schools, such as accounting, computer programming, schools for design, and secretarial training. However, only one-fourth of the students who attend a four-year college or university are girls.

The Work Force and the Education of Children

The number of working women has increased. While in the 1960s the working women were only young women, in the 1970s both young and older women were working. However, in the 1980s women of all age levels (young, middle-aged, and older) were working to help support their households. Many women went back to work after they had children, or after their children had entered schools, or after their children left home either to get married or to find a job to be on their own.

Because the cost of living had increased due to inflation, many women were compelled to get jobs as full-time workers. Before World War II, even though their living conditions were hard, women (i.e., wives) thought that they had to stay at home. Today, however, women's thinking has changed. The cost of education for their children is high, even though the number of children in each household has decreased. All parents would like their children to receive higher education. Sometimes the children have to attend *jyuku* (a kind of preparatory school for the entrance examination to high school). Returning home from school, a child goes to *jyuku* in the evening or at night. The tuition fees are not cheap. If they fail to pass the entrance examination to a college or a university, they must try again, hoping to succeed the next time. They must go to *yobiko* (another kind of preparatory school for those who want to enter a university or a college after high school). They must attend every day and it is expensive. To meet such expenses many mothers must work outside the home and earn additional income. Sometimes the newspapers report the sad news of a student who failed the entrance examination and tried to commit suicide.

Household Responsibilities

Because of the many electrical appliances that are being used in households, housekeeping chores are made easier for women. Thus it is possible for women to work outside the home and easier to earn an additional income. However, sometimes the mothers must leave a child at home without a babysitter. In Japan it is not the custom to hire a babysitter when the mother is away. Often the grandmothers take over this duty. Because children are alone in their homes, there are many reports in the newspapers about *kagikko* (a child who stays home alone after coming home from school). A boy may have the key to his home, while his mother is working. These children are usually called "key boys" (a term identical to the U.S. "latchkey children"). Sometimes infants who were left alone have died because of a fire in a closed (locked) room.

Good electrical equipment and the mother's going to work outside the home can produce two different consequences. The trend of grandmothers to take over the duties of the mothers for their grandchildren while the mothers are out working is positive. However, the effects of *kagikko* when there are no grandparents and a child dies by fire is tragic.

Elderly Population

The increased number of elderly persons is a serious problem in Japan today. Most aged individuals need the help from their children or money for their medical care. Suicide of elderly people sometimes happens because of their loneliness, chronic disease, weakness of their body, bad relationships with family members, or others reasons. All these situations represent a heavy burden on the women in their homes.

Children

The decrease in numbers of children in each household is a serious matter for the parents. It means that the children have no groups which are adequate in size and proportion for different ages. Group activities are important for learning socialization skills. When they have no adequate groups, they also have no time to play and chat with their peers in order to learn the skills that are necessary for interpersonal relationships. Furthermore, children are busy attending *jyuku* and therefore they have no time or place for group activities such as playing ball, because streets are busy with traffic by cars.

Since children have no opportunities to play with peers, they cannot learn to solve or settle disputes between peers by friendly interactions or to deal with feelings of aggression. In many schools there are numerous children who worry about such troubles, and then try to escape by suicide or by fights with knives against their peers. It was suggested that these unfortunate cases came about because of the lack of group activities.

INFANCY AND EARLY CHILDHOOD

Parent-Child Relationships

In Japan, a child is called *kodakara* (child treasure) and is well protected, sometimes even overprotected. After a birth many rituals are held: On the third day and on the seventh night parents, relatives, the midwife, and other people come together to celebrate the baby's well-being and to express thanks to *Ubugami* (the birth deity), because for a baby the first week is a dangerous time. Therefore after three days and after the seventh day, they celebrate. Then, after one month, the baby is brought to an *Ubugami* shrine. Usually the mother's mother brings the baby, who is especially beautifully dressed for this occasion. It is the baby's first outing and the first time for the baby to be exposed to the sun. On the hundredth day, the baby tries to eat ordinary food, the same as the family eats. This ritual is called *tabezome* (the first time for eating ordinary food), and brings enjoyment to the parents. *Shichi-go-san mairi* (going to a shrine when the children are three, five, and seven years old) is another important ritual for parents. For Japanese people, *Ubugami's* protection of the children is important. Throughout the entire life-span, going to a shrine is repeated, both for the children as well as for the parents themselves; they ask the deity to watch over them and express their thanks for the deity's protection.

Usually, the mothers stays with a child below three or four years old. However, as every household needs more income, many mothers go out to work in factories, supermarkets, or offices, either part-time or full-time. However, this is an additional burden for the mothers, both mentally and physically.

Since in Japan there are customarily no baby-sitters and if there are no grandparents in the home, parents take their children when they go swimming, to the movies, on picnics, or to sports activities, and other pastimes. If they have good neighbors they can get a neighbor to help take care of the children while they are away from home. In any case, caring for the children is the mother's responsibility. She carries the children on her back or puts them in a baby carriage. Since after World War II, fathers have helped mothers to carry the children. Frequently one sees fathers with a child in a backpack.

As a consequence of so many mothers working outside the homes, many children are enrolled in daycare centers from early morning to evening. In 1982, 12.6 percent of all six-year-old children went to such centers, and a total of 1,957,000 children stayed in daycare centers in that year. Their ages ranged from newborn infants to six-year-olds. They can stay in the daycare centers all day, while the kindergartens usually close at noon. It is interesting to note that in 1982 almost one-fourth of all six year old children were staying at home with their mothers, without going either to a daycare center or a kindergarten.

Most urban areas are crowded with buildings, pedestrians, and cars; consequently children cannot find a place to play. Therefore children go to either daycare centers or a kindergarten where they can play. However, many parents take their children to small parks or to playgrounds on the roofs of department stores or of supermarkets.

In many households, on May 5th for boys, and on March 3rd for girls, parents display dolls. Generally dolls are warriors in May, while in March they are mainly court ladies and gentlemen. These doll displays are traditional events in Japan, a carry-over from old times: *momono sekku* (the festival of the peach) for girls, and *tangono sekku* (the festival of the fifth month) for boys are happy times for children. Mothers offer sweet cakes to the children and invite the children in the neighborhood to see the dolls which are displayed on a shelf, or on several shelves in the living room. The national holiday *kodomo no hi* (children's day) serves to continue this old tradition.

Usually a baby sleeps near its mother, either on the same *futon* (mat), or on a separate *futon* during the night. Most preschoolers sleep in the same room as their parents. However, more frequently, many children today sleep in their own rooms. This is a new trend, following the U.S. style.

Sex-Typing and Socialization

Before World War II, boys' and girls' styles differed from each other with regard to their clothes and hair. But since the war, the differences have been minimized. Compared with the choices before the war, the range of color selections has widened; now boys wear red and pink, while girls choose black and blue clothing. Younger boys wear the clothes of their older sisters, who wear in turn their older brothers' clothes.

The purpose of *shitsuke* (the training or education of children at home) is to train and educate children as members of society for many years. The earliest instructions are given by the parents at home. *Shitsuke* is the training of preschoolers and has as its aim to make all-round good human beings, though it is not just an intellectual endeavor. The teaching of *shitsuke* by parents leaves its mark on children throughout their lives. Usually boys are taught to be brave, steadfast in hard times, show good etiquette and manners, and for the less vigorous to have a kind heart. Girls are told to be gentle and polite toward everybody, and have charming manners and pretty clothes. After the war all education in Japan became coeducational, except in rare cases. However, boys and girls are supposed to behave differently; boys are active and run energetically, climb trees, play with mud, sand, and water, while girls usually sit or squat to play with dolls and other toys. Generally, boys shout loudly, while girls speak relatively quietly.

Although in daycare centers and kindergartens children of both sexes are treated similarly, they behave differently. Perhaps such sex-stereotyping was established by their early *shitsuke*.

Listening to and obeying adult persons, as well as eating quietly without chatting are important for good manners in Japan. In daycare centers and kindergartens they learn many things, among them: group activities, the importance of keeping promises, following and keeping to the rules of games, and so on. However, tardiness is frowned upon. Today in Japan parents do not have enough time to spend with their children. Therefore such training in the daycare centers and in the kindergartens is very important for a good upbringing. Many fathers work and are away from home all day. Consequently many homes lack an atmosphere of masculine dominance that the father's presence creates.

Compared with the girls, boys generally prefer more physical activities in playing, story telling, looking at television programs, and so on. All boys prefer rockets, cars, ships, and airplanes, while girls choose beautifully dressed dolls and like to play "house."

Japanese bathing is different from the Western customs of taking a bath. The bathtub is filled with water. Then usually the father with the infant enter together. Either the father or the mother washes the children's bodies outside the bathtub in the bathroom. Sometimes it is the father who takes off the baby's clothes and then hands the baby to the mother in the bathroom. After washing the baby, the mother hands the baby back to the father, who dresses the baby again. Sometimes the father takes care of washing the older children. Parents who do not have a bathroom in their home usually go to a public bath, where there are two big baths. One is used by men (boys) and the other accommodates women (girls). While they are there the father sometimes hands the baby over to the mother after taking its clothes off. Later the child is returned to the father. During bathtime, the parents and the children chat with each other, as they do when they are going to the public bath and also when they are returning to their home. It is an important opportunity for interfamily interaction.

THE SCHOOL YEARS

The Educational System

After the war, the compulsory educational requirement was extended to a total of nine years: six years in elementary school and three years in middle school. After attending these schools, the students go to high school for three years, and then enroll in college for four years. The 6-3-3-4 system was decided on as the basic law of education for the development of healthy spirits and minds, which are consumed with the wish for independence, respect for accepted values, and love for truth and justice.

Educational Achievements

After graduating from middle school in 1985, 93.8 percent of all youngsters went to high school (these consisted of 94.9 percent of the girls and 92.8 percent of the boys). Almost all girls went to vocational training schools or junior colleges (which represent two-year programs). Today 24.5 percent of the students at colleges and universities are young women.

It is a Japanese custom that almost all young men and women who want to enter the business world must try to do so immediately after graduation from school, college, or university. And after joining a company or working in an office, they continue to work all life long, usually until they reach 60 or 65. Since graduation from a good school or college is important, almost all the young men and women try to enter a good school, as the school or college they enter may influence their entire life.

After completing their education, young men try to find jobs in a professional or skilled work capacity, while young women do not have the same opportunities. Therefore women usually enter offices, or work areas where they perform services. In general Japanese women think that when they marry, they will stop working at a job. However, recently this trend has been changing: Even after they get married many women are working.

Values and Interests

For school children the most important goal is to pass the examination to enter a good school or college, and after the education is completed, to find a good job. Before World War II young people worked hard and learned the necessities for building their future. They showed more respect to higher status than to money; usually intellectual life had more value than material things. Today, however, they think that the important thing is their private lives. They want to achieve a pleasant life without working hard. Pupils of the middle schools have interest in newspapers and reports of current events, such as a variety of social and community news (traffic accidents, suicides, etc.), the photo page, movies and theater, sports, comics, fiction, and so on. Adolescents who work spend their holidays or vacation days as follows: They go out and visit, watch television, listen to the radio, go to the movies, hike and fish, rest, participate in sports, games, and read newspapers.

MARRIAGE

Pattern of Mate Selection

A young man and woman are free to marry, based on their own decision. But before the war a young man and woman who wanted to marry had to go to the *koshu* (head of the household). It was the custom during the *samurai* period, when the *ie* (family members or clan) was important, that the needs of the individual members of the household were not neglected. Thus parents taught their offspring that choosing a good partner depended on their sharing the same economic and social status as the person under consideration. To find an eligible person was often difficult.

Then a *nakoudo* (go-between or matchmaker) was sought who brought the two households together. In doing this, they had to determine first whether the two households had the same social and economical level. Of course, even in those days, love matches existed in a way similar to the modern customs, but they were rare. Today, love matches are possible under the new law; but generally parents' customs and opinions do not change so quickly. Usually marriages follow the rules established by mediators or go-betweens. While young people have the right to do their own mate selection, there are not adequate opportunities available where they can meet eligible singles. The number of love marriages has increased as part of a modern trend. However, at the same time, the number of divorces has also increased.

Marriage Arrangement

Regardless of whether a young person makes the decision concerning the selection of a spouse or whether the marriage is arranged by parents based on the younger individual's wishes, the next steps are the same. First, a *yuinou* (ceremonial betrothal gift) from the bridegroom-to-be is presented through a go-between or emissary to the bride-to-be's household (the bride price, in anthropological terms). Sometimes this gift is presented in the form of money. The amount of the money gift as *yuinou* varies, based on many different conditions or local customs, for example, a man's age, the status of his job or position, his family's social and economical status in the community, and the status of the bride's family. Based on the amount of *yuinou*, parents of the bride must spend many times this amount on the new home for the bride and groom. The amount of *yuinou* plus the money which the bride's parents spend is based on common tradition of a given community that varies from place to place.

In the old traditional custom, the bride met her new husband at the wedding ceremony without ever having seen him before the ceremony, while today the usual custom is for the young groom to meet and walk together with his future bride before the wedding, even if the match was arranged by a matchmaker.

In the Japanese wedding ceremony, usually parents and relatives come together to celebrate the young couple's future life together. Almost all wedding ceremonies are performed in the *Shinto* manner. A *Shinto* priest reports to the god the names of the two young persons, and prays that the god may guard and protect them. Later the newlyweds and all their attendants drink *sake* from the same bottle. Drinking *sake* is an important part of the ceremony in Japan to seal the new relationship.

After the ceremony, a party is given to announce the marriage. To this celebration many friends from their job affiliations and their places of employment, from schools and colleges, and so on, are invited. Many young couples give their big party at a large hotel, or in some public hall. After the party many honeymooners fly to their destination for their honeymoon.

Families

Before the war, many young couples lived in the home of the husband's parents. However, since the war many young couples live by themselves. Today many couples who are working live in an apartment for convenience. Generally there are no old family members living with them, and usually they have only one or two children. Sometimes parents worry about what to do when their children get sick, because there are no members of the older generation to take care of them.

Divorce

Compared with the years before the war, the number of divorces is increasing. In 1980 the divorce rate increased to 1.51 percent, and the marriage rate dropped to 6.4 percent. Love matches for young men and women were increasing. Similarly, the number of divorces was increasing. Divorces that occur between five and ten years of marriage typically include 27.8 percent of all divorces; 16.2 percent of all divorces took place among couples who were married from 10 to 15 years. Those married less than one year have a higher rate. And a new trend registered an increasing numbers of older persons sought divorces (in 1979).

The listed causes of divorce were: incompatibility of the couple's personalities (56.5 percent by the husbands and 39.5 percent by the wives), extramarital affairs (24.3 percent by the husbands and 32.1 percent by the wives), wasting money (19.8 percent by the husbands and 38.5 percent by the wives), violence (2.9 percent by the husbands and 38.1 percent listed by the wives), as well as alcoholism, quarrels among family members, and separation/absence, among others.

PREGNANCY AND CHILDBIRTH

Attitude and Practices

After the wedding many parents, as well as the newlyweds, expect to have a baby soon. In former times a baby was an important key to a happy marriage for the young couple, because not having any children was a possible reason for divorce. In old Japan, the birth of a baby was necessary to provide continuity of the family name. Even today many parents prefer a boy. They remember an old proverb: *Ichi hime ni taro* (first a princess, and second a prince), which is interpreted as: a firstborn girl is easier to raise than a boy, because a girl is generally healthier and emotionally gentle.

When a woman is five months pregnant she starts to wear an *iwata obi* (abdominal sash). This is the first announcement of the baby to society. Before the war many women gave birth at home with the help of a midwife. Today almost all babies are born in the hospital.

Usually the mother of a pregnant woman prepares the expected baby's clothes, which are white or yellow; thus they are appropriate for either sex. Naming the child is important. The expectant father, or his father, selects the names. Very often the boy's name shares a common letter with his father; each Chinese letter *(kanji)* has a meaning, or meanings, such as strong, clear, good, bright, and so on. Many Japanese boy's names include these virtues, while girls' names are based on a different rule, usually the names contain beautiful sounds to pronounce, or a special letter, that means gentleness, beauty, and long life.

Many Japanese people think that for successful child rearing it is necessary to receive the protection of many different gods and spirits. Therefore, many parents and family members go to the shrine or temple before the birth of the baby.

Preparation for Childrearing

The young father and mother of the nuclear family may not have much experience in childrearing in the Japan of today. Before the war, there were older persons, especially an elderly woman, in every household, because women live longer than men. Young couples were glad to get some good suggestions, as well as some physical help with rearing the child. But that is not the case currently. While they gained independence, young parents lost another, more important point: good childrearing. Young couples try to find good substitutes. They listen to the radio, or watch TV baby programs on mental and physical health; they go to lectures in hospitals and public halls, and the like. Some lectures are especially prepared for these young parents. Books are also important sources of helpful hints.

In Japan, through the years, a grandmother was a good teacher of childcare in every household, but after the war there were changes in the customs. However, for the home without an older woman, there are no good substitutes in this society. Therefore there are many lonesome children in every home; these situations are in part the cause of current children's problems in Japan.

Mother-Infant Bonding

Mother-infant bonding is strong in Japan. A mother tends to think that her child is an extension of her body. While the baby is small, the mother carries it on her back, wearing a *nenneko* (Japanese cloth that covers mother and baby together; it is usually quilted in the winter). The baby covered by the *nenneko* is comfortable because its keeps him or her warm and the baby can feel the warmth of the mother's body. Usually the baby is given something sweet to eat or else holds a toy in its hand, such as a doll or a small pinwheel. Today many young mothers do not wear a *nenneko*; they use a baby carriage or circular walker instead, though sometimes the father carries the baby on his back.

Before the war, carrying the baby was a job for the mother. However, now fathers also carry the baby. Behaviors such as mother's quietly singing a lullaby, caressing and patting the baby, swinging the infant back and forth with both hands, and so on, are difficult to find these days in urban communities. However, at the entrance ceremonies to kindergarten, elementary school, high school, college and university, there are many mothers present. Of course at graduation ceremonies there exists a similar situation. While these observable phenomena have changed, the mother-infant bond still seems strong and lasting.

After their entrance to middle school, children gradually show signs of their increasing independence. They prefer to go out with their peers, even when their mothers want to do something for or with them, and the children reject that. In Japan there is a saying that weaning is difficult for a baby, but it is difficult for the mother when children grow apart and follow their separate ways.

Traditionally in Japan, child rearing was a major part of mother's duties for which no adequate replacement exists, while the children of today are given an earlier independence. For the hard work they do, outside their homes, mothers receive only monetary rewards. While Japanese women wish to keep strong bonds between themselves and their children, they must find other goals or aims for future happiness in life.

ADULT ACTIVITIES

In 1984, 35.6 percent of all employees were women. Of these 22.8 percent were between the ages of 20 and 24 years, and 13.4 percent were from 25 to 29 years old. In Japan, generally, young women and older women whose children are grown up work outside the home, while the middle-aged group works less frequently outside their homes. Among all female employees, 38 percent are unmarried, and 51.3 percent are married. The number of women workers in each category is distributed is as follow: office workers 32.9 percent, factory workers 22.5 percent, professional or skilled workers 13.7 percent, sales personnel 12.1 percent, and service workers (e.g., waitress or hostess, among others) 11.2 percent. Also in 1984, the average woman worker's wage was 51.8 percent that of a man's, and the International Labor Organization cautioned that "this ratio was unusual with regard to current world trends."

Many women need jobs to supplement the income for their household. Still, while the wages are low and labor conditions are not very good, the job market is small and applicants for the existing jobs are numerous; therefore any improvement in work conditions and salary increases are difficult to achieve.

Whether married or unmarried, many women today join health clubs, or participate in a variety of activities. All such activities cost money and add to the expenses.

Throughout Japanese history, there were reports that women passed their lifetime in misery. But nowadays women have a more pleasant and enjoyable life. Even though they are working with and for the husband, children, and any elderly person in their household, as well as for their own future, women's pleasures at present are not exceedingly great but provide a pleasant life; however, during the past, such cases were rare.

AGING

Rojin (old people) in Japan are individuals over 65 years. When people are over 65 years, they can receive a pension from the government (the annual income is less than 627,200 yen, which means if $1.00 equals 140 yen, the annual pension is $4,480). Of course the different amount received may vary in each case based on individual circumstances.

In 1980 the number of *rojin* was 9.9 percent of the total population (of 120,235,000 individuals). This number will increase in the future, which is a serious problem not only for every household, but also for the entire nation. Of all the *rojin*, 495,000 were bedridden, and among these, 366,000 lived at home, while 99,000 stayed in hospitals. With the increase in the number of *rojin*, whether in hospitals or at home, women's burden and duties became heavier.

According to Confucius and Buddhist philosophy, throughout the years women were taught *sanjyuu* (obedience to the three). It meant that a woman must first obey her father, then her husband, and after her husband's death, she must obey her son, conforming with the teaching of Confucius. This is an old tradition, though even today some women follow this doctrine and remain passive.

Japanese *rojin* of today prefer to live separately from their children. Yet currently 69.8 percent of the women live with their children, as compared with the 59.1 percent of men who do so.

When they have leisure time, *rojin* participate in sports and club activities, gardening, *go* (a Japanese game, similar to checkers), calligraphy, painting, arts and crafts, and listen to lectures on poetry, literature, or the classics, among others. There are numerous groups of *rojin* in cities, towns, and villages where shelters and rooms are provided for them. But the most serious and disturbing problems for the elderly (*rojin*) are money and diseases. *Rojin*'s suicide rates are continually increasing (1980). For example Japanese suicides are the third highest in the world (following Hungary and Austria), with 44.8 women and 51.1 men for each 100,000 persons.

There are many "silver banks," where records are being kept of *rojin* who have superior ability or knowledge in any field. If somebody needs some *rojin*'s knowhow or skill based on an application for assistance or consultation, the bank sends a qualified *rojin* to the applicant. For such services the *rojin* receives money as a remuneration, based on the regulations of the bank.

It is natural that there are many elderly patients who need medical care. Of the total for the nation, 22.8 percent of the *rojin* need medical care. In 1982 there were among the elderly population about 140,000 persons in *rojin*-homes (these are public welfare institutions). Another 10,000 elderly individuals were in private *rojin*-homes, where they had to pay the expensive rates for themselves, and still others were taken care of in hospitals. However, the majority of elderly people were in their own homes, where they received the care of their spouses or their children, which usually meant that it was the woman's job.

WOMEN TODAY: TRADITION AND CHANGE

In ancient Japan man visited a woman's house at night (*tsumadoikon* or marriage visit to a wife). Women aimed to receive the visit of man who had a higher status or class than they had, in order to raise the status of their household. Before the sixth century there were many women who had a high status in the political world; in fact, some rulers were empresses. An interesting parallel was the *amaterasuoomikami* (the highest being) in *takamagahara* (heaven, in Japanese mythology, where many gods and goddesses were living), who was a female. Women's status was not low in ancient Japan. However, after the influences of Confucius and the Buddhist religion and philosophy women's status changed and held a lower rank until today.

Women have always worked hard and had skills to do many things and perform numerous duties, but their hard work was hidden behind men's activities. Women remained in the background and worked unobtrusively; that was the appropriate manner for women.

After the end of the Meiji era new thoughts and customs intruded that came from the Western world. They taught that there was equality between man and woman. Many social movements were instigated to achieve women's rights for equality. Since World War II, women's status has clearly changed. The right for women to vote was first instituted in December 1945. Although State Universities did not admit women as students before the war, they have done so since the war. From then on, women were accepted as students.

"Women have power," as many people are saying. Nowadays, generally speaking, women are working and acting energetically in many different areas. The conditions for women are changing now gradually, though many elderly women even now continue in the traditional ways without any changes. One can find two different types of life-styles for women: one, mainly followed by the younger group, is toward a trend of modernity, and the other includes the older women, who lean toward the traditional ways.

CONCLUSION

Many Japanese women now actively work outside the home to get an income for their households, while they are enjoying the opportunity to participate in a variety of group activities. such as sports, arts and crafts, as well as many kinds of skills, and attend lectures. Japanese women want their children to receive higher education in order to be successful in business or a profession. However, some women show hesitation or are reluctant to pursue some activities openly. This is a traditional trend in Japanese women, which was the appropriate custom for many years throughout the history of Japan. However, at present women are trying to experience many new patterns of behavior. After they have tried out and sampled these new experiences, they can create new life-styles for the modern Japanese woman.

REFERENCES

Itasaka, G. (Ed.). (1983). *Encyclopedia of Japan*, 8 vols. Tokyo: Kodansha.

Keizaikikakuchou Toukeika (Economic Planning Agency, Statistics Bureau). (1985). *Kokumin Seikatsu Hakusho* (White Paper on the National Standard of Living). Tokyo: Ookurasho-Insatsukyoku. (Ministry of Finance, Printing Board).

Kouseishou (Ministry of Welfare). (1985). *Kousei Hakusho* (White Paper on Social Welfare). Tokyo: Ookurasho-Insatsukyoku. (Ministry of Finance, Printing Board).

Nihon Fujindantai Rengoukai (Japanese Association of Women's Organizations). (1985). *Fujin Hakusho* (White Paper on Women). Tokyo: Horupu Shuppan (Horupu Publishing Co.).

Soumuchou Seishounentaisakuhonbu (Management & Coordination Agency, Youth Affair Administration). *Seishounen Hakusho* (White Paper on Youth). Tokyo: Ookurasho-Insatsukyoku. (Ministry of Finance, Printing Board).

Soumuchou Toukeika (Management & Coordination Agency, Statistics Bureau). (1984). *Kokusai Toukei Youran* (International Statistical Data). Tokyo: Kousei Toukei Kyokai (Association of Statistics on Social Welfare).

Woman weaving a mat from pandanus leaves while another woman watches

Photo credit: Dr. Corey J. Muse

Girl (7 years) taking care of a sibling (3 years) and another child

Photo credit: Dr. Corey J. Muse

16

Women in Western Samoa

Corey J. Muse

Children in Western Samoa enter life with a humble prayer: *Ia tupu i se fasi*, "May he grow in a swamp."

Western Samoa is a South Pacific island nation of Polynesians, who dwell atop hard volcanic outcroppings covered by lush vegetation that belies the difficulty with which sustenance is wrested from the earth. Tree crops are rooted in topsoil a mere 50 centimeters deep, yet subsistence farming is the primary way of life for the majority of the 160,500 inhabitants. The soil is quickly leached of nutrients by constant warm temperatures, high humidity and high precipitation. It is in swamps that plants thrive best, and the prayer asks that newborn children, like the swamp plants, will have the nourishment necessary to thrive, grow strong, and mature without complications. What has often been described as idyllic simplicity is in reality a hardrock complex society with several levels of intercourse that can both enrich and confound the potential of the newborn.

In Samoa a newborn female faces a decidedly different path than a newborn male. Traditionally, when the umbilical cord was separated from the newborn female child it was buried under a mulberry tree to ensure her being industrious at household tasks (Mead, 1928); the division of labor and sex-typing in Samoan society was thus determined. The mulberry bark, the cloth from which tapa is made, is the ceremonial cloth of traditional value along with the *ie toga*, a delicately woven mat. In contrast, the umbilical cord of a newborn male child was planted under a taro plant or thrown into the sea that he might become a good farmer or fisherman. From this beginning women came to be assigned "work that is light, clean and focused on the central village and household areas. By contrast, work that is heavy, dirty or associated with the bush or other areas peripheral to the central village is more clearly men's work" (Shore, 1982). While this is a traditional division of labor, there are occasions when a role reversal is both possible and desirable, but the process of sex-role typing began at birth.

Infant babies sleep with their mother as long as they are nursing; they are at the mother's breast without great regularity—whenever they cry. When no longer nursing, however, an older "sister" is charged with the care and nurturance of the infant until it is four or five years of age or until the "sister" is old enough to take on heavier chores. Since the basic unit of Samoan life is the *aiga*, or extended family consisting of members by blood, marriage or adoption, there are often several "sisters" or "brothers" who can be given the responsibility of infant care. Life for the infant child is one of few constraints but nearly total constant care. Each family household may include both blood relatives and adopted members living in or near the family dwelling (*fale*), and each household or family is headed by at least one chief (*matai*) who is appointed by consensus of the adults and represents them in the village council. The *matai* is responsible for all the household members, overseeing family affairs, directing use of family land, and assigning tasks according to age and sex. Though *matai* hold great power over individual lives, often within the household age rather than relationship determines disciplinary authority. Mothers hold daughters responsible and older sisters hold younger sisters responsible; thus, the newborn is subject to every individual in the household until a younger child arrives. While feelings toward one another within the family are very strong, parent-child relationships are somewhat diffused since any older family member has the authority to discipline and shape a child's behavior. M. Mead (1928) accurately described the early training of small children as ranging from "indifference" to "non-malicious stoning" in which pebbles taken from the *fale* floor are tossed in the direction of children who might be disturbing adult conversation; however, no Samoan infant or child is without love and affectionate care from an adult.

Life for an infant is largely spent on the floor of the *fale*, for that is where much of Samoan life is conducted. Infants crawl or toddle about investigating the laps of adults seated there, or sleeping mats, food being served, games being played, business being conducted, and evening home worship services. The infant child's early training is simple. They must learn to be quiet, to be housebroken, and to know the rudiments of social intercourse. Certain ceremonial objects are not to be touched (e.g., the kava bowl and cup), and they must learn never to address an adult from a standing position, and to treat fire and knives with respect. Specific instructions on appropriate behavior are infrequent or absent; most early social behavior is learned primarily through observation. Indeed, the complex social structure, with its attending respect language, responsibility, and deference to authority, is learned by watching from afar. Much of what the infant child must learn constitutes behaviors that are to be avoided and these are enforced by loud admonitions and a few substantial cuffings. Most transgressions are quickly forgotten and when inappropriate behaviors persist beyond socially implicit age levels, they are met with more severe punishments and explanations that she or he "does not yet know."

While small girls are given the task of caring for the babies and younger children, some small boys may also be given that task if no girl is available; however, the duration of their responsibility is limited. Little girls must also learn to pick up litter, gather flowers to string, bring water, roll the pandanus leaves for weaving, weave simple toys for infants to play with, and put away sleeping mats each morning. Little boys are given more cooperative group tasks, often assisting older boys at the plantation or fishing. Mead (1928) concluded, arguably, that boys, because of group activities, organize quickly while the girls, because they are baby-tending and cannot accompany older females, are innocent of any skills that lead to efficient cooperation. Small girls must learn early that modesty is expected; genitalia and upper thighs are to be covered. Small boys may run about partially or wholly naked until eight or nine years of age except when going to school or church.

Samoans live most of their lives in a very public setting. The absence of walls in traditional Samoan houses encourages social interaction; indeed, social etiquette is highly differentiated and Samoan children in a traditional village become finely attuned to this complex social field and the importance of proper discourse. It is impossible for a Samoan to converse without knowing the necessary contextual discriminations required of the setting—whether they are speaking to a chief (*matai*), a village orator (*tulafale*), or a pastor (*faifai'au*), each of which requires role-specific language. Language, or literacy, as used by Duranti and Ochs (1983), is fundamental to what they call the primary socialization of children. Verbal ability is a highly desirable skill in Samoan culture. Most ceremonies are long events—heavily competitive verbal exchanges laced with historical and political etiquette. Children are expected to listen and observe the proceedings. Except in households where family members have been outside the islands, few Samoan children are exposed to children's books or stories, although elders often recite traditional Samoan myths or read Bible stories during the daily evening worship hour. Formal literacy instruction begins at age three or four, when children rise before sun-up to receive instruction under the tutelage of village pastors and their wives. Usually commencing with a Western alphabet and passages from the Bible, memorization and recitation are the dominant strategies for learning.

Once formal school begins, life for Samoan children becomes more regulated. They rise before dawn, prepare for school and arrive just as the sun appears above the horizon. The early morning hours are cooler, but the day warms rapidly and European-style schoolrooms become hot and humid by mid-morning. The school day ends shortly after noon and the children return to their homes where they must then complete assigned chores. When the leaves have been picked up, the coconuts harvested from the plantation, and other chores are finished, nearly all the children and youth in every village will find volleyball, cricket, or rugby games to participate in until the village *logo*, or gong, is rung or a conch is blown, signaling that the evening quiet or worship hour has begun. Families gather for prayers, worship, study, or family activities—often checkers or *suipi*, a fast-paced card game. Older children then complete what school work they may have or visit friends, sing songs, and play the guitar or ukelele. The sleeping mats are then rolled

out and mosquito nets hung; the lights often remain on all night, illumi-
nating the sleeping families. For adults there are usually choir practices,
worship services, or village meetings to attend and for some, trips into
Apia for music and dancing.

Compulsory attendance laws require children to attend village, district,
or denominational schools from age 5 to 17. The format and curriculum
are very similar to the New Zealand system of education. For four
decades the New Zealand government had administrative jurisdiction
over Western Samoa, chartered by the League of Nations. Western
Samoa became an independent Polynesian nation in 1962, a member of
the British Commonwealth in 1972, and a member of the United Nations
in 1977; much of New Zealand's influence remains evident today in
government agencies. Recent educational policies have led to changes
tailored more specifically to Samoan goals. Data from the Commonwealth Secretariat reports an adult literacy rate of 98 percent, though
most reading is confined to scripture and religious material, along with
newsprint. Among the younger generations educational attainment is
generally higher for females than males, a marked contrast with those
aged 40 and over. For example, among the 20-24 age group 67 percent
of the females had obtained upper secondary level leaving certificates,
compared with 55 percent of the males. During the 1971-81 decade the
proportion of school-age population in the 10-14 age group decreased
only 2 percent for females, but 18 percent for males. More females
attend school and remain longer than male students. Department of
Education data indicate that of the female students in secondary school
at Form V and beyond, 60 percent attend mission or parochial schools.
Of the more academically capable, those in upper form 5 and 6, three-
quarters attend parochial schools. Since 1979 the government has
conducted two- and three-year teacher training colleges, preparing
primary and secondary school teachers respectively (Thomas &
Postlethwaite, 1984). Teaching, as in many countries, has become
largely a woman's occupation in recent years. Seventy percent of the
1,458 primary school teachers and nearly half of the 458 secondary
school teachers in Western Samoa are women. More current data would
suggest an even larger ratio of women to men working as classroom
teachers today.

The explicit division of labor along gender lines is reinforced throughout the life-span. As young girls reach pubescence, their responsibilities
broaden to include other activities located near the central village such
as: (1) learning to weave practical items essential for household comfort
and, later, the more difficult and highly valued ceremonial *'ie toga*, or
fine mats; (2) assisting in the preparation of more specialized food;
(3) doing the family laundry; (4) learning the various aspects of looking
after village guests, dances, or ceremonial functions. Young boys,
meanwhile, tend the family *maumaga*, or farm, by planting taro,
harvesting coconuts and bananas, preparing and cooking the basic food
for meals and ceremonies, learning the ceremonial requirements for
village leadership, and serving the *matai* in various assignments.

Life in a Samoan village centers around the family economic, social, and spiritual needs. Understanding village life requires understanding the village structure and the function of the extended family. Local authority rests in the hands of the village Council of Chiefs whose responsibilities includes maintaining the *fa'asamoa*, or Samoan way, which places great importance on the dignity and achievements of the group rather than on its individual members. Each village will also have at least one Women's Committee. Originating during the 1920s these committees, led by the wife of the senior or ranking *matai*, include in their membership all the village women and girls who are no longer in school. From the beginning, the Women's Committee was charged primarily with the health and sanitation of the village, making certain the village water source remained unpolluted. However, more recently they are concerned with village presentability and making certain guest facilities are appropriate. In some villages Women's Committees now sponsor monthly maternal and infant welfare clinics, nutrition seminars, and engage in fund-raising activities for various school-, church-, or health-related projects. Much of the work is carried out through subcommittees. Committee members make regular inspections of village households in many villages, focusing on codes of cleanliness in and near bathing pools, waste disposal facilities, and latrines. In short, these committees are primarily engaged in looking to the quality of village life.

Other women's organizations include the *Faletua ma Tausi*, or Chiefs' wives, who, like their husbands, provide village-wide leadership of women's activities. The wives of untitled men may also be organized but, as B. Shore (1982) states, their function is less "corporate." Their group participation in the village weaving house is frequently correlated with that of the chiefs' wives. Perhaps the oldest and most distinct women's organization is the *Aualuma*, or village girls' group, which is confined to unmarried females born and reared in the village. The *Aualuma* functions primarily in ceremonies, entertaining, and looking to the comfort of village guests. Leadership in this organization is provided by the *taupou*, who is ideally the daughter or direct-line niece of the village High Chief. Shore (1982) concludes that "nowadays, many of the functions of the *aualuma* seem to have been assumed by the Women's Committee."

Where the life of women is centered on the quality of village life, it is perhaps slightly less utilitarian than the focus of male activities. It is certainly more on the aesthetic elements, putting things into proper order by containing disorder. Traditionally, women's work produced woven mats for domestic comfort and cleanliness in Samoan homes and, more importantly, for the absolutely essential Samoan exchange ceremonies. Great value is placed on the *'ie toga*, *'ie loga*, and *tapa* which are fundamental to hospitality and status during the investiture of titles, weddings, visiting guests, funerals, dedication of buildings, and inter-family or inter-village negotiations. A single *'ie toga*, of high quality may take as long as two years to weave. The *'ie toga*, or fine mat, is woven of very fine strips of specially prepared pandanus leaves; the result is a soft and very pliable mat. Truly superior fine mats may measure three by four meters and are very highly prized for their age and number of times they were exchanged during special occasions. The quality and number of fine mats a family owns are tangible evidence of family power and wealth. As the occasion demands, greater display is made—that is, at the marriage of the High Chief's daughter to the son of another High Chief many very valuable mats and tapa will be exchanged. Because of the constant exchange of mats, it is necessary for the women of the family to continue weaving new ones and young girls are trained by older family females to do this. Indeed, great family pride is taken in the ability of their women to weave exceptional mats. Traditionally, this skill and the continual weaving of fine mats was the central and most important activity of the village women; more recently, however, it is becoming less central as young women are finding employment away from the village and more attuned to a cash economy.

When entering Samoan villages, visitors will see Samoan women weaving together and enjoying the company of each other. Samoans, for the most part, do not like being alone. If they do like it, they seldom admit to it publicly. To be alone appears to be equated with being lonely and sociability is a strongly approved Samoan value. Indeed, Samoans are inclined to consider the social contextual conditions of a given experience to give meaning to it. There is no Samoan term parallel to the English word "self." Samoan personal identity is derived almost exclusively from external feedback rather than from internal motivations. (See B. Shore (1982) for an excellent discussion of this Samoan characteristic.) The emphasis is on perception of social relations and a concomitant and persistent social awareness of contextual relationships. In a well-run village, life is highly ordered; lives are protected by customary institutions and social relations. Role functions and expecta- tions are clearly understood. All villagers are subjected to explicit constraints on their personal behavior through village regulations, government laws, and, most importantly, language. The Samoan language is full of precise distinctions associated with rank and degrees of politeness and deference. Samoans are sensitive to nuances of status, rivalry, and rank; they are also very quick to show deference to clear superiors, but equally quick to take offense at perceived slights to their own position. Self-identity is the conditioned product of these social perceptions, relationships, and contextual references. Personal experi- ence is rarely discussed except in a social context, and a person is understood in terms of different sides of her or his personality, with social context shaping the perceived sides. Shore (1982) explains, correctly, that "there is no absolute reference point for personal identity outside any social context." They are very competitive even while being nearly totally committed to the *fa'asamoa*, which is based upon communal ownership and sharing. Of great importance to the *fa'asamoa* is loyalty and service to the extended family. Therefore, preferred activities are those in which other family members are participants, whether cooperative or competitive, and where feedback is made possible, particularly from family members. This is best illustrated in the traditional form of dance and the nearly exclusive preference for team sports or games as opposed to individual sports.

Though the preference for cooperative activity is the source for personal identity, gender tasks and responsibilities are pervasive in Samoan thought. Female activity is traditionally located near the places where they live, restricting the boundaries of interaction. Male activities are more aggressive, explorative, and require movement within and away from the village center, allowing wider boundaries. Girls are expected to remain in or near the home to help the other women, while boys are expected to be away and thus freely roam more widely and enjoy fewer restrictions. Girls, then, learn to associate a large set of complex attitudes and behaviors such as remaining in or near the village, modesty in dress, deportment, and etiquette; boys are relatively free of constraints. Of particular significance to Samoan youth are the complex cross-sex relationships that begin in early childhood between brothers and sisters and continue as a model for cross-sex relations throughout the Samoan life-span. The relationship between brother and sister, or cross-sex bond, is based on *alofa* (love), *fa'aaloalo* (respect), *ma* (shame), and *amio teuina* (self-control of behavior). This bond requires passiveness, avoidance of intimate contact, shyness, and lack of aggressive displays (Shore, 1982). Shore clarifies this relationship and generalizes to encompass all complementary relations:

> Sexual drives and acts are considered the quintessential example of aggression and impulse gratification. Many of the terms used to refer colloquially to sexual intimacy suggest this aggressiveness: *pi'i* (wrestle), *fai mea leaga* (do evil things), *fai le amio* (do the behavior). Others are merely neutral in this respect: *ta'aalo* (play) *toto le tiapula* (plant the taro shoot). The English expression "make love" would suggest the very opposite of sexual relations to a Samoan for *alofa* is frequently given as the very reason for avoiding sexual relations, at least before marriage. Even sexual relations between married couples, while obviously not disapproved of, are described in their functional aspect. They are, in their most polite euphemism, *fai 'aiga* (making a family).

All of these cultural applications are precisely the opposite to those a male has in relating to a sister; they are the justifications for the prohibition of incest. Samoans frequently condemn premarital sex as it demonstrates the lack of *alofa* for the partner. Girls are often generalized as sisters because of the extended family and therefore sexual contact between brothers and sisters is wrong.

The relationship between brother and sister is understood by the term *feagaiga*, a covenant bond which serves as a very forceful model for

Samoans from early childhood through the life-span. In this model, the sister's relation to her brother is to be *mamalu*, or dignified, while the brother's role requires showing her *alofa* and *fa'aaloalo*, or love and respect, through concern for her physical and social welfare. Both will avoid any direct contact with one another, and both will generally behave as if ashamed in each other's presence. Traditional behavior expectations of the brother was honor for his sister through service, care, and protection. He was expected to move about *(gaioioi)* in looking to her needs. She was expected to stay put *(nofonofo),* accepting his efforts and service. This uneven relationship is, as Shore (1982) puts it, one of "asymmetrical exchange, the sister providing the bond with dignity and public presentability, the brother supplying the energy, strength, and movement." In the presence of his sister the usually somewhat unconstrained brother controls himself, is shy and solicitous. The sister, whose welfare and chastity in particular are her brothers' concerns, is less inhibited, tending to be more assertive, demanding, and demonstrative toward her brother. A legitimate norm-reversal occurs in which although

> the sister may stand symbolically for dignity and passivity, it is the brother who is clearly the more passive of the pair in brother-sister encounters. It is through a generalization of their dignified role as sisters that Samoan women seem to gain a remarkable energy and assertiveness, which appears to contradict their symbolic significance. Likewise, it is the experience of men as brothers that renders them shy and deferential in situations. (Shore, 1982)

The shyness and deferential respect a male has appears to underlie all relations and is founded in the early brother-sister model. It is, however powerful, an unsteady model as the sister's assertiveness contradicts the otherwise dignified restraint expected of her, and the brother's shyness is energy contained rather than timidity or weakness. Given certain circumstances, shyness and restraint give way to violent reactions, particularly if the sister's brother catches her in intimate contact with a lover; the sister's dignity, and hence her brother's, has been compromised, provoking a violent verbal and physical reaction toward the lovers.

There are three forms of unmarried relationships between Samoan youth other than the brother-sister bond: the clandestine encounter, the published marriage announcement or elopement, and the *moetotolo*, or sleep crawling. Mead (1928) described all three forms in detail. More recent elaborations by D. Freeman (1983) and L. Holmes (1987) indicate quite different perceptions regarding marriage and the controversial sleep crawling, described by some as rape. All writers, however, agree that a certain amount of sexual freedom is enjoyed by Samoan youth, though probably no more than in most other contemporary cultures dominated by Christian moral precepts and traditional values centered on female chastity and virtue. Some U.S.-style dating occurs on a very infrequent basis. There is virtually no negative stigma associated with unwed motherhood and the offspring are always welcomed into the extended family and loved.

Samoan women marry at about 20 years of age and men at 25. Traditionally, some marriages in Samoa were arranged to consolidate political power and influence associated with male and female descent lines through family titles. Few, if any, arranged marriages occur today. More typically, courtship proceeds from clandestine rendezvous arranged by the boy's *soa*, or intermediary, to a more formal or public announcement as the couple becomes more compatible. The *soa* is a trusted friend whose function through the early stages parallels that of the *tulafale* for the *ali'i*, or chief. The *soa* speaks for the boy and stands guard against unwise decisions that could lead to social and physical dangers. Here, however, the parallel ends.

Following the formal announcement both families begin preparations for the marriage. This requires a traditional engagement period during which the families make preparations; the girl's family must see to the exchange of *'ie toga*, *tapa*, and sleeping mats, while the boy's must focus on the collection of money and making a wedding dress for the bride to wear at the wedding feast. Most weddings are first conducted in a civil ceremony before a judge and are then followed by a church or religious ceremony. The wedding festivities following the ceremony are occasions for speech-making by the *tulafale*, or talking chiefs, of each family. Speeches generally contain historical information, religious approval, and traditional admonitions; they are followed by dancing, singing, and feasting by both families. The exchange of wedding gifts, which are not given to the bride and groom, occurs later after both families have accumulated the quality and number of gifts appropriate to their status and family titles. The bride's family must bring numerous *'ie toga* and *tapa* to the groom's family, for the gifts are between families and the *'ie toga* is a measure of the female family's wealth in terms of labor by the women of the family. The male exchange, in the form of food and money, or *'oloa*, symbolically represents the direct product of material needs extracted from the earth through work. (For a complete discussion of the *toga* and *'oloa* see Gilson, 1970 and Shore, 1982). Shore writes that this formal exchange symbolizes the affine relation in which "*toga* constitutes a kind of dowry, moving with the bride from her group to that of the groom. *'Oloa* represents a kind of bride price, given by the groom's family to that of the bride." Inherent in the wedding reciprocal exchange is a complex set of intricate social factors regarding what is described as bride-side and groom-side political linkages. The Samoan maternal descent group is called *tamafafine*, while the paternal is called *tamatane*. The exchange of gifts at ceremonies such as weddings is a complementary exchange as opposed to symmetrical as it forms an alliance between the *tamafafine* and *tamatane* descent groups. It is, in C. Levi-Strauss' (1966) terms, complementary because it is ritual rather than competitive. R. Gilson (1970) explains that "marriage itself conveyed no absolute right to political support, but once a child was born of a union, bridging the two linkages by virtue of his dual descent, conditions for the formation of an interlinkage alliance were especially favorable" (p. 45).

Thus the bride is a probationary member of the groom's *aiga* and fully incorporated only after producing a child. The *'ie toga* and *'oloa* are symbolic of the affiliations and the political alliance between them; they are neither competitive nor disjunctive.

The majority of people in Samoa sustain themselves by subsistence and some cash-crop farming. A subsistence economy is virtually wholly dependent on the amount of usable land space, and Samoa is no exception. The Samoan islands lie between 12° and 15° south of the equator and just east of the International Dateline. Consisting of 3 main islands and 14 smaller ones, the archipelago, stretching over 600 miles, is of volcanic origin and rises sharply from a narrow coastal plain to abrupt mountain peaks. The surrounding ocean, coral reef, and rising coastal plain provide the primary source of food; men and women are often seen gathering seafood from the reef. The major land area for agriculture is confined to the coastal plains, with successive growth areas set aside for crops congenial to the terrain. However, the mountainous topography and basalt rock make farming a most difficult occupation. In 1899, seven islands of eastern Samoa came under U.S. jurisdiction when Germany, the United Kingdom, and the United States of America resolved a dispute over rights of claim. The first European contact had been made by the Dutch explorer Jacob Roggeveen in 1722, but settlement did not occur until 1832, 110 years later, when John Williams of the London Missionary Society landed intent on converting the islanders to Christianity. Arriving in what is now Western Samoa, Williams was greeted warmly not for his religion, but in the manner in which any visitor would be greeted according to Samoan custom. The Samoan way requires an open and warm hospitality, offering food and comfort to those weary from travel. Williams was very successful and his form of Protestant Christianity was soon well established among the families of Samoa. From the 1840s, Germany, the United Kingdom, and the United States of America, intent on developing and protecting their commercial and economic interests, often exploited internal rivalries between important traditional Samoan families. Political and economic interests of these major nations intensified, leading to the signing of conventions which gave administration of the Western islands to Germany and left the Eastern islands in U.S. hands. The people of Samoa were infrequently consulted. Between 1900 and 1914 the German administration established large commercial cocoanut plantations on Upolu, the second largest island and most densely populated. These plantations significantly contributed to the economic development of the country and effectively influenced the existing subsistence economy. The copra industry had little immediate effect on the social structure of Samoan village life. Though copra was to become the major export commodity, bananas and cocoa were added at a later time.

In 1914 New Zealand was given a mandate by the League of Nations to administer the islands and guide them to independence. Nearly 50 years later, in 1962, Western Samoa became the first South Pacific island nation to achieve independence. Eastern Samoa, or American Samoa, remained a territorial trust administered through the U.S. Department of the Interior. Though the sister islands were separated having common origins, they are now substantially different, with the dominant influence of the past decades clearly evident in their formal governance. Culturally and linguistically, however, they have remained remarkably unified, reflecting in part the kinship and political alliances that have persisted even while the islands have been administratively separated. The persistence of the *fa'asamoa* allows the Samoan people to move between islands frequently and adjust to differences rapidly and comfortably. The *fa'asamoa*, or Samoan way, remains the underlying foundation on which political governance rests and social intercourse flows, both in the islands and in foreign lands.

In 1983 population data in Western Samoa indicated a low annual growth rate of 0.8 percent, significantly lower than the previous census data, which was attributable to a continuing high outmigration to overseas destinations. Outmigration on an extensive basis began to accelerate in the mid-1960s; by 1976 national estimates reported that more than 27,000 Western Samoans had migrated to New Zealand alone. During the 1974-83 decade, net outmigration averaged nearly 2,700 per annum to New Zealand. In 1983 immigration officials reported that 45 percent of the outmigrants were females, of whom nearly half were seeking better employment opportunities. Accurate outmigration data to the United States of America are difficult to substantiate. Western Samoans are required to obtain entry visas in American Samoa prior to departure for the U.S. west coast and Hawaii; however, many obtain various entry permits initially and then change their status after arrival by virtue of their concept of family membership and relationship. Church and school records indicate large communities of both Western and American Samoans holding U.S. passports and visas in west coast cities in excess of 125,000. MacPherson and Pitt (1974) identified increased opportunities for position improvement, social mobility, and education for their children as the primary motivation for leaving Western Samoa. In terms of impact on population size, outmigration has reduced the potentially high population increase in Western Samoa that would have resulted from the combination of a high birth rate and a low death rate in 1975 to the existing moderate levels in 1986.

As in many developing countries the age structure in Western Samoa is characterized by a young population, and the proportion under the age of 15 appears to be declining. This age group, which comprised just over half the total population in 1971, had fallen to 44.3 percent in 1981. At the other end of the age scale, the number and proportion of people over 60 has been rising; the overall dependent population remains high. Forty-seven percent of the total population is female. During the decade 1971-81 the proportion of women of childbearing ages (15-44) increased by 15 percent. Therefore, other things being equal, this would have been conducive to a rise in the number of births and the crude birth rate; however, potential was not realized as there was a decline in the fertility rate. Women aged 26-29 had an average of 2.1 children in 1981, as compared with 2.7 and 3.2 during 1976 and 1971, respectively.

At the time of the 1981 census there were approximately 87,000 persons in Western Samoa in the 15-60 age group—or potential labor force—which reflected an 11 percent growth from 1976. The potential labor force has been growing more rapidly than the total population in spite of outmigration. Participation in the monetized sector of the economy increased only slightly for males, but increased dramatically for females. According to the Asian Bank data the reverse is true in the subsistence sector. Those in the subsistence sector are "working primarily to grow, gather or catch food to eat," while those employed in the monetized sector work for wages or salaries. There has been a continuing trend of labor moving from the subsistence into the monetized sector, due largely to growing numbers in the 15-19 age group pursuing some form of education. Since a larger proportion of females were continuing through secondary schools, a concomitant increasing number were moving from activities in food production to service and commercial activities. At the time of the 1981 census, 19 percent of the females in this age group described themselves as engaged in education or training and most of the remainder declared themselves as working in household duties.

The continued importance of agriculture in the overall economy is reflected in the fact that nearly two of every three males are working in food production and related aspects. The number of females is much smaller and decreasing. The major increasing occupational opportunities for females, consistent with their educational achievement, lie in professional, technical, or teaching areas. Though women are moving to the monetized sector of the economy, their achievement is not reflected in top management positions in Western Samoa; the number of women at middle management levels in private enterprise and public service in both Western and American Samoa is significant, however. There has been no substantial increase in the number of women participating in national politics over the last ten years. Only two women hold seats as full members of parliament in Western Samoa, nine women are recorded working as medical doctors, and there are large numbers of women in unskilled and semiskilled wage labor positions. One unmeasured wage labor area is that of domestic services, where many women are also employed. Their contribution to the non-wage sector of subsistence and commercial agriculture is of great significance, but remains essentially unquantified.

Though two-thirds of the male labor force in Western Samoa work in agriculture as small farmers cultivating land near the villages to grow root and tree crops for consumption and cash-cropping, relatively few engage in farming aimed at commercial exporting per se. Even fewer females engage in this activity. Decreasing world markets and inflated transportation costs have significantly curtailed wider participation by either sex. The proportion of females engaged in agriculture-related industry in 1981 (16 percent) was less than half the corresponding number ten years previous; females engaged in social and personal service industries, however, grew to 54 percent during the same time period.

The people of Western Samoa are the largest essentially pure Polynesian group in the Pacific, though the population includes other Pacific islanders, some Chinese, and Europeans. The basic unit of Samoan life is the *aiga*, or extended family, headed by at least one high chief, or *matai*, who is appointed by consensus of the extended family. Nearly 10 percent of the population hold *matai* titles and of these, 400 are women. The *matai* are given responsibility for directing the use of family land and overseeing other family affairs. They hold enormous power over individual lives. To a large degree the status and social position of most women is determined by their location and the dominant life-style of a particular village. Women living in or near Apia, in non-traditional villages, often work in Apia as wage earners, many having migrated from rural villages where wages are not associated with daily work. These urban women usually maintain the social practice of belonging to a women's group by joining civic or service organizations. The social status of rural women, more so than urban women, is highly influenced by the traditional social stratification system based on the ranking of their husbands in the village hierarchy. Rural Women's Committees are concerned with improving the quality of village life; they are neither unemployed nor economically dependent, for their responsibilities are clearly defined. Women's Committees are structurally subordinate to the village council; however, they are effectively autonomous as their activities and duties are almost always respected by the men who generally refrain from intervening in their activities (Schoeffel, 1978). The organization and social structure effectively provides for the extended family and villagers. Carefully defined formal and informal social relationships prevent the rigid classification of "rural poor" or "disadvantaged" in Samoan culture for virtually no Samoan is without a home, work responsibility, and/or food. According to the 1981 census, about 20 percent of the total households in Western Samoa are headed by women; however, this group is not seen or recorded as disadvantaged because they are absorbed into the environment of the extended family with all its support systems in the islands and with expatriates in the United States of America and New Zealand.

As in other developing countries, a relatively high fertility rate existed in Western Samoa, such that the government took steps to influence the potential population growth. A national policy was adopted which established a Family Planning Program aimed primarily at women. Traditional attitudes, both male and female, militating against the application of family planning have persisted. The success of the program has been limited, particularly in rural areas where instruction on family planning has been sporadic. The more significant aspect of the program included a carefully explained educational presentation with a comprehensive rural emphasis aimed at changing traditional attitudes about large families providing the necessary plantation labor. Another national policy encouraged women to develop various incentive schemes that would enable them to pursue economic goals while still maintaining their traditional concerns about the quality of village life. To date this aspect of the policy has been but partially implemented.

The Government of Western Samoa adopted a number of policies that affected employment and development opportunities for women such as equal employment opportunities for both sexes. As in many economically dependent island countries, legislation aimed at creating jobs has been necessary, particularly as the rise in general educational level demanded increases in jobs consistent with the training and skills women in particular have achieved. Since a higher proportion of females than males are completing secondary education requirements, the need for new jobs for women becomes all the more crucial as they move from village subsistence sectors to the monetary sector of the economy.

A multisectoral approach centering on women was written into the *Government of Western Samoa Fourth Five-Year Development Plan, (1980-84)* which was designed to provide an appropriate mechanism for the integration of women more completely into the national development process. Rural women were especially encouraged to participate as widely as possible. The government sponsored technical and advisory services in such diverse areas as maternal and child health education programs, gardening, and mariculture industry. Women were, and are, encouraged to submit proposals for government-funded projects in rural development, marketing, and trade cooperatives. The lack of expertise, leadership, and the traditional Samoan social hierarchy impeded the success of cooperatives, whether staffed by males or females.

Policies establishing rural development programs often serve to disadvantage women in many developing societies because women generally are seen to perform essentially non-commercial productive services in or near their homes. This is especially true in Western Samoa where women traditionally centered much of their work indoors, such as weaving and sewing. Planning projects supported by rural development funding tend toward the acquisition of skills, knowledge, or technology that are associated with male productive tasks rather than female. In Western Samoa the contribution of women to subsistence and cash-cropping carried less prestige and, reflecting the traditional division of labor along sexual lines, was viewed as being of less importance. The increasing monetization of the economy has begun to change this condition, as women are assuming a greater role in providing supplemental family incomes. Home-produced handicrafts for both domestic and tourist trade, sold at government markets, have now become a substantial part of the weekly schedule for women in rural villages. Indeed, some women now hold labor roles complementary to men in marketing, agriculture, fisheries, forestry, and government service.

The two major thrusts of the Rural Development Program in Western Samoa, aimed at the village level, are economic (agriculture, fishing and small business, and social; these involve changes in village infrastructure and provision of social services), and organizational activities of village life. When it awards support of rural project proposals the Samoan government considers the nature of the village organization making the proposal and its potential ability for implementing the project. Two factors affect project approval: first, the land tenure system which encourages village projects that are suitable and commensurate with traditional land divisions, but which do not create controversy or litigation between families over land titles that usually accompany *matai* titles; and second, whether projects to be undertaken are extraneous to the functioning village leadership and will *avoid* long-term use of substantial land resources.

The rural development projects in general are based on communal participation, consistent with the traditional village council form of local government whenever possible. The Women's Committees and youth organizations have participated effectively by submitting their own proposals. Women are actively encouraged to submit project proposals and since 1977 they have engaged in various agro-based projects such as livestock raising and gardening. Of the total number of projects undertaken 21 percent have been women's group proposals and, of these, half have been poultry projects. This is a desirable activity because it requires minimal land use and avoids displacing women from their traditional home and family responsibilities. Women involved in poultry egg production have achieved a measure of self-sufficiency that has led to a reduction in import expenditures at both the local and national levels. The success of these projects is attributed to an effective training program and the assimilation of information into useful manuals that are made available to women in villages (Andres, 1980). Of equal interest is the growing number of small crop projects popular among women and youth groups.

Though successful, women in rural settings work under difficult social and structural constraints, according to Natarajan (1983). The women often lack technical expertise in some projects, for example, a communal cattle production project that requires several trained women participants. In some women's projects there has been little evidence of relating project costs to project revenues or, put simply, the lack of financial management skills. The lack of leadership qualities and skills led to the failure of other projects as well. The strong influence that village social hierarchies impose on women has contributed to the failure of otherwise plausible projects, particularly as related to land tenure and ownership rights. The commercial success of some women's projects may also be viewed by some village males as potentially undermining their traditional authority, threatening the existing social and economic balances within the village or district. There is evidence that new adaptations are occurring in village life, adaptations brought about by the growing monetized economy which fosters greater individualism and the lessening of communal ownership and sharing. Sharing is a cornerstone of the *fa'asamoa* so highly valued and protected by village elders. Despite some changing attitudes toward individualism, communal projects remain the preferred mode over individual projects. Certain advantages accrue from submission and approval of communal projects; perhaps most important is that communal projects allow the contributions of all women in the group without impeding their duties to either the project or to their families.

The Department of Agriculture has recognized and encouraged the potential contributions of women toward agricultural production through rural development programs specifically. Agriculture officials have provided women with extension service training in cash cropping of cocoa, copra, and passionfruit. Younger women have been very responsive to this opportunity. Through extension service a program in home economics has also been promoted whose topics have included improving domestic roles, better family nutrition, and women's gardening projects. The latter have become highly visible and productive, with over 700 women producing vegetables for family consumption. Garden projects are small vegetable gardens located adjacent to the family dwellings rather than deeper in the bush, and near water resources. The women construct and protect these gardens with natural wooden barriers, allowing them to control their own vegetable production. Surpluses have been taken to market for family income or purchase of other family commodities.

Extension services have markedly improved village awareness of nutritional alternatives to the limited traditional Samoan diet. During recent years the incidence of infant malnutrition in Western Samoa has increased, causing alarmed medical and nutritional experts to conduct seminars and conferences focused on improving the understanding of village women toward better nutrition, new ways of preparing traditional foods, newly introduced non-traditional vegetables and fruits, and better health hygiene.

In Samoan society prestige increases with advancing age. Elders are respected for their knowledge of the *fa'asamoa*. Presumed to be wise because of their experience and knowledge, the aged are occasionally called upon to give advice to the *matai*. Children are responsible for their elderly parents; usually the sons are responsible for the care of their parents by providing them with food and money, and daughters may take them into their own households to care for them. The elderly are given priority in many daily activities. Having raised large families they are fed first, given duties involving less physical labor such as tending infant grandchildren and weaving mats or thatch for the houses. Old *matai* spend countless hours conversing with one another while rolling and braiding coconut sennit into the vitally important rope used for lashing together the beams of a house or outriggers on a canoe. Old men seem to have less to do than old women but may, as L. Holmes (1987) reports, "often be seen assisting older women in household tasks such as weeding, or making blinds and thatch." Old women are the family genealogical respositories of the family ties, assisting the Council of Chiefs when necessary in making sure appropriate recognition of status and rank is given. Old women continue the traditional making of pigment for tattooing so essential to a young man's preparation for an eventual title. The candle nut burning for tattoo pigment is a ritual taught to younger women by older women and is similar to the function of old men who meet in a *fa'asauga* to discuss the traditional Samoan myths and legends, educating younger men seated nearby. The older women also serve as repositories for traditional medicines and their appropriate applications.

Death usually occurs at home in the village. It is looked upon as another natural event and thus grief is not excessive. The body is prepared in full view of village friends and family while the village *logo* (bell) announces the death. Dressed in white, the body rests upon a white sheet placed on a pile of sleeping mats located at the north end of the oval *fale*. The women of the family sit behind the body to watch over and care for it until the interment 24 hours later. Shortly after the logo announces the death a village choir will arrive, seating themselves in the house. A *tulafale*, talking chief, and member of the choir will give a speech for the dead following the singing of hymns by the choir. In response to the speech, the family *tulafale* gives a speech of gratitude to the choir. The choir then sings another hymn before departing.

The women of the house remain with the body and do not sleep, showing their personal attachment for the deceased. Funerals include the exchange of *'ie toga* and *tapa* from friends, family, and distant relations. Grave sites, usually located near the family house, are decided upon by the family head and are dug by family members and friends. The body is carried to the grave by household members and choir members. The body is laid to rest wrapped in sleeping mats, the sheet upon which the body lay, and the *tapa*. Life began for the women with the mulberry bark cloth and weaving of mats, and life's last ritual includes the same items. Christian services may be conducted by local pastors. Funeral services for women are similar to those of untitled men, which differ from that of titled men only for the number of *'ie toga* exchanged as gifts and the elaborateness of the burial marker. While the funeral services are conducted, the more distant members of the deceased's family cook the food, which is distributed immediately after the funeral ceremony and which is then followed by an exchange of fine mats. Special shares of food are set aside for the *matai*, *faifaiau* (pastor), relatives, friends, and village households. A period of mourning is usually observed which lasts about one year; after that the family head calls an official end.

REFERENCES

Andres, P. (1980). *Evaluation of microprojects in Western Samoa: The lack of linkages.* Paper no. 10. Apia, Western Samoa: University of South Pacific.

Asian Development Bank. (1985). *Western Samoa agriculture sector study: Background and sector review,* vol. 2. Apia, Western Samoa: Asian Development Bank.

Duranti, H., & Ochs, E. (1983). Literacy instruction in a Samoan village. In B. B. Schefflin (Ed.). *Acquisition of literacy: Ethnographic perspectives.* Norwood, NJ: Ablex.

Freeman, D. (1983). *Margaret Mead and Samoa: The making and unmaking of an anthropological myth.* Cambridge, MA: Harvard University Press.

Gilson, R. (1970). *Samoa 1830-1900: The politics of a multi-cultural community.* Melbourne: Oxford University Press.

Government of Western Samoa. (1980). *Development Plan IV 1980-1984.* Apia, Western Samoa: Office of Prime Minister.

Government of Western Samoa. (1981). *Report of the census of population and housing.* Apia, Western Samoa: Department of Statistics.

Holmes, L. (1987). *Quest for the real Samoa.* South Hadley, MA: Bergin and Garvey.

Levi-Strauss, C. (1966). *The savage mind.* Chicago: University of Chicago Press.

MacPherson, C., & Pitt, D. (1974). *Emerging pluralism: The Samoan community in urban New Zealand.* Auckland: Longman and Paul.

Mead, M. (1928). *Coming of age in Samoa.* Middlesex: Penguin Books.

Natarajan, N. (1983). *Rural development projects and women in Western Samoa.* ILO study. Apia, Western Samoa: University of the South Pacific.

Schoeffel, P. (1978). Gender, status and power in Samoa. *Canberra Anthropology, 1*(2), 69-81.

Shore, B. (1982). *Sala'ilua: A Samoan mystery.* New York: Columbia University Press.

Thomas, M., & Postlethwaite, T. (1984). *Schooling in the Pacific islands: Colonies in transition.* New York: Pergamon Press.

Alice Anne Carey scuba diving from the Four Seasons Barrier
Reef Resort in the Great Barrier Reef

Photo credit: Dr. Justin P. Carey

17

Women in Australia

Brian R. Costello and Janet Lee Taylor

Whether genteel aristocrat or impoverished convict, the first Australian woman shared a common goal with her menfolk—survival. Hence the term, "Aussie Battler." She entered combat with a hostile physical and social environment, different from anywhere in the world. Life on the island continent of Australia, with its huge expanse (it is the size of North America) had the added difficulties of communication because of the country's isolation. Although many of her sisters overseas had made similar pioneering voyages, the women who went to Australia traveled to the other end of the earth. Australia was "down under." The sea voyage from England was long and arduous—a treacherous and heart-rending nine months on the high seas only 200 years ago.

European settlement grew from the explicit need to establish a self-sufficient penal settlement colony for England, a new "dumping ground for convicts" because the United States of America had rebelled. The Australian woman evolved through painful exploitation, an unquestioned feature of her early heritage. Later, she blossomed internationally through suffrage to become the first woman in the world to win the vote. Helen Reddy's moving composition, "I Am Woman," which was adopted by the United Nations for International Women's Year (1984), gives a powerful rendition of her unique achievements. Reddy also wrote another song that gained international acclaim, "That Ain't No Way to Treat a Lady."

The Australian woman came from England, the United States of America, Ireland, China, Scotland, Wales; indeed, she came from everywhere.

In 1851 a second wave of settlers arrived during the Gold Rush to find the new "El Dorado" where fortunes were to be won through panning, sluicing, or even stumbling over the mullock heaps of Victoria's Ballarat or Walhalla Gold Fields. The cities of Sydney and Melbourne, like the Gold Field towns, teemed with new arrivals. Australia advertised for women. Because communities grew so quickly, women entered a new stage of social development; with wealth came the desire and need for learning and culture. There was a new culture, thriving and driven, uncertain and overwhelming. Women had emerged from their relatively lowly existence to become land owners and proprietors of small factories and shops. Schools, largely staffed by women produced an influential focus solidly based on traditional ideals of the family. Other women emerged as outback cattle- or sheep-station owners. Together with their husbands they forged a family morality similar to the U.S. pioneers. A sense of worth and achievement had been shared in overcoming hardships, bonding the family unit and community within a Christian philosophy. Freedom was the keynote and religion underlined that freedom as a prime motivating force. (Costello, 1982a)

INFANCY AND EARLY CHILDHOOD

With such high mortality rates generally experienced in those early years of settlement, Australian women have continued to develop priorities in prenatal care. The National Mothers and Babies Association provides educational programs and support together with the Infant Health Care System, which is provided by local government for early neonatal development and monitoring. All mothers are able to receive prenatal care covered by the National Health Program (Medicare) and provided without charge. Infancy and neonatal care have also been given priority through the establishment of daycare centers, allowing working mothers to continue with their careers. While in the early 1950s it was considered inappropriate for married women to work and rather than confine themselves to childrearing and home duties, an exceptional change has evolved such that nowadays the converse applies. The provision of daycare centers illustrates this point. Some centers are provided by local government while others are maintained through private enterprise. Creches are considered to help mothers and children in maintaining a higher standard of living but essentially, all women have the choice of whether they wish to work or not. Women need comprehensive support services to allow them equal access to full participation in the life of the community and in education, training, and the labor force. Women still do most of the parenting and most of the domestic work in the house. While childcare is essential for all parents, women in particular have, through their Advisory Councils, pointed this out to state and federal governments. Capital expenditure of up to 4.8 million dollars by the Victorian state government attracts 5 million dollars in recurrent funding from the federal government. This initiative has provided for badly needed childcare places and provided new jobs.

Parent-child relationships thrive as a result of tender loving care as they do in any country. Through contributing to the quality of life, Australian women have forged a frontier in childcare provisions which simultaneously offer them more access to further opportunities, be these in employment, training, or education.

ACHIEVEMENTS AND CAREER OPPORTUNITIES

From the 1870s to 1900, outback women possessed qualities different from their city counterparts. The situation was problematic because the type of work they did either enhanced or degraded their status. They were "help-mates" or "slaves." "Fictional and documentary accounts abound with explanations of how women's farmwork easily became the occasion for oppression" (Lake, 1985). The 50 years leading up to federation in 1901 assumed a particularly colonial character because the population was predominately emigrants from England, Ireland, and Scotland. Overall, women, some widowed and some married, participated in a surprising range of labor in this period. According to the 1861 census, women worked in such occupations as printers, cattle dealers, bricklayers, bullock drivers, shepherds, and overseers (Baynton, 1902). "Battling just to live in make-shift homes, from farm laborers to gold miners, women were prepared to be adaptable in searching for ways to support themselves and contribute to the subsistence of the family" (Grimshaw, 1985). This characteristic hallmark is still evident today as part of the Australian woman's inheritance, whether a recent refugee arriving last week from less fortunate countries, migrant, or second-generation Australian.

State governments have instituted action plans to improve career opportunities for girls and women. They have removed legislative barriers that prevented women from entering sectors of the labor market and strengthened the position and role of women in the public sector, particularly those in the nursing work force. The Equal Opportunity Act statistical returns reveal that women have achieved increased representation in senior executive positions, as their employment as administrative and professional staff rose from 22 percent in 1985 to 24 percent in 1986. Women now occupy 11 percent of senior management positions. Female representation in non-administration and non-professional categories of the public service has remained, however, at 48.5 percent. On average, female applicants are significantly more successful than male applicants in achieving selections for positions with salaries greater than $20,000.

Further incentives have been given priority, such as resources to develop the Women's Employment Strategy, working parties to report on legislative restrictions, community employment programs, home-based employment projects, Migrant Employment Advisory Units (Women's Policy Co-ordination Unit, 1984).

Australian women must be considered within the context of the country's varying landscapes, to which they have adapted very well.

It is clearly seen that Australian women, having migrated from so many distant shores, have developed varying life-styles. Many of these are culturally based; because they have come from over 60 different countries, one cannot generalize about such a cosmopolitan population. Their achievements are, however, another matter. Being the first women in the world to gain the vote, with New Zealand, Australian women for the first time had a say in the running of their country. They wanted a "fair go" and got it. They prided themselves on living in a society that aimed to give everyone a fair go, but unequal treatment of women and minority groups led the government to pass the Equal Opportunity Act in 1984. The Act defines discrimination on the grounds of: status—which includes sex, marital status, impairment, race, parental status, childless status, and de-facto relationships—and private life, which refers to lawful religious and political beliefs.

Women have successfully promoted equal opportunity through newspapers, videos, posters, the Equal Opportunity Forum, and education programs. Australian women have achieved much by skillfully using both the political and legal systems. This has entailed a lengthy process, but in essence it has provided them even further opportunities and achievements such as access to education (Women's Policy Co-ordination Unit).

THE SCHOOL YEARS

In Australia, all children are given the right to a free education from the ages of 5 through 15 years. Primary and secondary education is legally compulsory for everyone. The majority of children have an opportunity to attend preschool and kindergarten. Tertiary education in Australia is comparatively free should people wish to enter graduate or postgraduate degree courses on a full-time or part-time basis; a Higher Education Contribution Scheme (HECS) requires full-time students to pay, as also sports and union/administration charges apply. Technical and further education vocational programs and technical orientation programs are also offered, virtually free of charge.

In Victoria, there is a move toward increased coeducation through the development of postsecondary schools, replacing the single-sex high schools and technical schools. In this way, girls enter technical courses previously provided only for boys. In Victoria, 25 technical schools became coeducational. The curriculum branch of the Education Department now has a Women and Girls Curriculum Committee to ensure that all curriculum material at primary and secondary level adequately cover education for girls. "Growth in senior high school participation is part of a national trend which will almost certainly continue. Although governments have made planned efforts to encourage participation, the growth probably reflects a general cultural change connected to social and economic changes" (Kirner, 1990).

Given the way in which Australian society has structured the biological imperatives of childbearing into sexual divisions of labor at home and in paid work, women have responded to the trade-off with a compromise between traditional and innovative destinies. The problem is not so much a question of absolute female powerlessness but one of balancing limited and conflicted potency in both domestic and public domains. The most disabling aspect of this socialization of girls is that young women may make the trade-off when their resources in both domains are minimal.

There has been a shift in vocational interests. In a recent study (Costello, 1987), it was revealed that tenth-year female students express an increased preference for mechanical career possibilities, in comparison with literary or clerical careers. A recent study showed that 7 or half of the 14 scores on ACVIIA, male students scored significantly higher than females: Mechanical, Scientific, Management, Agriculture, Crafts, Law/Military and Engineering. Only on three of the scores did female students score *higher* than male: Education, Medical, and Clerical (Costello, 1990).

Women, as parents, teachers, and students, are encouraged to become involved with decision-making processes at all school levels. It is usual for women to participate in school councils where they have strong representation. Ministry Committees on Multicultural and Migrant Education have undertaken research to establish the needs, experiences, and aspirations of girls of ethnic background as a basis for further planning.

For many adult women, access to education is essential. Important avenues are the small Technical and Further Education Providers which include neighborhood houses as well as the larger colleges. These smaller providers are now recognized in the education budget, which consolidates their importance. The Federal Government Participation and Equity Program guidelines encourage schools and Technical and Further Education Providers to analyze and assess the extent to which girls and young women share access to all programs offered by schools, and include the special needs of girls in the mainstream of education resources.

WOMEN IN THE RURAL AUSTRALIAN WORK FORCE

How could women be expected, when living in the bush, to remain in the "sphere of separateness" from the male, when they literally have to "breathe through their noses the same dust likely to fly upwards by their husband's movement, should they happen to be standing next to him?" That is, of course, when he is not away working. Partners who live in the bush still form a congruent relationship, painful and loving, in the midst of the awful hot winds that blow in summer and the "fearful dust-storms." Our women still survive despite the same cruel elements and they are greatly respected, often even above the career woman who is now very successful in professional life.

Ethnic Work Force Components

The Italian migrant women are a case in point. Bear in mind that the experiences, cultures, and traditions of women from northern Europe will be different from those of women who migrated from Italy and

Greece. These are dissimilar yet from cultural differences exhibited by Australian migrant women from the Middle East and Asia. There exists a popular misconception in the Australian community that migrant women do not participate in unions, school activities, or the community generally. Feminists generally insist that it is a submission to the patriarchal authority which prevents their participation in the work force and the women's movement.

The perceived view of patriarchal dominance of migrant families, held by Anglo Saxon feminists, might not offer a full explanation of the migrant woman's voicelessness. The women's movement draws much of its support from a socioeconomic group that is mainly middle class. A balance in views should be perceived by the reader when considering views of the silent majority, rather than the sensationalist articles that indeed highlight the plight of women in the work force. There are women, like men, who are very happy in their jobs and would not want them any other way.

ACHIEVEMENTS FOCUSED ON WOMEN'S VALUES

By the year 1943, Australian-type feminism had a history all its own, older than the British Commonwealth's efforts. The first female members of the Federal Parliament were Dame Enid Lyons of the United Australia Party in the House of Representatives, and Dorothy Tangey of the Australia Labour Party in the Senate. It was a time when the demands of war admitted Australian women, in or out of uniform, to do jobs traditionally denied them in all callings. But a new deal for women was not part of the postwar world. Even in 1972 there were only three women in the Australian Senate and none in the House Of Representatives. Dame Margaret Guilfoile served between 1973 and 1983. By 1984, six women were in the House Of Representatives (Australia, 1987).

Between the years 1981 and 1985 the number of mothers in one-parent families who were not in full-time work increased from 175,700 to 205,200. This statistic must be considered within the wider perspective of the family generally. There have been unsettling influences from unexpected variables such as changes through the Family Law Act (1975). A gradual alteration of values dependent on questions such as, "can we survive as a single-parent family?" have obviously influenced decision making. (Costello, submitted).

Provisions of additional childcare agencies representing a "collective childcare" view have been questioned in terms of the woman single parent (Costello, 1980). Women are concerned about the effects of extramarital relationships on children, and so too are men. There are definite changes within Australian societal mores, reinforced through the fear of AIDS.

A misconception has been attributed to Australian women. Certainly, there are women who oil themselves in the hot sun and follow stringent diets while others go hungry. These same women contribute to funds such as World Vision. Those who are well endowed with money somehow suffer threat sensitivity apart from the overwhelming need to contribute to those less fortunate. Without doubt, Australian women are "charitable" (Costello, 1980). It is erroneous to suggest that the Australian woman does not care because she is passionately intent on bettering the plight of all women everywhere. She can be perceived as an admixture of cultures; fortunately, she reflects a common denominator in her charity. She is perceived as a "quiet achiever."

ABORIGINAL WOMEN

Aboriginal women have always played an extremely significant role in the life of their people. An Aboriginal woman has been appointed supervisor of Aboriginal Education Services in the Department of Education, the first Aborigine and the first woman to hold such a senior position in the department. Her appointment reflects the government's belief that Aboriginal people must be involved in all levels of decision-making, particularly in Aboriginal education. The Victorian Aboriginal Education Consultative Group (VAECG), whose executive and membership is largely female, advises on Aboriginal education. Aboriginal women are the only group of women specifically selected for the Victorian Women's Advisory Council.

WOMEN'S ACHIEVEMENTS IN AUSTRALIA

Between 1947 and 1971 Australia welcomed 2,855,000 migrants. Only four in ten were from the British Isles. Half were from continental Europe and these were comprised of (in percentages): Italians 11.7, Greeks 7.7, Yugoslavs 6.3, Dutch 4.6, Germans 3.9, Poles 3.5, and Maltese 2.4 (Australia, 1987). It was seen that Australia's immigration policy changed, resulting in fewer people coming from England and the British Commonwealth in general.

Carolyn Chisholm, Australia's first women's rights advocate, achieved so much while still supporting Australia's colonization by the British and as a result founded the Family Colonisation Loan Society, which organized and financed the immigration of families to Australia. By increasing the number of women in Australia, the birth rate also increased. Chisholm was a phenomenon, reinforcing women's foothold in Australia. Her portrait is found on the Australian five-dollar bill, the only woman other than a monarch to be so pictured anywhere in the world. It is claimed that Australian women have many role models like Chisholm.

Australia has one of the world's best current female authors: Colleen McCulloch. She is no "soft touch" or "soddy nosed wet conformist." McCulloch can swear with the rest in a new idiom, proclaiming sharp ideas that confront the establishment but with gentility. She knew she could do it! (Measured in U.S. dollars McCulloch's work has been bought for over $800 million, a world record.) Colleen McCulloch is an author to watch closely. Her remarkable books include *The Thorn Birds* and, more recently, her novel, *A Creed For The Third Millennium.*

While Australia might not claim many international female scientists, its women celebrities include poet Judith Wright, songsters Olivia Newton John and Colleen Hewitt, the fashion designer Prue Acton, and olympic swimmer Dawn Fraser. Others, like Dame Joan Sutherland, the great soprano, exemplify Australian female talent at the highest degree.

Australia's women are changing. Previously, they adopted career interests that were literary, but now they are moving toward mechanical and computational career interests that are not necessarily associated with "clerical" careers (Costello, 1988). In the past, women's roles were confined to the house, but this is no longer so. A new breed of women has evolved. Australia has some "tall poppies" who were once cut down, like Dawn Fraser.

MARRIAGE OR NONMARRIAGE

While marriage once offered a type of traditional respectability, and still does for many, with perfumed apple blossoms and confetti, there has been a gradual change within Australian culture. A trend has begun for couples to attain a level of "respectability" when simply living together in a type of trial marriage, should they wish.

Generally, women traditionally have looked toward the security of marriage; but during the last 20 years, they have increasingly entered the work force and presumably gained a higher level of financial independence so that previous ties do not always apply. Perhaps this was precipitated by a breakdown of traditional values and mores as quietly witnessed by the churches in dwindling attendance and vocations, or possibly the radical sexual revolution spearheaded by Germaine Greer.

Suddenly, women were no longer confined to looking up medical dictionaries or attending "kitchen teas" for new ideas. There was an influx of information on previously considered taboo subjects, and this came through a popularised style. Various women's magazines published explicit articles on female sexuality, unlike anything released for the general public before. These began to question such ideas as the male's techniques of love-making and even his knowledge of the sexual act or whether indeed he understood the female anatomy. Women were now invited to rate their husband/lover. (Costello, 1982a)

These changes within the family are a necessary precondition for the expansion of women's roles. Most women are, or become, mothers. Inextricably connected, then, to the woman's work force conditions and status is the issue of childcare, which by and large has been all too inadequately dealt with by government, business, and unions alike.

"In 1982, as reported by the Bureau of Statistics, four out of five women who were rearing children were actively employed in the work force." (Amato, 1987) However, between 1969 and 1982 divorce increased by 39 percent.

Neck-to-knee bathing costumes may have been in vogue during the Victorian period but the fashions very obviously changed in the 1960s. Both men and women seemed to enjoy this new facet of women's liberation, which was reinforced by the media with special reference to overseas trends, especially those in the United States of America. The Hite Report provided further impetus but, quite unlike the work of Masters and Johnson or even that of Kinsey back in the 1950s, it had a greater effect because Australia now had television.

In the late 1960s, Australian women started to "burn their bras." In the early 1970s, "blue" films evolved to R- and X-rated films. In the 1980s, we even had "streaking." No longer was sexuality confined to the male club and even the male "strip-tease" has expanded to female audiences by the late 1970s. No longer did federal censors appear to use their scissors. It was earlier contended that films such as "Last Tango In Paris" should not have passed the Australian officialdom, who by that time appeared somewhat bureaucratically impotent, "scissors and all."

THE ALTERING FAMILY—A TRAUMATIC EXPERIENCE

During the Great Depression of the 1930s, millions of men were thrown out of work. As factory doors closed against them, many plunged into extremes of despair and entrenched guilt, their egos shattered by the pink lay-off slip. Eventually, unemployment came to be seen in a more sensible light— not as a result of individual laziness or moral failure, but of giant forces outside the individual's control: the maldistribution of wealth, myopic investment, runaway speculation, inept trade policies, or government resistance. These, and not personal weaknesses of laid-off workers, caused unemployment. In most cases, feelings of guilt were naively inappropriate (Costello, 1982a).

WOMEN TODAY: TRADITION AND CHANGE

Today, once more, egos are shattering like egg shells. Now, however, the generalized threat-sensitivity or guilt is associated with the fracture of the family rather than the economy. As millions of men and women exit the strewn wreckage of marriage, they too suffer the agonies of self-blame. However, we might address the question of marital breakdown as a consequence of macroeconomics and personal financial hardship, once again.

When a tiny majority is involved, the disintegration of the family may reflect individual failure. But when divorce, separation and other forms of familial disaster overtake millions of people at once, the causes must involve more than just personal ones. The fracture of the family today is, in fact, part of the general crisis of industrialism—the crack-up of all institutions despised by the Second Wave. It is part of the ground-cleaning for the new Third Wave socio-sphere. And it is this traumatic process, reflected in our individual lives, that is altering the family system beyond recognition. (Toffler, 1980)

An article by Paul R. Amato (1987), highlights several aspects of a study of children and families:

Most people realize that prolonged and intense conflict between parents is not good for children. Our findings support this common perception— but also provided a few surprises.

Marital conflict was also found to have a negative impact on children's self-esteem. However, the effect was particularly strong for young girls, but it was not observed for young boys. This finding may be related to previous research showing that girls become more upset than boys when overhearing adults fighting—"Mum and Dad are fighting because I have been bad!"

The finding that young girls are particularly vulnerable to conflict in the family has one worrying implication. Boys tend to play up when they have problems and often receive attention for this reason. But girls who experience depression and feelings of low self-worth are likely to be quiet and well behaved. For this reason young girls from high-conflict families, although at risk, may not be receiving the attention they need from teachers, counsellors and parents. (Amato, 1987)

"Given that one in three marriages in Australia will end in divorce and this is a very conservative estimate, one wonders whether children today see any value in marriage whatsoever" (Amato, 1987). By 1979 over 70 percent of divorces were filed by women. The first author of this chapter was previously awarded the National Distinguished Award for helping children of divorced/separated parents, which had previously been awarded to Walt Disney, for being able to keep the children happy through distraction during times of their ultimate conflict: separation and divorce. We need a form of distraction so that children and parents might be able to adjust to such a severe problem that is presently portrayed in the media. It is okay to be divorced or separated! (Costello, 1982b). Perhaps in time we might think about that, and not just in Australia.

In the 1940s, divorce in Australia was literally unheard of, but in the 1950s there were a comparative few. In the 1980s, divorce has somehow grown acceptable. It is estimated that three out of five families in the major cities are single-parent families.

THE SINGLE-PARENT FAMILY

With so many women entering the category of single parents, funds were immediately made available through pensions or benefits for one-parent families. Pensions were also provided for unmarried mothers and these were called "Supporting Mothers Benefits." The plight of the single parent has been well recognized in Australia, perhaps more so than in any other country.

Many divorced women have remarried. In 1975 there were 10,282 and by 1985 (in ten years) this figure had grown to 23,240. Conversely, there has also been a decline in divorce from 44,088 in 1982 to 38,752 in 1986 (Australian Bureau of Statistics, cited in Kilmartin, 1987).

SOME CONCLUSIONS

The Australian woman is powerful and proud, gentle and warm, but very practical. She watches and waits, and then "pounces like a tiger," not so much emotionally as with a refined and dynamic organizational or political process, lest anyone question her hard-won independence. Her heritage is based on deprivation and past depression. She may still suffer fools sometimes but no longer as readily.

Women have often been credited with pronounced abilities to talk, perhaps endlessly when perceived by men generally; however, it seems the Australian woman has organized this talking into a practical and political modus operandi.

Australian women have entered the sciences as well as the humanities. They are no longer looking for equality because they have made their mark in law, politics, and medicine. They have exceeded the comparative expectations of other nationalities through their grassroots and academic perseverance in this "lucky country." After only 200 years, they have achieved a great deal.

The Australian woman is a product of her inherent qualities and physical environment, within matrices of psychosocial influences. She stands strong in the face of adversity and oppression, and she rightly dares anyone to "stain the wattle with blood." She is unlike many of her international counterparts because she speaks up and we are not used to that. We must either listen to what she has to say or suffer the consequences because she is usually right, using a mixture of rational logical argument and powerful emotive sentimentality, born out of her suffering.

In summary, the Australian woman's lot is by far the best in the world. However, she is not satisfied with the status quo because she sees so many areas where she should and will be involved. In a democracy such as Australia, where anyone can have a say, women will somehow gain previously inconceivable equality, subtle and yet sure, without inferences of "momism," while maintaining a delicate balance with their menfolk in a delicate balance that looks threatening now.

Australian women will probably not launch outlandish campaigns although some fringe "alternative life-style" feminists might wish to do so. Instead, they will continue to put across their points of view by working in government as well as by talking or consulting with their husbands, brothers, and sons. Surely, Australian women rock the cradle of the world, and they know it, here in the new El Dorado which they have made for themselves!

REFERENCES

Amato, P. R. (1987). Results of the Australian institute of family studies. Children in families study: Some highlights. *AIFS Journal,* No. 17 January.

Argus Newspaper. (1854). Melbourne, Vic.: Bendigo Advertiser. November 27.

Australian Bureau of Statistics. (1981). Labour force status and other characteristics of families. Canberra: Australian Government Printer. Cat. No. 6224.

Australia. (1987). *A historical library.* Sydney, N.S.W.: Fairfax, Syme, & Weldon Publ.

Baynton, B. (1902). *The chosen vessel.* London: Bush Studies, Duckworth Publ.

Beverage, J., & Shute, S. (1982). *Working women.* Sydney, N.S.W.: Iron Manager.

Cheetham, J., & Costello, B. R. (1979). *Parent power.* Melbourne, Vic.: Macmillan, Sun Books.

Costello, B. R. (1980). The single parent and effects on relationships. National Convention : Parents without partners. Adelaide, S. A. (Abstract).

Costello, B. R. (1982a). A psychological analysis comparing computerised psychological assessment: Divorced/separated women with happily married women. Unpublished Doctoral dissertation. International College, Los Angeles.

Costello, B. R. (1982b). Applications of computerised psychological and educational assessment in South Australia. *Journal of International School Psychology.*

Costello, B. R. (1987). A comparison of vocational interest between male and female 10th year students: For Langwarrin Secondary College. *College Student Journal.* Vol. 22, No. 2.

Costello, B. R. (1988). ACVII: Australian computerised vocational interest inventory. XXIV International Congress of Psychology (Abstract). Sydney, N.S.W.

Costello, B. R. (1990). The Australian computerised vocational interest inventories. *Journal of Education,* Vol. 110, No. 4.

Costello, B.R. The Australian computerised marriage assessment profile. *Journal of Instructional Psychology.* (submitted)

Grieve, N. (1984). *Australian women feminist perspectives.* Oxford University Press.

Grimshaw P., McConville, C., & McEwen, E. (1984). *Families in colonial Australia*. Sydney, N.S.W.: George Allen & Unwin.

Kilmartin, C. (1987). Is the proportion of sole mothers dependent on social security really increasing? *Australian Institute of Family Studies Newsletter* ISSN 0818-0229. No. 18. Melbourne.

Kirner, J. E. (1990). The prospect for public education in Victoria. *Journal of Education*, Vol. 110, No. 4.

Lake. (1985). *Families in colonial Australia*. Sydney, N.S.W.: George Allen & Unwin.

Lawson, H. (1986). *Henry Lawson's short stories*. Melbourne, Vic.: Penguin.

Ministerial review of postsecondary schooling. (1985). *Report,* Vol. 1, Melbourne, Vic.: Victorian Government Printing Office.

O.E.C.D. (1989). *Pathways for Learning*. Paris: OECD/CERI.

Toffler, A. (1980). *The third wave*. London: Pan Books.

Women's policy co-ordination unit. (1984). *The 51% Minority*. Melbourne, Vic.: Government Printer.

Index

109, 110, 111, 112-114,
117-122, 124-129, 135, 143,
145, 146, 148, 150-152, 154,
155, 156, 157, 163, 165,
177-181, 184, 185, 190,
191-195, 200-202, 206, 208,
210-213, 216, 218, 223-225,
232, 233, 235, 240, 243,
245-247, 248
El-Abd, A. A., 131, 114, 119
El-Ghandour, A., 123, 124, 131
El-Mamoun, N. A., 116, 131,
El-Meligui, E., 124, 131
El-Nimeiri, Gaafar Mohammed
(President of the Sudan), 112,
113
El-Sayed, A. M., 119, 131
Elizabeth II *(Queen of G.B.),* 1
Elvin, V., 161
Emin, Ardashes, 85
empty nest, 13, 102
empty nest syndrome, 13
Equal Rights Amendment, 3
Erikson, Eric, 149
Eskimo, 20-21
Etzion, D., 102, 105

F

Fahmy, N., 123, 131
Fahys, J., 25
Feldman, S. A., 21, 25, 21
female circumcision, 115-118,
129, 139,
Fernandez, L. C., 13
Feshbach, S., 5, 15
Flemming, A. L., 6, 15
Floyd, W., 14, 15
Freeman, D., 228, 239
Friedan, B., 12, 15
Friedman, A., 102
Fyzee, Asaf A. A., 123, 131

G

Gafni, Y., 101
Galal el-Din, M. E., 113, 114,

121, 125, 129, 131
Gardiner, H. W., 178, 181
gender-role behavior, 7
Gilson, R., 229, 230, 239
Giraldo, O., 30, 37
glasnost, 80
Glebov, O., 79
Godoy, Lucila, 34
Good, T. L., 7, 16
Goode, W. J., 8, 16
Gorbachev, Mikhail *(President,
USSR),* 80, 82
Gore, M. S., 153, 158
Greer, Germaine, 249
Grieve, N., 253
Grimshaw, P., 244
Guilfoile, Dame Margaret, 247
Gulhati, L., 155, 158
Gutek, B. A., 35, 37
Gutmann, D., 145, 158
Guttentag, M., 83

H

Habiballa, M. 121, 132
Halsell, G., 79, 85
Hammond, D., 176, 186
Hamzawi, R. A., 125, 126, 131
Han, F.L.K., 202
Hanks, J. R., 176, 186
Hanks, L. M., 176, 186
Hasan, A., 164, 172
Hatshepsut *(Queen of Egypt),*
108
Hayes, M., 7, 15
Hazleton, L., 90
Herring, H., 27, 37
Hewlett, S. A., 9, 16
Hirschman, C., 182, 186
Ho, K. J., 21, 25
Hoffman, L. W., 16, 11
Holmes, L., 228, 238, 239
Horner, M. S., 7, 13, 16
Houseknecht, S. K., 11, 16
Houssain, A. B., 116, 131
Hurst, M., 10, 16
Hyde, J. S., 4, 8, 9, 12-14, 16

Perón, Juan D., 33
Perón, Eva *(Evita)*, 33, 34
Pitt, D., 239, 232
polygamy, 110, 111, 123, 124, 139, 198
Postlethwaite, T., 224, 240
Potter, S. H., 180, 182, 187
Prachuabmoh, V., 187
Pratap, P., 148, 158
pregnancy, 10, 11, 13, 32, 48, 60, 63, 69, 73-75, 83, 84, 94, 95, 98, 112, 124-126, 135, 136, 138, 139, 153, 168, 181, 183, 185, 214
Prophet Muhammed, 113, 115, 118, 121, 123
puberty, 7, 116, 117, 139, 149, 150, 176, 179, 195, 224
puberty ceremony, 116
public bath, 211

Q

Quay, H. C., 6, 18

R

Radai, F., 93, 105
Ramayana, 144
Ramzi, N., 123, 131
retirement, 65, 76, 84, 102, 112, 192, 201
Rich, T. A., 6, 15
Richman, N., 11, 17
Rindfuss, R., 182, 186
Rivera, A. N., 35, 37
Rizkalla, M., 126, 127, 129, 132
Robinson, J. P., 9, 17
Rodgers, W. L., 11, 15
Roggeveen, Jacob, 230
roles *(masculine, feminine)*, 2-4, 6-9, 11, 13-14, 21-24, 28, 32-36, 39-43, 45-49, 52, 56, 58, 60, 64-66, 70, 76, 85-87, 90-92, 95, 96, 98, 101-104, 108, 109, 111, 112, 114, 128, 130, 145, 147-153, 156, 157, 162,
176, 180, 181, 184, 185, 189, 191, 193, 194, 196, 200, 201, 221, 223, 226, 228, 235, 237, 244, 248, 249
Rosenberg, B. G., 8, 17
Rosenblum, L., 4, 16
Rossi, A. S., 10, 17
Rubin, L., 13, 17
Russo, N. F., 10, 12, 17
Ryback, D., 178, 187

S

Safir, M. P., 92, 96, 105
Saghayroun, A. A., 125-127, 129, 132
Sakesna, V., 164, 173
Satti, Z. A., 121, 123, 124, 132
Schoeffel, P., 234, 240
Schwartz, P., 2, 15
Seager, J., 2, 17
Secord, P., 83, 87
sex-typing, 3, 42, 58, 96, 163, 191-192, 210, 221
sex-role socialization, 3, 4, 6, 13, 14, 149, 152, 153, 221
Shafer, N., 13, 17
Shah, N. M., 178, 182, 184, 187
Shalaq, A., 132, 121, 123, 124
Sharawi, Huda, 110
Shepher, Joseph, 98
Sherman, J. A., 4, 17
Shore, B., 221, 225-230, 240
Shute, S., 253
Sikes, J. N., 7, 16
Sillman, N., 102, 105
Silvern, L. E., 7, 17
Singh, A. K., 160, 173
Singh, U. P., 181, 186
single-parent families, 3, 10, 251
single parent, 9, 247, 252, 253
Sinha, S., 160, 173
Sita, 144, 148
Smith, M. C., 141
Smith, P. C., 185, 187
Smith, R. E., 12, 17

Contributors

LEONORE LOEB ADLER received her Ph.D. in Experimental Social Psychology from Adelphi University. She is the Director of the Institute for Cross-Cultural and Cross-Ethnic Studies and a Member of the Faculty in the Department of Psychology at Molloy College. Dr. Leonore Loeb Adler is President of the Social Psychology Division and Past President of the Academic Division, of the New York State Psychological Association, and is a recipient of the N.Y.S.P.A. Kurt Lewin Award and the N.Y.S.P.A. Wilhelm Wundt Award. A former Treasurer of the International Council of Psychologists and a former President of the Queens County Psychological Association, she also served on the Board of Directors of the Eastern Psychological Association for several years; she is a Fellow of Division 35, of the Psychology of Women, of the American Psychological Association. For six years she was the Managing Editor of the *International Journal of Group Tensions,* and is currently on its Editorial Board. A member of the Executive Board of the International Organization for the Study of Group Tensions, Dr. L. L. Adler is involved in several cross-cultural and cross-ethnic research projects. She has attended and organized psychological conferences, workshops, colloquia, and symposia nationally and internationally. She has published over 50 professional papers and chapters, and is the author, editor, or coeditor of eight books.

RAMADAN A. AHMED received his M.A. from Alexandria University in Egypt and his Ph.D. from the Karl Marx University, Leipzig, D.D.R. (East Germany), specifically in a cross-cultural context, investigating the cognitive development of children from different cultural, national, and socioeconomic backgrounds. Dr. Ramadan A. Ahmed is affiliated with the Faculty of Arts of Cairo University Khartoum Branch in the Sudan, where he is an Associate Professor of Psychology. He was recently a visiting Faculty Member in the Department of Psychology at Kuwait University in Safat, Kuwait. Before embarking on a professional career in psychology, Dr. Ahmed received a law degree and worked as a lawyer for the Egyptian Government. His present research activities include studies in developmental and social psychology, such as the perceptions of age-related activities, attitudes toward family members, and moral development. Dr. R. A. Ahmed has presented his research and participated at international psychological congresses, conferences, conventions and symposia. Among his other professional affiliations, he is a Member of the Advisory Board of the Institute for Cross-Cultural and Cross-Ethnic Studies, Molloy College.

RUBEN ARDILA is Professor of Psychology at the National University of Colombia in Bogota. He obtained his Ph.D. degree in Experimental Psychology at the University of Nebraska in Lincoln. He has worked in Colombia while visiting many countries for academic purposes. Dr. Ruben Ardila is the Founder and Editor of the *Latin American Journal of Psychology*. He has published 130 scientific papers and more than 20 psychology books, some of which have been translated into English, Russian, and German. His description of a scientific utopia, *Walden Three* (1990) was recently published in the United States of America. Dr. Ardila participates in many professional activities, and is a Member of the Advisory Board of the Institute for Cross-Cultural and Cross-Ethnic Studies, Molloy College.

LEE CARPENTER received her M.A. degree in Comparative Literature from Pennsylvania State University, and is a Ph.D. candidate in the Department of History at Pennsylvania State University. She is employed as an Editor at the Institute for Policy Research and Evaluation.

BRIAN R. COSTELLO received his Ph.D. in Clinical Psychology from the International College in Los Angeles, California. He has been teaching since 1962, specializing in Health Education. In 1973 he was awarded the highest Australian Federal Grant for Special Education and Community Counselling Provision in Victoria, Australia. He has lectured in psychology at the Victorian Institute of Social Welfare and at the South Australian Institute of Technology. An author of several books and numerous articles, Dr. Costello has presented research papers at Munich, Germany, for the United Nations; at the University of California, Los Angeles; at Princeton University; and in New York City at the American Psychological Association Convention; as well as at Australian Psychology and Education Conventions. Dr. Brian Costello is the originator of the first Australian Computerized Vocational Guidance Program (ACVII); he is the Director of the Cassel Research Centre (Australia) and now researches computerized neuropsychological biofeedback.

FLORENCE L. DENMARK received her Ph.D. in Social Psychology from the University of Pennsylvania. She was the President of the American Psychological Association, 1980-1981; the Eastern Psychological Association, 1985-1986; the New York State Psychological Association, 1972-1973; the International Council of Psychologists, 1989-1990; and Psi Chi, the National Honor Society in Psychology, 1978-1980. In addition, she served as Vice President for the New York Academy of Sciences and the International Organization for the Study of Group Tensions, and is currently a Member of the Advisory Board of the Institute for Cross-Cultural and Cross-Ethnic Studies, Molloy College. Dr. Florence L. Denmark has been the Thomas Hunter Professor Psychology at Hunter College of the City University of New York, and at present is the Robert Scott Pace Professor of Psychology at Pace University, where she is the Chair of the Department of Psychology. She has authored or edited eight books and has written numerous chapters and articles.

MARGARET FISCHER holds degrees from Seton Hall University, San Diego State University, and the University of Washington, where she received her Ph.D. in Psychology. She also attended the University of Maryland's overseas branches, the University of Paris, France, and the C. G. Jung Institute in Switzerland. Currently she is completing an M.B.A. degree at the University of Alaska. Dr. Fischer has worked as an instructor in Okinawa, Germany, Turkey, and France. After completing her doctorate, she was a Professor at Purdue University, the University of California, Massachusetts State Colleges, and the University of Alaska. Since 1978 Dr. Fischer has worked as a Psychologist at the Alaska Psychiatric Institute. She served as Member of the Alaska Board of Examiners of Psychologists. Dr. Fischer has been a Member of the Board of Directors of the International Council of Psychologists (ICP), and a Columnist for the *International Psychologist*. She has recently been elected President-Elect of ICP. Dr. Margaret Fischer has been an Alaskan resident for the past 12 years. Her interests in Cross-Cultural Psychology grew out of her work with Arctic natives.

NAOHIKO FUKADA, Professor Emeritus at Doshisha Women's College, received his Ph.D. from Doshisha University in Kyoto, Japan. Currently he is a Professor in the Department of Environmental Planning at the Osaka University of Arts. His main research interests are in the area of Personality Testing, Drawing Behavior, and Cross-Cultural Studies. Dr. Naohiko Fukada has published many articles in professional journals, as well as in dictionaries and encyclopedias. He has also contributed several chapters to books, and has translated seven books from English into Japanese. His book on the *Experimental Study of Drawing Behavior* was published in 1989. Now he is working on the publication of other books as well.

HARRY W. GARDINER is Professor of Psychology at the University of Wisconsin-LaCrosse. He received his M.A. from the University of Hawaii and his Ph.D. from the University of Manchester in England. He has been engaged in training, teaching, and research in Europe, Asia, and the United States of America. Dr. Harry Gardiner has published more than 60 articles in professional journals and has presented research papers at numerous international meetings. He is coauthor of *Child and Adolescent Development* and currently is working on *Understanding Cross-Cultural Psychology*.

ORMSIN SORNMOONPIN GARDINER was born in Potaram, Thailand. She is Assistant Professor of Mathematics of Winona State University. She received her B.Sc. (Honours) from Chulalongkorn University in Bangkok, Thailand, where she taught physics for several years. Her M.Sc. in Electrical Engineering was conferred by the University of Manchester, Institute of Science and Technology in England. Professor Ormsin Sornmoonpin Gardiner is currently conducting a cross-cultural study of math-achievement by students in Thailand and the United States of America.

HALINA GRZYMALA-MOSZCZYNSKA received both her M.A. in Clinical Psychology and her Ph.D. in Social Psychology from the Jagiellonian University in Cracow, Poland. Dr. Grzymala-Moszczynska is currently teaching courses in the field of the psychology of religion at the Institute for the Science of Religions at the Jagiellonian University. She is completing a project on the therapeutic and pathogenic aspects of religious systems and a cross-cultural project on the world views of youth.

DAFNA N. IZRAELI was born in Canada and immigrated to Israel in 1963. Her Ph.D. is from Manchester University in England. She is Associate Professor of Sociology and Past Chairperson of the Department of Sociology and Anthropology at Bar Ilan University in Israel. Dr. Izraeli cochaired the First International Interdisclipinary Congress on Women—Women's Worlds: the New Scholarship. She edited a Special Issue of the *Israeli Social Science Review* on Women in Israel (1989). Her books include: *Women's Worlds: From the New Scholarship* (with Marilyn P. Safir, Martha S. Mednick, and Jessie Bernard), *Women in Management Worldwide* (with Nancy Adler), and *Dual Earner Couples: A Cross-National Perspective* (with Susan Lewis and Helen Hootsman).

USHA KUMAR received her Ph.D. in Counseling/Clinical Psychology from the Ohio State University. After a two-year Internship at the University of Michigan Counseling Center, she returned to India and joined the Faculty of the Department of Humanities and Social Sciences at the Indian Institute of Technology, Kanpur. Dr. Usha Kumar is currently Professor of Psychology at the Indian Institute of Technology, where she pursues research in the development of Indian women, and in cross-cultural comparisons of the middle-age crisis of managers. Dr. Kumar is also a consultant to many Indian companies in the area of human resource development, and is a former Member of the Advisory Board of the Institute for Cross-Cultural and Cross-Ethnic Studies, Molloy College.

HARRIET P. LEFLEY, is a Professor of Psychiatry, Office of Transcultural Education and Research, University of Miami School of Medicine in Miami, Florida. She attended the University of Chicago and Roosevelt University, Chicago, where she received her B.A. in Psychology and her M.A. in Clinical Psychology. She obtained her Ph.D. from the University of Miami, specializing in Cross-Cultural and Community Psychology. Since 1973 she has been a Faculty Member of the University of Miami. She has been a Resident Consultant in Social Research to the Government of the Bahamas, Program Evaluation of the New Horizons Community Mental Health Center, Director of the University of Miami's Cross-Cultural Training Institute for Mental Health Professionals, and Director of the Collaborative Family Training Project. Dr. Harriet P. Lefley has been involved in cross-cultural research, service, and training for more than 20 years. She has published six books, and is the author of over 100 scientific papers, journal articles, and book chapters on cultural issues in mental health service delivery, community mental health models, and family support systems for the mentally ill.

KATHLEEN LOWENSTEIN is Deputy Principal and has taught at Allington Manor School and Therapeutic Community, Hampshire, England, for over 11 years. Allington Manor is a residential school for children with emotional, learning and behavioral problems. As a role model, Kathleen Lowenstein has raised the standard of behavior of the youngsters who have been placed in the school, after being rejected by their previous schools and their families. She is the righthand person to the Director of Allington Manor School, her husband Ludwig Lowenstein.

LUDWIG F. LOWENSTEIN, M.A., Dip. Psych., Ph.D., is Director and Consultant Psychologist of Allington Manor and Therapeutic Community in Hampshire, England. He was born in Germany and is a citizen of the United States of America. He is the former Chief Educational Psychologist for Hampshire, and served as Visiting Professor at the University of Khartoum. Dr. Ludwig Lowenstein is the author of numerous books and articles on Education and Psychology; he is the former Editor-in-Chief of *School Psychology International* and former Director of the International Council of Psychologists. He is presently a member of the Advisory Board of the Institute for Cross-Cultural and Cross-Ethnic Studies, Molloy College.

NIHAR R. MRINAL received his Ph.D. from the Indian Institute of Technology is Kanpur, India. Currently he is a Faculty Member in the Department of Psychology at Nagpur University. Dr. Mrinal is a Fellow of the Indian Association of Clinical Psychologists and a Life Member of the Indian Science Congress Association, Calcutta. He is a Member of the Advisory Board of the Institute for Cross-Cultural and Cross-Ethnic Studies, Molloy College and a Member of the International Council of Psychologists. Dr. Mrinal is active in Cross-Cultural Research and has developed three Psychological Tests. He has published and presented over 30 research papers, both nationally and internationally.

COREY J. MUSE is Professor of Education at Whitman College, Walla Walla, Washington, where he has been since 1966. He began his association with Samoan culture in 1960, when he went to Western Samoa as a Guidance Counselor. After receiving the doctorate at Brigham Young University, he returned to Samoa on several occasions to lead student tours. Dr. Corey J. Muse gathered research data and has also photographed the birds of the regions, which he published with S. Muse in a book titled *The Birds and Birdlore of Samoa.* His research focus in Samoa has centered on cognition and learning.

NMUTAKA AGNES OBY OKAFOR was born in Nigeria and holds a Nigerian Certificate in Education in French (Credit Level) from Alvan Ikoku College of Education, Owerri. She served in the National Youth Service Corps, and taught in High School in Nigeria. Since coming to the United States of America, Ms. Okafor has received a B.A. Magna Cum Laude in Psychology and French from Lehman College of the City University of New York and received Departmental Honors in both disciplines. Ms. Okafor holds an M.A. in Educational Psychology from Fordham University. She is currently pursuing studies at the French Institute in New York. She has presented a paper at a Cross-Cultural Conference at the Institute for Cross-Cultural and Cross-Ethnic Studies, Molloy College. She is a Member of Psi Chi, (the National Honor Society in Psychology) and the International Council of Psychologists.

MARILYN P. SAFIR received her Ph.D. in Clinical Psychology from Syracuse University. She is Director of Women's Studies and Associate Professor in the Department of Psychology at the University of Haifa in

Israel. She was a leader of the Israeli Feminist Movement in the early 1970s. Professor Safir was appointed Director of the National Commission for the Advancement of the Status of Women in 1986 by then Prime Minister Shimon Peres. Dr. M. P. Safir organized and chaired the First International Interdisciplinary Congress on Women in 1981, at the University of Haifa; served on the organizing committee of the Second International Congress, held in Groningen, Netherlands, in 1984; the Third Congress, held in Dublin, Ireland, in 1987; and the fourth Congress, held in New York, the United States of America, in 1990. She has coedited *Women's Worlds: From the New Scholarship* (with Martha S. Mednick, Dafna Izraeli, and Jessie Bernard), *Sexual Equality: The Israeli Kibbutz Tests the Theories* (with Michal Palgi, Joseph L. Blassi, and Menachem Rosner), *Calling the Equality Bluff: Women in Israel* (with Barbara Swirsky), and published numerous chapters and articles.

LAUREL SCHWARTZ worked as Research Assistant for Dr. Florence L. Denmark while she was a student at Hunter College of the City University of New York.

UMA SINGHAL is Chairperson of the Department of Psychology at BAKPG (Bhagwandin Arya Kanya Post-Graduate) College in Lakhimpur-Kheri, India. She has both an M.A. and a Ph.D. in Cross-Cultural Psychology from Kanpur University. Her areas of interest are Cross-Cultural and Community Psychology, and she is active in Cross-Cultural and Cross-Ethnic Research. Dr. Uma Singhal is a Member of the Advisory Board of the Institute for Cross-Cultural and Cross-Ethnic Studies, Molloy College. She is the author of several tests in Hindi and the coauthor of various chapters in books. She is the Resource Person for several social work organizations.

KATHLEEN MAURER SMITH is Assistant Professor of Sociology at Molloy College, as well as Adjunct Assistant Professor at Hofstra University. She received her M.A. in Sociology from Adelphi University and is currently a Ph.D. Candidate at the City University of New York Graduate School. Professor K. M. Smith was one of the founders of the Community Research Institute at Molloy College and serves as one of its Associate Directors. In addition, she assisted in the establishment of a curriculum for Molloy College's Alcohol and Drug Addiction Counselor Education Program. Her present research focuses on women alcoholics, alcoholism and the family, and the portrayal of gender, age, and ethnicity in the media.

HAROLD TAKOOSHIAN received his Ph.D. from the Graduate School of the City University of New York in Social/Personality Psychology. A Social Psychologist on the Faculty, Division of Social Sciences at Fordham University, he researches Social Issues, including Feminism. In 1987 he served as a U.S. Fulbright Scholar to the Soviet Union, where he taught or studied in four cities for four months, and collected Soviet women's views on feminism. From 1983 to 1985 he was also Visiting Professor at three South American Psychology Programs. Dr. Takooshian received the New York State Psychological Association's Kurt Lewin Award, from the Social Psychology Division of this Organization. He is also a Member of the International Council of Psychologists, and his research publications deal with many current social issues.

JANET LEE TAYLOR received a B.A. in Criminology and Psychology from Melbourne University, Australia. She is presently interning as a Clinical Psychologist and has accepted the position of Research Assistant at the Cassel Research Centers in Australia and in the United States of America.

LUCY C. YU received her Ph.D. from the University of Michigan. She is Associate Professor in the Department of Health Policy and Administration, and Senior Research Associate in the Institute for Policy Research and Evaluation at The Pennsylvania State University. Dr. Yu's research has been in the following areas: Policies on the support of aged parents among Chinese Americans and Chinese in the United States of America; behavior therapy for urinary incontinent elderly in long-term institutions; chronic illness among the elderly; cognitive and functional status of institutionalized elderly; and occupational stress among office workers and health care providers. Dr. Yu has published widely and contributed chapters to several books.

LENA ZHERNOVA graduated from Moscow University, Faculty of Journalism, in 1980. For several years she worked for the *Newspaper of Moscow Writers*, where she was the Editor-in-Chief. Then she was affiliated with the Soviet Lenin Children's Fund. Her special interests include modern Soviet Literature, and the Problems of Women and Children. Ms. Lena Zhernova is the author of numerous articles, published in different newspapers and magazines. She is a Member of the Professional Union of the Journalists of the USSR.